Research on Meeting and Using Standards in the Preparation of Teachers

Teacher Education Yearbook X

Edited by

Edith M. Guyton and Julie D. Rainer

KENDALL/HUNT PUBLISHING COMPANY
4050 Westmark Drive   Dubuque, Iowa 52002

T 46095

Copyright © 2002 by Association of Teacher Educators

ISBN 0-7872-8901-9

Library of Congress Catalog Card Number: 2001094325

Kendall/Hunt Publishing Company has the exclusive rights to
reproduce this work, to prepare derivative works from this
work, to publicly distribute this work, to publicly perform this
work and to publicly display this work.

Printed in the United States of America
10 9 8 7 6 5 4 3 2 1

Teacher Education Yearbook X

EDITORS

Edith M. Guyton, *Georgia State University, Atlanta*

Julie D. Rainer, *Georgia State University, Atlanta*

EDITORIAL ADVISORY BOARD

Violet Allain, *James Madison University, Virginia*

David M. Byrd, *University of Rhode Island, Kingston*

Donna M. Gollnick, *National Council for Accreditation of Teacher Education, Washington, D.C.*

Susan Kent, *Ohio State University at Newark*

Gwendolyn Middlebrooks, *Spelman College, Atlanta*

Karen McClusky, *Harrisburg Illinois Public Schools, Harrisburg*

D. John McIntyre, *Southern Illinois University, Carbondale*

Sandra J. Odell, *University of Nevada–Las Vegas*

Mary John O'Hair, *University of Oklahoma, Norman*

Melba Spooner, *University of North Carolina, Charlotte*

EXECUTIVE DIRECTOR

Lynn Montgomery, *Association of Teacher Educators, Reston, Virginia*

Contents

Division 4: Perspectives from Accrediting Agencies   195

Foreword

*A word means precisely what I choose it to mean,
nothing more and nothing less.*

Humpty Dumpty, in Lewis Caroll's *Through the Looking Glass*

Allen R. Warner

Allen R. Warner is Professor, College of Education, University of Houston and President of the Association of Teacher Educators (ATE). He is Past Chair of ATE's Leadership Foundation for Teacher Education, elected as a Distinguished Member of ATE, and is the recipient of five Presidential Service Awards from five different ATE presidents.

Few words impact contemporary education more than *standard*. We are now several decades into education's *standards movement*, a period during which virtually every professional educational organization (and most public policy bodies) have enacted statements of expectations for students and for their teachers. We talk of setting high standards, and engage in public debates over who should have the authority to set standards and to enforce them.

Our discourse has taken a rather remarkable turn. While other professions are accountable for meeting procedural standards, educators are more and more asked to be accountable for results. That is not the case with physicians or lawyers. If a physician is accused of malpractice, the issue is not whether the patient lived or died, experienced remission or continued suffering (product accountability). The physician is expected to show that (s)he followed practices (processes) generally accepted by the profession as a whole in similar cases. For a lawyer called to task, the issue is *not* whether the client was convicted or acquitted (product accountability) but whether the practitioner abided by the rubrics established by other professionals. Educators, however, are increasingly called by public policy to be responsible for results—to a great degree, because we have not yet reached agreement on standards of professional practice.

It may be useful to pause for a moment to reflect on the exegesis of the term *standard*. As S. I. Hyakawa so eloquently reminded us a half-century ago in *Language in Thought and Action,* words carry powerful connotations that go far beyond their denotations. Expanded dictionary definitions of *standard* point out that earlier in the growth of civilization, the *standard* was the symbolic rallying-point (often a banner) for an army in the heat of battle. The most honored position in those armies was the standard-bearer, an individual chosen by virtue of courage and steadfast nature to carry the standard. The standard-bearer was usually defenseless because the duty of raising the standard high (and keeping it high) was so essential to victory that the responsibility took priority over personal safety.

The collective mythology of every culture is filled with images of heroes who held the standard high and did not allow it to fall. Conversely, major cultural symbols of victory are the capture of the standard of the opposing force, and raising one's own standard over the territory of the other. The Iwo Jima Memorial in Washington, D.C., is among the most ubiquitous of such symbols for the United States—a massive image of six Marines raising the flag (successor to the banner).

The point of this (perhaps overly) militaristic discussion is that standards *can* be far more than words. Standards can represent rallying points, *if* enough people are willing to rally around them. *Willing* is the operative term here. If standards in our contemporary parlance are not rallying points, they remain words. And those words lack the meaning, power and impact that could otherwise be achieved.

In this 2002 yearbook of the Association of Teacher Educators, editors Edith Guyton and Julie Rainer and their contributors explore standards for individual teacher educators, the impact—or lack of impact—of standards, the continued growth of standards for programs that prepare educators for entrance to the profession, and raising standards for individual educators through the work of the National Board for Professional Teaching Standards. The major challenge ahead is whether we, as educators, have the courage and fortitude to rally around standards that are professionally sound, professionally established, and professionally enforced, to assure the best teachers for all our children.

Introduction

Edith M. Guyton

Julie D. Rainer

Edi Guyton is Associate Dean of the College of Education, Georgia State University. In that position, she is the Director of the Metropolitan Atlanta P-16 Community Council. Dr. Guyton is a Professor of Early Childhood Education. She recently served as President of the Association of Teacher Educators. Her scholarship and publications are in the areas of teacher education, constructivist teacher education, and multicultural education. She was an editor of the *Handbook of Research on Teacher Education* (Macmillan, 1996). She is the editor of the Association of Teacher Educators Standards for Field Experiences in Teacher Education (2000).

Julie Rainer is an assistant professor in Early Childhood Education and currently coordinates the Educational Specialist Program at Georgia State University. Her research interests include teacher development, constructivist theory and mathematics education. She has published articles in a variety of journals including *Action in Teacher Education, The Journal of Teacher Education, and Teaching* and *Teacher Education*. She is currently a member of NCATE Board of Examiners, and chair of ATE's Commission on Constructivist Teacher Education.

The standards movement in education has gained momentum and is a major force driving educational change. In all academic endeavors, educators are developing performance-based standards and assessments that make clear what the outcomes of education are. Teacher education is involved in this reform movement in two ways. Teacher educators are including how to teach to high standards in the teacher education curriculum. Teacher educators also are using standards to inform research and practice. The most prominent of those standards come from the National Council for the Accreditation of Teacher Education (NCATE), the Interstate

New Teacher Assessment and Support Consortium (INTASC), the Association of Teacher Educators (ATE), and the National Board for Professional Teaching Standards (NBPTS). National groups also have content/subject area standards for teachers, as do most states.

Teacher educators must grapple with several issues regarding standards. How do we align standards, curriculum and instruction? How do we get teachers involved in and competent in standards based education. Which standards are the best ones to use? How can we show the impact of standards on learning? This yearbook addresses some of those issues.

Research on teacher education standards is in an early stage. Much of the literature tends to be descriptive. As is evident in this book, research tends to be on the development of standards-based teacher education. In its next stage, the research should focus on the effects of standards based education on teacher education students and on the pupils they teach.

The research reports are divided into three sections. The first section deals with research on standards for teacher educators, the Teacher Educator Standards developed by the Association of Teacher Educators. One article describes the development of standards in this country and in Holland and the other describes research on the use of the standards. The second section focuses on research on the impact of standards on teachers and their beliefs and performances. The third section includes research involving NCATE and INTASC standards.

The yearbook is designed to provide teachers and teacher educators with current research and practical guidelines for implementing research. The conceptual framework of the yearbook is based on a triadic definition of scholarship: the production of knowledge, the interpretation and synthesis of knowledge, and the application of knowledge. Each year, research reports based on a significant topic to ATE members are solicited for publication in the yearbook. All research reports are blind reviewed and reports are published in divisions. A responder, a recognized scholar in the field, reacts to papers selected for each division.

In addition to the research reports, we have included invited articles from leaders in the standards movement. You will find articles by Elizabeth Castor and Gary Galuzzo of the NBPTS and Art Wise and Jane Leibbrand of NCATE. We believe that their perspectives add contextual depth to the yearbook.

We hope this edition will inform your own journey in standards based teacher education and research on this phenomenon. The authors have presented us with interesting projects, and the respondents have presented us with stimulating ideas regarding teacher education standards research.

ACKNOWLEDGEMENT

As editors, we would like to acknowledge that this work could not have been done without the valuable contribution of Christi Bowen. We also wish to thank Elaine Persons, Sharon Enujioke, and Don Steele for their help in putting together this book.

Division

1

Standards for
Teacher
Educators

Overview and Framework

Gwendolyn H. Middlebrooks

Gwendolyn H. Middlebrooks is an Associate Professor of Education at Spelman College. She has been an active member of ATE for more than twenty years. Her research focuses on Teaching in Urban Settings. She is a graduate of Spelman College, Springfield College, and the doctoral program in Curriculum and Instruction at Georgia State University.

Globally, standards are used for selecting and judging quality. According to Rath (1999), they specify the amount of each variable that is needed to decide whether a criterion has been met. They are definitely used as tests of quality, and educators, as well as people in other professions, are cognizant of the need to use them for determining excellence.

Teacher educators in higher education are accustomed to the development and application of standards institution-wide, in the education unit and programs, and with teacher candidates. They maintain professional affiliations with accrediting organizations to guarantee quality education for all learners and ensure the appropriate application of standards to institutions, education units and programs, teacher candidates, and first year teachers. The Commission on Colleges applies institution-wide standards for accreditation to the Colleges/Universities at ten (10) year intervals. The Interstate New Teacher Assessments and Support Consortium (INTASC) provides standards for assessing first year teachers. The National Board for Professional Teaching Standards (NBPTS) provides assessments for accomplished teachers who want to be recognized for their excellent performance as Master Teachers or Board Certified Teachers. Redesigned National

Council for the Accreditation of Teacher Education (NCATE) 2000 Standards for accrediting units that have teacher preparation programs. State Departments of Education or Professional Standards Commissions use standards to approve teacher preparation programs in the education unit. National standardized test score requirements impact students interested in teaching careers and are specifically applied to teacher candidates in the areas of program admission, retention, and completion. Standards specific to each State are used for certification of public school teachers to ensure that all instructional personnel maintain a level of quality in knowledge of content and in communication and pedagogical skills. These may include undergraduate degree, teaching field preparation, grade-point averages at specific phases of the program, and appropriate performance levels on standardized tests.

Though these standards for education units and programs, teacher candidates, and first year teachers are currently used to improve the quality of educational opportunities in our nation's schools, they exclude standards specifically applicable to the skills and competencies of teacher educators. They ignore the potential impact that teacher educator knowledge and skills may have on the preparation of teachers and ultimately the education of our nation's youth.

In past years, without national standards for quality faculty in Teacher Education, selection of college and/or university teacher educators was based on criteria established for all faculty. Selection criteria mainly focused on academic degree and in-field preparation, with little or no consideration for characteristics of qualified teacher educators. According to Goodlad (1989) (1990), teacher education has not been a priority for college presidents. Not only did the public criticize schools and teacher educators, but deans and professors of arts and sciences were also critical of education departments, schools, and faculty.

This blatant negative climate of criticism and lack of support for teaching, teacher educators, and teacher education surfaced before 1969 and continued for many years. It is interesting to remember that this was a period of time when national standards for teacher candidates and education units were minimal, standards at the state departments of education for education programs were simplistic and less than rigorous, and standards for teacher educators did not exist. Many curious researchers were stimulated by the public criticism of teaching and teacher education and conducted research to unveil causative factors and recommend solutions to the problems. Though findings were critical of the preparation of teacher educators, changes subsequent to their research for the purpose of improving teacher preparation and teaching and learning in schools focused on the development and use of standards not applicable to teacher educators.

Counelis (1969) and Walberg (1969) believed a solution could be found by focusing on the college teacher educator, and they examined teacher educator preparation and productivity. Among their findings relative to teacher educators was evidence of little published research, lack of preparation in the scientific process, minimum ability, and broad preparation. Counelis recommended that education be defined and recognized as a field of study. Walberg believed the absence of scholarly activity in schools of education placed them in danger of losing qualified faculty to more attractive careers in education. He recommended that they make efforts to recruit and retain talented faculty and prepare college teachers of education in basic research directed at advancing knowledge, learning, and teaching.

Research conducted by Raths, and Katz (1985) indicated that teacher educators generally did not conduct research because they disliked the research process. They were incapable of engaging in scholarly discussions and communicating with science faculty and seldom received outstanding awards. They were born into lower middle and middle class families void of education at the college/university level. They attended "non-elitist" four year state colleges, had work experiences in the elementary and secondary schools, engaged in part-time study in pursuit of the master's and doctoral degrees and completed pragmatic dissertations.

Ducharme and Agne (1982) conducted research and reached similar conclusions. But in general their findings indicated that teacher educators were second rate. Most were first generation college educated, attended low prestige institutions located close to their homes, in pursuit of second rate education degrees, and accepted low prestige jobs as elementary and secondary school teachers (Ducharme and Agne, 1989).

Watts (1984) advocated required certification for all teacher educators. He believed that the principle of individual certification should be applicable to college faculty who prepared teachers. He believed teacher educators should be individually required to meet specific criteria to ensure that they had appropriate knowledge and skills to prepare teachers. According to Watts, appropriate practitioner skills for first year teachers were not evident in instruction by teacher educators. He suggested that the statements referenced to quality of faculty by NCATE and State Departments of Education were inadequate and weak. He recommended the establishment of a national certification system for teacher educators. He suggested that the American Association of Colleges for Teacher Education (AACTE) take the initiative for developing standards and criteria, and he recommended the steps or process for accomplishing this task. He specified that requirements for initial certification of teacher educators should include an earned doctorate in education, completion of a minimum of three years of successful teaching experience at the elementary or secondary level, and an acceptable score on a standardized, comprehensive examination of pedagogical knowledge.

More than twenty years ago, standards were raised to solve the problem of the teacher shortage and improve the professional status of teaching (Orlosky, 1988). It was believed that rigorous standards would improve the reputation of education, attract more and well-qualified individuals to the teaching profession, and improve teaching performance. The greatest fear was that rigorous standards might encourage potentially competent teachers to avoid the profession, result in fewer certified teachers, and classrooms filled with teachers prepared through alternative certification programs.

The current standards movement focuses on "output" and outcomes-based candidate performance standards (Andrew and Schwab, 1993, Wise, 1998, Cochran-Smith, 2001). However, in the midst of this emphasis on performance standards, educators began discussing and examining the relevance of the preparation of teacher educators to the performance of teachers in classrooms.

Currently, education deans and department chairpersons at institutions of higher education that seek NCATE approval of their education units, use the NCATE 2000 Standard for Faculty Qualifications, Performance, and Development in the Unit (Wise and Leibbrand, 2001). The standard is used to screen candidates for faculty positions in teacher education and to clearly indicate that teacher educators are expected to model the effective teaching practices that their teacher candidates must demonstrate in classrooms. Although this is a national standard, it does not have an impact on education faculty nationwide because many institutions don't seek NCATE approval for their teacher preparation programs and do not use the NCATE standard to ensure the quality of their teacher educators.

Blackwell and Diez (1999) recommend using standards for assessing the knowledge and skills of teacher educators in specific master's degree programs in higher education. They also recommend that teacher educators model teaching practices. They believe standards are needed because teaching skills and methods used by teacher educators may not be consistent with National Board standards for developing classroom teachers. According to Diez (1996) teaching models also are important for developing appropriate teaching practices. She believes future teachers must experience appropriate teaching models during their years in K–12 schools and during their undergraduate years, because these experiences will assist them in constructing images of their roles as teachers and improve their teaching skills.

Carney (2000) supports the development and incorporation of technology standards into the accreditation process and modeling by teacher educators. Her paper presented evidence that new teachers can improve their proficiency in the use of technology, if faculty in teacher education model and integrate technology into their teaching practices. Courses in teacher preparation programs provide ideal opportunities for the integration of technology.

Currently, educators assist in development and utilization of standards to improve teaching and learning at all levels in teacher preparation programs. Teacher educators have experienced more than twenty years of efforts to elevate the teaching profession in the eyes of the nation. It is apparent that when standards are incorporated into assessment processes, the public is assured that quality exists in teacher education and the teaching profession. Standards are accepted and used by teacher educators to indicate the competences pre-service students must acquire and demonstrate. Teacher educators are faced with a challenge to assess their competencies based on a specific set of standards that define quality preparation for teacher educators. Though Andrew (1997) cautions an overemphasis on the use of standards and assessment in teacher Education, developing and using standards for teacher educators means that standards for determining quality will be available for everyone and all aspects of the teacher preparation process.

The following two chapters represent bold efforts by teacher educators to develop and use standards applicable to their own performance. Teacher educators have always had the responsibility of guiding the growth and development of teachers who will fill the classrooms in our nation's schools. But they have traditionally fulfilled that responsibility by using standards developed and mandated by other organizations. Chapter one details the extensive process used by the Association of Teacher Educators (ATE) to develop seven standards for assessing the quality of the performance of teacher educators in United States, and how those standards influenced the development of standards for teacher educators in Holland. Chapter two discusses how team teaching practices were used by teacher educators to model the seven standards. The chapters affirm our confidence in the quality and value of standards and their appropriateness for teacher educators.

References

Andrew, M.D. (1997). What matters most for teacher educators. *Journal of Teacher Education*, May–June, 48, (3), 167–176.

Andrew, M.D. and Schwab, R.L. (1993). Outcome-centered accreditation: Is teacher education ready? *Journal of Teacher Education*, May–June, 44, 3, 176–182.

Blackwell, P.J. and Diez, M. (1999). *Achieving the new vision of master's education for teachers.* NCATE/NBPTS Partnership for Graduate Programs. Washington, DC: NCATE, 1–41.

Carney, J.M. (2000). *What do preservice teacher educators need to know about technology?* Using ISTE/NCATE standards to define and develop competencies. International Society for Technology in Education: Washington, DC, 1–20.

Cochran-Smith, M. (2001). Higher standards for prospective teachers: what's missing from the discourse? *Journal of Teacher Education*, 52,3, 179–181.

Counelis, J. S. (1969). The professoriate in the discipline of education. To be a phoenix: The education professoriate. *Phi Delta Kappa, Inc.* 21–23.

Diez, M. (1996). Who will prepare the next generation of teachers? In L. Kaplan and R. A. Edelfelt (Ed.), *Teachers for the New Millennium* (pp 20–35). California: Corwin Press, Inc.

Ducharme, E. and Agne, R. (1982). The education professoriate: A research based perspective. *Journal of Teacher Education*, 33, 30–36.

Ducharme, E. and Agne, R. (1989). Professors of Education: Uneasy Residents of Academe. In R.Wisniewski and E.R. Ducharme (Ed.), *The professors of teaching: An inquiry* (pp 67–86). Albany: State University of New York Press.

Goodlad, J. (1989). *Educating educators.* Britanica Encyclopedia Britanica Educational Corporation. Video Cassette.

Goodlad, J. (1990). *Teachers for our nation's schools.* San Francisco: Jossey-Bass.

Interstate New Teacher Assessment and Support Consortium, (1998). *Model standards for beginning teacher licensing.* Washington, DC: Author.

National Board for Professional Teaching Standards (1994). *What teachers should know and be able to do.* Washington, DC: Author.

National Council for Accreditation of Teacher Education (2000). *Professional standards for the accreditation of schools, colleges, and departments of education.* Washington, DC: Author.

Orlosky, D.E. (1988). *Society, schools, and teacher preparation: A report of the commission on the future education of teachers.* Washington, DC: ATE and AACTE.

Raths, J. (1999). A consumer's guide to teacher standards. *Phi Delta Kappan,* October, 136-142.

Raths, J.D. and Katz, L.G. (1985). *Advances in teacher education.* Norwood, N.J. Ablex Publishing Corp.

Walberg, H. J. (1969). Training education professors for the future. To be a phoenix: The education professoriate. *Phi Delta Kappa, Inc.* 102–103.

Watts, D. (1984). Teacher educators should be certified. *Journal of Teacher Education*, 35, 30–33.

Wise, A. (1998). NCATE 2000 will emphasize candidate performance. *Quality Teaching*, 7(2), 1–2.

Wise, A. and Liebbrand, J. (2001). Standards in the new millennium: Where we are, where we're headed. *Journal of Teacher Education*, 52,3, 244–255.

Wisniewski, R. and Ducharme, E.R. (1998). *The professors of teaching: An inquiry*. Albany: State University of New York Press.

Walking Our Talk
as Educators
Teaming as a Best Practice

Terri L. Wenzlaff, Lorraine Berak, Katherine C. Wieseman, Ann Monroe-Baillargeon, Nancy Bacharach, and Paula Bradfield-Kreider

Terri L. Wenzlaff has been a high school classroom teacher and principal, K–12 curriculum director and district professional development director. She has taught at a Mid-West land grant university and currently is the Teacher Education Program Director at Western State College in Gunnison, Colorado.

Lorraine Berak has been an elementary classroom teacher, principal, and K–12 Curriculum & Staff Development Director. Prior to joining Central Michigan University where she is an Associate Professor, she owned a private consulting company. Her research focuses on effective teaching strategies, team development, integrative team planning and curriculum integration.

Katherine C. Wieseman, an Assistant Professor at Western State College, Colorado, formerly taught middle school science for eleven years in urban and international schools. Her research interests lie in standards-based curriculum reform, interdisciplinary approaches to education, and equity issues in science education, preservice teachers' ideas of the nature of science.

Ann Monroe-Baillargeon is an Assistant Professor in the Education Department of Nazareth College in Rochester, New York. She teaches primarily in the undergraduate dual certification program and works with local schools to provide faculty development. Her qualitative research continues to explore collaborative teaching relationships at all levels, elementary–higher education.

Nancy Bacharach is currently a professor in the Department of Teacher Development at St. Cloud State University in St. Cloud, Minnesota. Nancy's research interests lie in collaborative efforts in teaching and preparing teachers, multiage classroom structures and pedagogy, professional development schools, and alternative teacher licensure.

Paula Bradfield-Kreider was a classroom teacher for 14 years and currently is an associate Professor at St. Cloud State University. Her research interests include the culture of teaming, critical communities, and strategies to promote perceptual changes in teachers' abilities to advocate and provide meaningful learning environments for all children.

ABSTRACT

Reform in teacher education is necessary to meet the increasing array of standards used in teacher education programs. The Association of Teacher Educators (ATE) has described a vision for the qualities of master teacher educators—a set of seven standards for teacher educators that emphasize best practices, inquiry and scholarly activity, reflection, leadership and responsibility, collaboration, advocacy for excellence and equity, and improvement of the teacher education profession. Effective team teaching practices in teacher education can be a means for meeting the ATE standards. This manuscript presents ways that teaming practices model the ATE standards. Teaming is a way to improve teaching, learning, and contribute to the improvement of teacher education.

Introduction

Educational reform in teacher education is necessary to meet the changing needs of educators and to respond to an increasing array of standards used in developing teacher education programs. The Association of Teacher Educators (ATE) is one of several organizations (e.g., Interstate New Teacher Assessment and Support Consortium, National Board for Professional Teaching Standards, and the National Council for the Accreditation of Teacher Education) that have developed standards having implications for teacher education. ATE's vision for the qualities of master teacher educators are delineated as seven standards for teacher educators (ATE, 1998). The standards feature modeling of best teaching practices, inquiry and scholarly activity, reflection, leadership and responsibility, collaboration, advocacy for excellence and equity, and an orientation toward improvement of the teacher education profession. The complete standards are available in the Houston, et al. chapter in the book.

The purpose of this article is two-fold. Based on an interpretation of the literature that discusses terms related to teaming and its definitions, an operational definition of teaming is proffered. Second, the article provides a perspective on how current teaming practices in teacher education can be one way to enact the ATE Teacher Educator Standards and to demonstrate the qualities of master teacher educators.

We begin by establishing a need for research and discussion of this topic, exploring definitions and reviewing the literature on teaming in higher education. Then we briefly describe how teaming can promote the ATE teacher educator standards. The standards provide a methodological guide for organizing the data sources. We share four "stories" (data sources) about current teaming practices in teacher education. Preceding each story is a portrayal of specific ATE standards that emerged from analyzing the method of teaming in the story (results/conclusions). Each story communicates dilemmas and merits of teaming in higher education. The last section, Implications of Teaming and Standard 7, illuminates how teaming can serve as a significant way to improve teaching, learning and contribute to improving the teacher education profession.

We, the authors, represent a group of teacher educators who have engaged in teaming at our respective institutions. We propose that teaming in higher education can be one way of "walking our talk" to demonstrate the seven ATE standards.

The Importance of Teaming

Traditional teacher education may not be preparing teachers for the new roles they are being asked to assume. Increasing demands to teach students at a variety of learning levels and to respond to the social and psychological needs of all students (Pugach & Johnson, 1990) require changes in teacher education. The current reform movements necessitate that teachers learn new ways of teaching and unlearn some very familiar ways of working with students (Cohen, 1991). Davern and Schnorr (1991), Villa, Thousand, Stainback and Stainback (1992) and Warger and Pugach (1996) posited that one fundamental change in the role of teachers is through teacher collaboration. Monroe-Baillargeon (1999) found that teacher educators seeking to prepare professionals to meet the educational needs of an increasingly diverse student population must include learning opportunities in collaboration. Collaboration is no longer an optional part of school life but an essential feature (Villa, Thousand, Nevin, & Malgeri, 1996). We believe that collaboration is the foundation for teaming.

Teaming Terms and Definitions

The various definitions applied to the teaming concept can be confusing. Words used interchangeably in the literature include collaboration, "collaborative teaching" (Angle, 1996), "co-teaching" (Dieker & Barnett, 1996) "team teaching" (Pugach & Wesson, 1995) and "collegiality" (Little, 1990). Friend and Cook (1996) defined collaboration as "a style of direct interaction between at least two co-equal parties voluntarily engaged in shared decision making as they work toward a common goal" (p. 6). Pugach and Johnson (1995) provided a more fluid definition of collaboration—a collection of activities that exist along a continuum spanning the range from teachers developing solutions together to specialists prescribing solutions in the infrequent instances when unique expertise is needed. Trump and Miller (1973) defined co-teaching "as an arrangement in which two or more teachers plan, instruct, and evaluate in one or more subject areas using a variety of technical aids to teaching and learning" (p. 354). Co-teaching is more than putting two teachers together and expecting them to deliver content. Team teaching is not an end result, but is a process involving teachers working together from the beginning planning stage to the end effort (Woodward, 1990).

Based on a synthesis of the definitions encountered in the literature, we propose an operational definition for teaming:

> Two or more individuals (educators) who come together in a collaborative relationship for the purpose of shared work and for the outcome of achieving what none could have done alone. These individuals bring to the process and the relationship their areas of expertise and experience. The values of shared decision-making and interdependence form the foundation for the shared work.

Forms of Teaming in Higher Education

Teaming in teacher education focuses on collaboration between professors in higher education and/or partnerships between institutions of higher education and K–12 schools. Teaming in teacher education can generally be characterized in two models. The first model is one in which isolated teaching and team teaching are used concurrently to integrate content and explore common strategies across courses. In this model, professors teach their specific courses at a commonly scheduled time. At regularly scheduled intervals, the professors and students meet to explore the integration of content area knowledge and to examine pedagogical knowledge common across the topics of instruction (Bakken, Clark & Thompson, 1998; McDaniel & Colarulli, 1997; Wilson & Martin, 1998). In this model, the professors collaboratively plan, implement and evaluate a course outline for the topics covered in the individual courses and determine the content and pedagogy of the shared classes.

The advantages identified by faculty who have used this model, the "dispersed team model" (McDaniel & Colarulli, 1997), include mentoring, sharing expertise, reflective teaching and expanding instructional practices. These authors have claimed that this model is one way to make teaming in higher education cost effective. The disadvantages of this model for faculty is an increase in planning time and a need for shared philosophies, open communication and flexibility.

A second model of teaming in teacher education is one in which two professors co-teach two related courses simultaneously (Davis-Wiley & Cozart, 1998; Winn, Messelheimer-Young, 1995). Both professors are involved in ongoing planning, teaching and evaluation of the courses. They are present at each class meeting, although at times one may lead the instruction while the other adds comments. At other times, both instructors may co-teach the entire lesson.

Due to the increased amount of time collaborating, all of the advantages identified in the dispersed team model are increased in this model. Professors have more opportunity to provide mentorship while learning through reflective teaching. Likewise, the disadvantages are greater. As the amount of time spent in co-planning and evaluation is increased, the need for developing and maintaining an effective collaborative relationship is critical.

In the isolated teaching of courses students often construct fragmented knowledge bases and seemingly make little or no connection between information presented in different courses. The greatest advantage of both models is that co-taught courses can provide students with a broader content knowledge base (Preskill, 1995) and a clearer relationship between theory and practice (Lenn and Hatch, 1992). In teacher education the integration of content area knowledge and pedagogical knowledge is critical for student success and development of their pedagogical content knowledge.

Teaming as a Way of Promoting the ATE Teacher Educator Standards

Based on the operational definition of teaming stated earlier, teaming is one way to promote the ATE teacher educator standards. The following subsections denote overall themes found in the stories (data sources) pertinent to the standards. The process of generating each story is consistent with Guba and Lincoln's (1989) idea of the "hermeneutic cycle." While all four stories reflect all of the ATE Teacher Educator Standards, each story exposes one or two standards more than others.

ATE Standard 1   Teaming provides a natural vehicle to *model best practice.* Teacher educators can model integration across curricular areas because they are engaged in it, and preservice teachers learn how to engage in integrated instruction because they are immersed in it (see Lorraine's story).

ATE Standard 2   Teaming provides a unique perspective on *scholarship.* Scholarly inquiry into how teaming is modeled and how teacher educators with diverse perspectives collaborate can serve as a basis for scholarship. This process has the potential to impact and broaden the perceptions held by preservice teachers (see the Lorraine, and Katherine/Terri stories).

ATE Standard 3   The accountability of working within a team increases awareness of *professional growth,* perceptual and conceptual gaps, and how culture, first language, gender and sexual orientation contribute uniquely to the work of educators and growth of teamwork. Notions of our own practice broaden as team members bring diverse perspectives to a teaming interaction (see Nancy and Katherine/Terri stories).

ATE Standard 4   Teaming can be a strong way to embrace *diversity* when educators model how they resolve differences in a respectful and accepting manner. The foundations of a strong teaming relationship welcome diverse perspectives (see Ann/Joan's story).

ATE Standard 5   Teacher educators who team value *collaboration across educational entities.* They can contribute to work done at various levels such as schools, state education agencies, professional associations and communities (see Ann/Joan's story).

ATE Standard 6   An effective team can advocate for *high quality education* for students. A team with multiple knowledge bases is able to model a variety of best practices leading to excellence and equity in education (see Nancy's story).

ATE Standard 7   The intent and purpose of this standard, improvement of teacher education, is inherent in each of the stories that follows. This standard is more explicitly addressed in the implications section of this chapter.

Lorraine's Story

The story reflects the heart of *modeling professional teaching practices that demonstrate knowledge, skills, and attitudes reflecting the best available practices in teacher education* (Standard 1). Within the story teacher educators integrate curriculum to encourage critical thinking and problem solving and use a variety of instructional methods matching learning objectives with student needs. *Inquiring into and contributing to one or more areas of scholarly activity that are related to teaching, learning, and/or teacher education* (Standard 2) is evident in course development as a response to broaden the perceptions held by students.

Beginning Journey to Integration and Teaming

"I really liked how these courses were integrated. It made it easier to see how the courses connected. The three instructors worked well together and made the class fun."

"I really liked the practice and teaching of integrating each subject. This is going to be a very helpful tool when I do get to the classroom."

"The integrated part of the course was very beneficial. All three of the instructors provided extended knowledge in other content areas."

These quotes are from three students who participated in an integrative semester of course work, the basis for this story. Before this semester my colleagues and I had been preaching about best practices including integration, collaboration, cooperative learning, interdisciplinary curriculum approaches, and thematic lessons, but we rarely modeled these strategies in our university classrooms.

The impetus for implementing this integrative semester was, as a response to the NCATE standards, a request that faculty model best professional practices in teaching. At the time, I was working with an elementary education program that was part of a consortium of colleges and universities providing undergraduate degree programs to people who were unable to relocate and finish a degree on campus. It occurred to me that these students would profit from a newly designed integrative approach. I asked two other faculty members to participate in integrating and delivering their courses as a team.

With a bit of trepidation, lots of questions, and great enthusiasm we started our planning process. As we all embraced constructivist principles, we considered our task a "work in progress." We learned more about each other than we ever thought possible during many meetings. To our surprise we discovered our philosophies varied about almost everything! Headed for defeat, we sought solutions for the emerging problems. We employed strategies such as brainstorming, curriculum mapping, venn diagramming, conflict resolution strategies, and humor. Retrospectively, this aspect of the process was extremely frustrating, but worthwhile.

By the end of our planning period we had: identified a name for our new course, designed a syllabus, identified key questions, coordinated assignments, discussed assessment practices, developed a course rubric, designed a process for student input, and mapped out key concepts. Additionally, we adopted the use of a lesson plan template to be used planning our weekly lessons. With determination and a feeling of accomplishment, we were ready to face the students.

We agreed to attend all classes when possible. The students were thrilled with the team taught course although a bit confused. Questions such as: "Who is really the teacher?" "How are you going to grade?" "What do you mean you want us to have input into what we are going to study?" were the focus of the first class session. To help the students feel more connected and secure we assigned them a "teacher email buddy" who dialogued with a specified group of students.

In addition to participating in all class sessions, we met before and/or after each class to modify, adjust, and reflect on events that occurred while teaching. We learned that flexibility was a key component for success and that we could not integrate everything. We also decided to let the students "see" us disagree in a professional way when we had different viewpoints, a strategy many students noted in the final evaluation as being very positive.

We constantly worried about "covering our content" and students not getting all our "pearls of wisdom." This fear was unfounded because students actually learned all they needed to learn as was evidenced by their exams, final projects, actual classroom teaching and their journal reflections. We all profited by hearing the major concepts presented in each other's class sessions, by watching different styles of teaching, and observing students' perceptions as we interacted with the students. Most importantly, we were able to change our paradigm about what we believed was the way our classes had to be taught.

Nancy's Story

In this story faculty members are *inquiring systematically into, and reflecting on, their own practice and demonstrating commitment to lifelong professional development* (Standard 3). Learning to team with faculty possessing different perspectives contributed to becoming *informed, constructively critical advocates for high-quality education for all students, public understanding of educational issues, and excellence and diversity in the teaching and teacher education profession* (Standard 6).

Excellence Through Different Perspectives The university where I work received a grant to merge a regular and special education teacher preparation program. One major hallmark of this program was that teaming occur in over 75% of the coursework. The goal was to have a regular and special education professor work together on the planning, teaching, and evaluating of as many courses as possible. Prior to this program, the two departments, although located in the same building, rarely interacted with each other. This new program provided the opportunity to cross the invisible, yet amazingly strong, boundaries that separated us.

As a teacher education faculty member, I teamed with a faculty member from the special education department. With the charge of teaming a course, my special education colleague and I began planning. We were very tentative, each of us afraid of putting forth an idea. Our background differences, one constructivist and one behavioral, were evident as we talked about what we each felt was essential for the students to know. By prioritizing, we were able to choose the most important elements for the syllabus.

While each of us took the "lead" for a specific topic, we agreed to attend every class session and to participate as fully as possible. The first few class periods were nerve-wracking. I was used to being the "professor" by myself. Another faculty member in the room made me conscious of every word, question, and experience I provided the class; my partner was also hesitant. However, barriers were broken through an invitation to comment or student questions. As it became evident that we respected each other's ideas/thoughts, the class began to be "our" class. By mid-quarter, we felt comfortable sharing the teaching and by the end of the quarter, it seemed as if we could almost finish each other's sentences.

A partner's presence and contributions has made me a better teacher. It has forced me to think through different perspectives. Even now I ask myself how my special education colleague would comment about a topic. I have experienced great professional growth and increased understanding of the "other" discipline. While I have benefited from teaming, the biggest beneficiaries have been the students. At times, they felt confused and torn between two divergent perspectives, but they emerged with more knowledge and an ability to look at issues from multiple paradigms. They also benefited from having teaming modeled for them, rather than just being discussed.

Katherine/Terri's Story

This story highlights a relationship between Standards Two and Three. Standard Two is prevalent through course revisions that address students' perceptions, ATE presentations and scholarly writing about teaming. The identification of a metaphor is evidence of a commitment to reflection, inherent in Standard Three. The metaphor of a marriage is used to describe the evolving relationship of teaming partners.

Teaming Is Like a Marriage Metaphor is not only is a powerful way to integrate one's understanding but it is also a way to express this understanding. After pondering several possibilities, the Katherine and Terri team agreed that teaming is like a marriage. Both are relationships that, for there to be harmony, "success" and growth, demand a structurally sound and well intertwined network of qualities. These qualities need to be part of the persona of each individual and include open-mindedness, patience, responsibility, respect, trust, communication, and a commitment to interdependence.

No one marriage is like another. Likewise each teaming relationship is unique. The Katherine and Terri team is certainly different from other teaming relationships of which we have been members during our years of being teacher educators. We credit the uniqueness of this teaming relationship to the differences in our life experiences, personalities, areas of expertise, professional experience in higher education and position in the tenure hierarchy, professional responsibilities and teaching philosophies.

We believe that a marriage is a response to needs in one's personal life, such as companionship, convenience, love, and/or the perpetuation of power. One enters into a marriage with some form of a dowry, traditionally as material wealth. As time passes, and influenced by the partners' choices, the marriage evolves. Likewise, needs in one's professional life provide an origin for teaming. A shared value of interdependence, a desire for mentoring, and professional development goals are some needs in the professional realm that can lead to teaming.

The Katherine and Terri team came into existence in 1998 for the purpose of teaching a curriculum design and assessment course for secondary preservice teachers. Katherine had recently obtained a doctorate in science education. Her experiences had been in a department in which the dominant culture emphasized individualism. She valued interdependence, collaboration, and the idea of a community of learners. When Katherine became a faculty member in a department of teacher education, she wanted to promote these values and desired to be mentored. Terri, a more experienced member of the higher education world, chair of thè teacher education program and instructor of the course, was willing to mentor the new faculty member and team the course. Because this responsibility was not part of Terri's already full load of administrative and teaching duties, she felt that she could not always be there and often felt like she didn't know the students or was not connected to the course content.

In the fall of 2000, the course became part of Terri's load. We have a more equitable sense of ownership and commitment to the teaming relationship. We are constantly revising course content and materials and teaching strategies in order to update our instruction. We model how curriculum development and teaching can be improved by, in class sessions with our students, making public aspects of our planning process. The teaming relationship is giving us opportunities to inquire systematically into and reflect on our practices. We work closely with high school teachers and secondary preservice teachers to plan interdisciplinary units taught by the secondary preservice teachers. One outcome of this partnership has been professional growth and a strong sense of collegiality among teachers, preservice teachers and teacher educators. Another outcome is that we and the high school teachers submitted a manuscript about the K-16 teaming and interdisciplinary planning and teaching process and made conference presentations.

Ann/Joan's Story

The two individuals comprising this team *provide leadership in developing, implementing and evaluating programs for educating teachers that embrace diversity, and are rigorous, relevant, and grounded in accepted theory, research and best practice* (Standard 4). This college-school partnership is the story of educators who *collaborate regularly and in significant ways with representatives of schools, universities, state education agencies, professional associations, and communities to improve teaching, learning and teacher education* (Standard 5).

Story at School #50 This story of professional collaboration involves a teacher education department and School #50 in Rochester, New York. The story began with a much more personal connection, a collaborative relationship between the two individuals who represent these institutions, myself a professor in teacher education and Joan, an instructional support teacher at School #50. This story is about the integration of the professional and personal elements of our collaboration. Our professional relationship with ever changing characteristics of the people involved has evolved over time. It has also been affected by the dynamic contexts in which we work.

The framework for our relationship was established before I arrived. My predecessor forged a collaborative relationship with School #50 in the creation of a site based teacher education program. When my predecessor retired, Joan was asked to be a member of the interview team. I remember vividly the uncertainty that I felt when she, an unknown individual to me, walked into the room for my interview. Joan's role on the team clearly was to determine if I was to be her next teaching partner. Her affirmation determined the future of our collaborative relationship.

As a new faculty member I learned the depth of the partnership between my predecessor and Joan. My challenge was to earn Joan's trust. As part of the trust building process we met several times before the beginning of the semester to plan our classes and to familiarize me with the culture of School #50.

As I began my collaborative teaching at School #50 I felt confident that our planning meetings had successfully established a strong relational foundation. I was soon to discover that although my primary teaching relationship was with the teacher, a broader collaborative relationship was with the school. Under the watchful eye of the school librarian, in whose space I was teaching, I realized that my professional content knowledge and pedagogical skills exposed to scrutiny as well as the quality of my institution. This burden seemed at times a heavy load to bear. Through mutual positive praise and a shared commitment to quality teacher education, Joan and I nurtured our collaborative relationship. We have come to understand that our collaboration affords us the opportunity to provide students with learning opportunities that neither of us could have provided alone.

The elements of our relationship make it work; we value each other professionally. We seek each other's input on our individual teaching and collaboratively discuss and critique students' progress as well as our own. When discussing the class and the students' understanding of the content, we also discuss each other's presence and the need to provide opportunities for the other to interject. We each value having the other in the room because it gives us an opportunity to give and receive objective feedback. This situation points to the importance of checking in about the relationship even after years of working together.

We have not allowed the walls of our classroom to limit our learning. Presenting what we have learned at teacher education conferences has provided us an unmatched time to talk, laugh, and dream about our program. We care for each other professionally and respect the tenuous balance of our multiple roles as educators and mothers. Now, I cannot imagine preparing pre-service teachers in any other way.

Implications of Teaming and Standard 7

While teaming is not new to the teacher education community and is often touted as a best practice, we rarely observe it in practice or discuss how it can *contribute to improving the teacher education profession* (Standard 7). Based on the emergent themes from the stories, we recommend that teacher educators go beyond talking about teaming. Teacher educators must be committed to and model teaming so preservice teachers observe and experience forms of team planning and teaching.

In order for a teaming relationship to be successful, teacher educators must demonstrate respect, sensitivity, flexibility, and compromise. Additionally, we must research the effect that teaming has on pre-service teacher attitudes and future practices. We have learned that teaming is difficult. It is not rewarded by tenure and promotion committees and is often not provided for in faculty loads. Despite these challenges, we believe that it is a way to contribute to improving teacher education as a profession as well as a way for walking our talk as educators.

REFERENCES

Angle, B. (1996). Five steps to collaborative teaching and enrichment education. *Exceptional Children, 29*(1), 8–10.

Association of Teacher Educators. (1998). *ATE Standards for Teacher Educators.* [Online]. Available: http://www.siu.eduldepartments/coe/ate/atestand.html

Bakken, L., Clark, F. & Thompson, J. (1998). Collaborative teaching: Many joys, some surprises, and a few worms. *College Teaching, 46*(4), 154–57.

Cohen, D. K. (1991). Revolution in one classroom (or then again, was it?). *American Educator,* Fall, 17–23.

Davern, L., & Schnorr, R. (1991). Public schools welcome students with disabilities as full members. *Children Today, 20*(2), 21–25.

Davis-Wiley, P., & Cozart, A. (1998, November). *Are two instructors better than one? Planning. Teaching and Evaluating a Deux.* Paper presented at the Mid-South Educational Research Association, New Orleans, LA.

Dieker, L., & Barnett, C. (1996). *Effective co-teaching. Teaching Exceptional Children, 29,* 5–7.

Friend, M., & Cook, L. (1996). *Interactions: Collaboration skills for school professionals* (2nd ed.). White Plains: Longman.

Guba, E.G., & Lincoln, Y.S. (1989). *Fourth generation evaluation.* Thousand Oaks: Sage Publications.

Lenn, E., & Hatch, J. (1992). *Making a kindergarten methods course make more sense: A teacher and professor team up.* Paper presented at the National Association for the Education of Young Children, New Orleans, LA (ERIC Document Reproduction Service No. ED 352 189).

Little, J. W. (1990). The persistence of privacy: Autonomy and initiative in teachers' professional relations. *Teachers College Record, 91*(4), 509–536.

McDaniel, E., & Colarulli, G. (1997). Teaching in the face of productivity concerns: The dispersed team model. *Innovative Higher Education, 22*(1), 19–36.

Monroe-Baillargeon, A. (1999). *Depending on others: A qualitative study of collaborative teaching teams in inclusive classrooms.* Unpublished Dissertation, Syracuse University, Syracuse, NY.

Preskill, H. (1995, March). *Using critical incidents in teaching HRD: A method for fostering critical reflection and dialogue.* Paper presented at the Academy of Human Resource Development, St. Louis, MO.

Pugach, M., & Wesson, C. (199S). Teachers' and students' views of team teaching of general education and learning disabled students in two fifth-grade classes. *The Elementary School Journal, 95*(3), 279–295.

Pugach, M. C., & Johnson, L. J. (1990). Meeting diverse needs through professional peer collaboration. In W. Stainback, & S. Stainback (Eds.), *Support networks for inclusive schooling* (pp. 123–138). Baltimore, MD: Paul H. Brookes.

Pugach, M. C., & Johnson, L. J. (1995). *Collaborative practitioners, collaborative schools.* Denver, CO: Love.

Trump, J. L., & Miller, D. F. (1973). *Secondary school curriculum improvement.* Boston, MA: Allyn and Bacon.

Villa, R. A., Thousand, J. S., Stainback, W., & Stainback, S. (1992). *Restructuring for caring and effective education.* Baltimore, MD: Brookes.

Villa, R. A., Thousand, J. S., Nevin, A. I., & Malgeri, C. (1996). Instilling collaboration for inclusive schooling as a new way of doing business in public schools. *Remedial and Special Education, 17,* 169–182.

Warger, C. L., & Pugach, M. C. (1996). Forming partnerships around curriculum. *Educational Leadership, Vol. 53,* 62–65.

Wilson, V. A., & Martin, K. M. (1998, February). *Practicing what we preach.* Paper presented at the Association of Teacher Educators, Dallas, Texas.

Winn, J., & Messenheimer-Young, T. (1995). Team teaching at the university level: What we have learned. *Teacher Education and Special Education, 18,* 223–29.

Woodward, R. (1990). The teacher trainer: A practical journal mainly for the modern language teacher trainers. *The Teacher Trainer, 4,* 13–15.

National Standards for Teacher Educators
The Story of Two Nations[1]

W. Robert Houston, J. Jurriën Dengerink, Robert Fisher, Bob Koster, and D. John McIntyre

W. Robert Houston is Professor, Moores University Scholar, and Executive Director of the Institute for Urban Education, College of Education, University of Houston. He is editor of the first edition of the *Handbook of Research on Teacher Education*, Past president of the Association of Teacher Educators (ATE), and Chair of the Commission on Teacher Educator Standards. In 1997 he was honored as ATE's first Distinguished Teacher Educator.

Jurriën Dengerink worked for a short time as history teacher in secondary education. Since 1981, he has served as an internal consultant for cooperation projects in the field of higher education and for the administration and management of teacher education institutes. He is currently with the Free University in Amsterdam. He is one of the coordinators of the national Dutch project "Towards a Standard For and Registration of Teacher Educators."

---

[1]The authors are indebted to members of the Commission, all of whom are co-authors of the description of the work on the American standards over a nine-year period. Members of the Commission were: Robert Alley, Wichita State University; Susan Arisman, Frostburg State University; Beverly Busching, University of South Carolina; Evelyn DiTosto, College of Notre Dame of Maryland; Sheliah Allen Dorton, Gaston, Indiana; Rose Duhon-Sells, Southern University; Roy Edelfelt, University of North Carolina; Richard E. Ishler, University of South Carolina; Leonard Kaplan, Wayne State University; Phyllis H. Lamb, University of Toledo; Dale Scannell, Indiana University-Purdue University-Indianapolis; and Joseph Vaughan, U. S. Department of Education.

Robert L Fisher is Professor of Education at Illinois State University. His specialty areas are the education of teachers and school/university partnerships. He has worked with NCATE, National Science Teachers Association, and the state of Illinois in the development of standards for teachers.

Bob Koster worked as a social science teacher in secondary education for twelve years. During that time he supervised student teachers during their teaching practice. Since 1992, he has worked as a teacher educator, educating student teachers during their post-graduate university teacher education program. He also educates groups of teacher educators in supervision skills and works on a thesis with the subject 'Competencies of teacher educators'. He is one of the coordinators of the national Dutch project "Towards a Standard For and Registration of Teacher Educators."

D. John McIntyre is Professor in the Department of Curriculum and Instruction and Associate Dean for Teacher Education and School Partnerships at Southern Illinois University Carbondale. He is a Past President and Distinguished Member of ATE. His research interests are in the area of teacher development and field and clinical experiences.

S tandards have become the hallmark of products, professionals, services, and just about everything in modern life. They form the basis for the school curriculum, for teacher licenses, and for the organization of schools and universities. Agencies such as state departments of education and the Southern Association of Colleges and Schools monitor schools on the basis of standards; the National Council for the Accreditation of Teacher Education (NCATE) accredits teacher education based on standards. The Interstate New Teacher Assessment and Support Consortium (INTASC) has identified assessments for first-year teachers and is working with states to implement standards and assessments. The National Board of Professional Teaching Standards (NBPTS) has specified standards for master teachers. Professional associations and learned societies linked with the Alliance for Curriculum Reform have developed standards (both content- and pedagogy-based) that apply both to PK–12 students and to new and experienced teachers. A number of states are aligning their efforts with national standards (primarily NBPTS, INTASC and NCATE) in specifying standards for teacher licensure.

These and all other standards were developed and honed based on some conceptual basis by an association or agency that supported their development and later publicized their usefulness. The validity of any set of standards depends upon the process upon which they are developed, their relevance and usefulness to those being assessed, the purpose of the assessment, and the value placed on them by all those involved.

It was inevitable that the standards movement would be applied to those who educate teachers for the classrooms in which other standards are being applied. This is the story of two sets of standards for teacher educators, one developed in the United States and the other in Holland. Their design and conceptual basis, the processes that guided their development, studies conducted, and their ultimate design provide useful insights into the process by which standards in any area are generated.

The Association of Teacher Educators (ATE) explored standards for teacher educators and their use in certification beginning in 1992 with the appointment of a national Task Force on the certification of master teacher educators and continued through 2000 with the publication of a set of standards for teacher educators. In Holland, the national office of education began exploring standards for teacher educators in 1997, basing in part their standards and development on those already used by ATE.

The American Story

Teachers are licensed by the state in which they teach and may demonstrate advanced knowledge and skills through national professional certification by the National Board for Professional Teaching Standards. Teacher educators are responsible for teaching these teachers yet are not certified by any review body.

WHO ARE TEACHER EDUCATORS?

Teacher educators are identified as those educators who provide formal instruction or conduct research and development for educating prospective and practicing teachers. Teacher educators provide the professional education component of preservice programs and the staff development component of inservice programs. Teacher educators may be categorized as:

- Faculty in higher education who provide course work and conduct research as described by NCATE as professional studies, including clinical experiences
- Personnel in schools who provide instruction or supervision of clinical experiences of prospective teachers
- Personnel in schools who administer or conduct instructional activities designed to provide advanced professional study for teachers

- Personnel from other agencies who design, implement, and evaluate professional study for teachers (e.g., state department certification officers, U.S. Department of Education personnel, researchers in R&D centers, and professional association leaders).

The development of standards for teacher educators has helped to distinguish the role of teacher educators from the role of other professionals in the education of teachers. Presentations about the ATE Standards for Teacher Educators have always generated intense discussions that begin with a broad interpretation of the term. For example, everyone agrees that the college instructors who teach content courses for prospective elementary teachers have a high level of influence on what those future teachers will do in teaching those disciplines to young children. Subsequent discussion then distinguishes the role of this individual from the university professor who engages the future teacher in planning and implementing instruction in the classroom. The content instructor is not expected to conduct research in the field of teaching, conduct workshops for teachers on how to teach, or attend ATE conferences.

EXPLORATION OF PROFESSIONAL CERTIFICATION

The Task Force spent its first year studying professional certification. It distinguished between a *license,* which is a permit to teach issued by state agencies, and *certification,* which is a recognition of special expertise by professional bodies. The standards and processes of other professional groups were explored, and a process adopted to study and make recommendations concerning certification of teacher educators.

An early decision was made to focus on certification, not licensure, and to recognize expert teacher educators—persons with recognized contributions to the development of teacher education as well as of teachers—rather than initial certification of teacher educators. The certification is comparable to the *diplomate* in some fields, membership in Academies in science and medicine, and the *master teacher* described in the National Board for Professional Teacher Standards.

Several principles guided the early work of the Task Force. First, this certification should be desirable and voluntary. Second, it should recognize that the expertise of teacher educators goes beyond that of teachers and requires specialized study on the education of teachers. Third, it should apply to teacher educators employed in a wide range of institutions (e.g., schools, universities, state and national agencies, private firms, and research organizations). Fourth, such certification should apply to those teacher educators who contribute to any phase of teacher development including preservice preparation and inservice education. Fifth, standards and criteria should contribute to both assessment and assistance.

The Task Force decided that it was more important in its initial efforts to focus on the development of the standards and how they could be used by teacher educators in addition to their use as a certification system.

Development of Standards

The Task Force considered different strategies for developing the standards, finally deciding that a set of standards would be developed by the Task Force and then circulated to the professional community for comment. The initial draft of the standards were conceptualized during the fall 1993, formulated at the ATE Conference in February 1994, and refined during the following months. Eight standards were identified as hallmarks of the proficient teacher educator.

DELPHI STUDY OF INITIAL SET OF STANDARDS

In October 1994, the first round of a Delphi was mailed to a number of distinguished educators, inviting them to participate in the development of standards for teacher educators. Over one hundred responded with recommendations that greatly strengthened the entire enterprise.

The second round of the Delphi, mailed in November 1994, included revised standards from the first round. As part of the second round, participants rated the eight standards in terms of importance. To assure variability among standards already judged to be important, a *forced-choice rating system* was devised in which respondents distributed ratings as follows on a five-point scale:

> Two of the standards could be rated 5
> One of the standards could be rated 4
> Two of the standards could be rated 3
> One of the standards could be rated 2
> Two of the standards could be rated 1

Table 1 lists the draft standards that were reviewed by the respondents, the mean rating, and the rank.

TABLE 1

Draft Standards for American Teacher Educators

Standard	Mean Rating	Rank
Master Teacher Educators		
1. Model exemplary professional teaching practices.	3.81	2
2. Inquire into one or more areas of scholarly interest that expand the knowledge base for teaching, learning, and/or teacher education.	2.92	6
3. Demonstrate the knowledge, skills, and attitudes reflecting the best available research and exemplary practice in teaching and teacher education.	4.23	1
4. Inquire systematically into, and reflect on, their own practice and demonstrate commitment to lifelong professional development.	3.04	5
5. Provide leadership in developing, implementing, and evaluating programs for educating teachers that embrace diversity, and are rigorous, relevant, and grounded in accepted theory and research.	3.35	4
6. Collaborate regularly and in significant ways with school, university, state education department, professional associations, and community representatives to improve teaching, learning, and teacher education.	3.56	4
7. Serve as informed constructively critical advocates for high quality education for all students, public understanding of educational issues, and excellence and diversity in the teaching and teacher education professions.	2.27	7
8. Contribute to improving the teacher education profession.	1.58	8

The second round of the Delphi also included draft indicators, evidence, and modes of assessment for each standard. Participants were asked to review the revised standards and sharpen the listing of (a) indicators of proficiency for master teacher educators on each standard, (b) evidence that would support proficiency, and (c) the modes by which proficiency would be assessed. These became the first iteration of revised standards, indicators, acceptable evidence, and modes of assessment.

A preliminary report of findings, *Certification of Teacher Educators* (published in February 1995) provided the substance for a long working session by the ATE Delegate Assembly. The Delegate Assembly voted to accept the standards in principle and charged the Task Force to continue refining standards, hold open hearings during the following year across the country, and explore ways to extend the standards.

OPEN HEARINGS AND CONFERENCES

The standards gained considerable national attention during the following two years through open hearings, presentations at national meetings, and articles in the national press. The initial set of standards was analyzed by a series of open hearings and conferences. Educators analyzed the standards in ten state open hearings, including Arkansas, California, Georgia, Iowa, Kansas, Louisiana, Michigan, New York, Texas, and Virginia. ATE's Board of Directors and its Delegate Assembly analyzed the standards and the process by which they were developed during 1995 and 1996. Presentations were made at the National Association of State Directors of Teacher Education and Certification Conference, ATE annual meeting, and the American Association of College for Teacher Education conference during 1995 and 1996. The standards were publicized nationally in three articles: "ATE Circulates First Draft National Standards For Master Teacher Educators," *Teacher Education Reports,* March 9, 1996; "Final Report Issued by ATE Task Force on Certification of Teacher Educators," *Teacher Education Reports,* May 2, 1996; and "Teacher educators implored to "lead" in improving training," *Education Week.*

Through these public examinations, the standards were subjected to intense review, resulting in a series of positive and negative attributes that are summarized in Table 2.

BROADENED MISSION

Based on findings in these hearings, ATE expanded the mission of Task Force in February 1996. The new Commission on Teacher Educator

TABLE 2

Attributes of Standards

Positive Attributes of Standards and National Certification

1. The concept of certification for teacher educators is worthwhile and important. It can only help to "professionalize" teacher education.

2. The definition of teacher educator as involving research, practice, education, and experiences is appropriate.

3. These standards as a means of standard-setting can be very useful to department chairs, deans, and teacher educators themselves. They can help develop an academy but probably will not have a measurable effect on prestige of the profession.

4. Can be helpful in tenure and/or promotion decisions.

5. Voluntary aspect is important.

6. Indicators and evidence are broad and encompassing. Well-written and well-envisioned document.

7. Standards appear thorough and comprehensive.

8. Process puts us in a similar situation to new teachers as they undergo review for licensure and certification.

9. Process will service to hold us accountable to our students, our critics, and ourselves.

10. They establish expectations for quality performance.

11. They publicly recognize excellence in a variety of agreed-upon dimensions of quality.

12. They recognize the distinctiveness of the teacher educator.

Negative Attributes of Standards and National Certification

1. Teacher educators from small colleges could not meet these standards because of too many responsibilities, time and monetary constraints.

2. More emphasis is needed on involvement and collaboration with PK–12 educators.

(continued on next page)

TABLE 2 (continued)

3. Cooperating teachers whose primary role is not teacher education yet spend 1/2 or more of the school year working with preservice teachers would not have the opportunity to earn the Master Teacher Educator title.

4. Process of certification appears very time consuming and demanding; documentation will involve much paperwork.

5. Not enough emphasis on the teacher educator's relationship with the preservice teacher.

6. Egalitarian stance of teacher educators is opposed to another stratification level for educators; is divisive, may be used as employment criteria, and adds one more level of bureaucracy to being a professional educator.

7. This process puts in place a "bookkeeping" mentality.

8. Standards appear to represent the status quo rather than the dynamic and changing roles of teacher educators, including the redefinition of exemplary practice because of alternate educational systems.

9. Although definition of teacher educator lists possible inclusion of inservice agencies and state department people, the standards are tailored for research institutions.

10. Fear that standards would become mandatory by some states, and institutions would be forced to adhere to them.

11. Certification is not accepted by the academic community in universities, therefore this certification moves teacher education out of the academy and into the ranks of practitioners.

12. Standards constrain individualism and creativity.

Standards focused less on certification of master teacher educators and more on the standards by which teacher educators could be assessed. Activities included refining the standards based on input and assessments, a simulation involving the standards, a national conference on teacher education standards, a broadly distributed brochure on the ATE standards, and a national award for a Distinguished Teacher Educator to be presented each year by ATE.

REFINED STANDARDS

During their development, strong and consistent recommendations resulted in two major changes in the standards. One standard was deleted, most were edited for clarity, and their purpose was broadened beyond certification to include teacher educator initial and advanced study, awards and honors, and job descriptions. The current Standards for Teacher Educators are listed in Table 3.

TABLE 3

Current American Standards for Teacher Educators

1. Model professional teaching practices which demonstrate knowledge, skills, and attitudes reflecting the best available practices in teacher education.

2. Inquire into and contribute to one or more areas of scholarly activity that are related to teaching, learning, and/or teacher education.

3. Inquire systematically into, and reflect on, their own practice and demonstrate commitment to lifelong professional development.

4. Provide leadership in developing, implementing, and evaluating programs for educating teachers that embrace diversity, and are rigorous, relevant, and grounded in accepted theory, research, and best practice.

5. Collaborate regularly and in significant ways with school, university, state education department, professional associations, and community representatives to improve teaching, learning, and teacher education.

6. Serve as informed, constructively critical advocates for high quality education for all students, public understanding of educational issues, and excellence and diversity in the teaching and teacher education professions.

7. Contribute to improving the teacher education profession.

To provide further definition to each of the standards, Commission members compiled lists of indicators of achievement and potential sources of evidence for each standard. Table 4 lists the standard, indicators, and sources of evidence for Standard 1. The full set of standards, indicators, and sources is found on the ATE Web site at *http://www.siu.edu/~ate/standards/atestand.html*.

TABLE 4

Illustrative Standard for Teacher Educators, Indicators and Sources of Evidence

Master Teacher Educators:
Model professional teaching practices which demonstrate knowledge, skills, and attitudes reflecting the best available practices in teacher education.

Indicators	Potential Sources of Evidence
Master Teacher Educators • Model effective instruction, reflection, and evaluation for prospective and practicing teachers. • Demonstrate and encourage critical thinking and problem solving among teacher educators, teachers, and prospective teachers. • Promote practices that enhance both an understanding of diversity and instruction that meets the needs of society. • Regularly revise courses taught to incorporate recent materials, including technology.	• Evaluations and/or statements from students, peers, and supervisors • Video and/or audio tapes of teaching • List of courses taught, with syllabus and assessment of each course, block, or series of activities • Instructional materials developed • Testimonials of mentoring of peers, current students, or former students • Teaching awards, recognition

(continued on next page)

TABLE 4 (continued)	
Indicators	Potential Sources of Evidence
• Consciously encourage and challenge students to be reflective practitioners.	• Documentation of changes in teaching based on recent findings from research and practice
• Use a variety of innovative instructional methods; matching learning objectives with student needs and appropriate teaching strategies.	• Logs or other written evidence of activities in classrooms during past two years
• Mentor novice teachers and teacher educators.	• Journals of reflective examination of own practice
• Apply specialized knowledge and processes of inquiry which are central to teacher education.	• Documentation of effectiveness of past students as model teachers
• Interpret developmental phases of becoming a teacher in a culturally and economically diverse society.	• Scores on tests of knowledge of central concepts in teacher education and subject matter of candidate's discipline
• Demonstrate an understanding of the influence of school context and culture upon teacher education.	• Written philosophical statement that reflects underlying knowledge and values of teacher education
• Demonstrate currency of knowledge regarding issues critical to education, and especially teacher education.	• Courses, experiences, case studies that reflect the best research and exemplary practice
	• Video or audio tapes of presentations, teaching episodes, or other experiences that reflect best research and exemplary practice
	• Other evidence as appropriate to the candidate's role and responsibilities

Use of the Standards

Once the standards were developed, the Commission recognized the need not only to publish the standards, but also to identify ways for the standards to be used to influence the education, function, and evaluation of teacher educators.

SIMULATION BASED ON STANDARDS

To help teacher educators examine the variety of purposes for the standards, a simulation workshop was developed. The manual developed for the workshop contained the ATE Standards for Teacher Educators, a matrix that calls for the workshop participant to reflect on each of the standards as they complete the exercises, and seven exercises that cause the participant to use the standards in a variety of situations.

- Exercise 1—Participants engage in a discussion of identifying teacher educators
- Exercise 2—Participants examine a resume of a teacher educator to determine the extent that the standards are reflected in the resume
- Exercise 3—Participants examine a doctoral program to determine how it can be modified to enable the graduate to meet the standards for teacher educators.
- Exercise 4—Designers of a Professional Development School consider how to define the teacher educators in the PDS.
- Exercise 5—A committee considers how to create a Staff Development Program for Teacher Educators
- Exercise 6—Participants consider the use of the standards by school administrators

The full text of the manual including the exercises is available on the ATE web site at *http://www.coe.ilstu.edu/rlfisher/manual.html.*

NATIONAL AWARD FOR DISTINGUISHED TEACHER EDUCATORS

Based on the standards, ATE initiated a special award for senior teacher educators who had made important life-long contributions to the profession, the *Distinguished Teacher Educator* award in conjunction with Wadsworth/ITP Publishing Company. The award was established "to recognize and honor those individuals in higher education or state departments of education who have advanced the profession of teacher education. The standards are used as the basis for recognizing those persons who have made significant contributions to educational thought and action. Each nominee submits a portfolio that is organized around the seven standards. Each portfolio is then reviewed by members of the Distinguished Teacher Educator Selection Committee to determine each nominee's contribution to the profession as measured against each standard. The award is issued annually at the ATE national meeting.

NATIONAL CONFERENCE

In June 1998 the National Academy on Alignment of Standards for Teacher Education, initiated by the Commission on Teacher Educator Standards nearly two years earlier, was convened in Washington, D.C., sponsored by a dozen organizations, and attended by over 300 participants. The conference brought together the groups that were developing standards for professional educators and those that were implementing such programs. The purpose of the two-day conference was to stimulate the alignment of teacher education programs at the institutional and state levels with national standards. The goals of the National Academy were:

- Clarify and analyze national standards. National leaders of standards reform will assist participants in understanding the context and substance of their standards.
- Examine the implications for teacher education of K–12 standards promulgated by professional associations and learned societies.
- Explore the role of standards in public policy, state licensing processes, national accreditation, and public credibility.
- Analyze the processes and content of teacher education programs based on national standards.
- Address state adaptations of national standards through several case studies that illustrate different conceptual approaches in licensure/ accreditation.

Colleges and universities were encouraged to send teams of faculty and administrators to begin working on the planning and implementing of programs that were aligned to professional and content standards. Major speakers from national organizations involved in developing standards addressed the participants. In addition, institutions that had or were in the process of aligning national standards to programs presented small-group sessions. These small group sessions not only presented practical suggestions for aligning programs to standards but also encouraged exchanges between presenters and participants that explored the strategies, barriers and opportunities that exist when redesigning current programs around standards. It was generally agreed that a second National Academy should be planned focusing on the issue of performance assessment of standards.

EXTENSIVE EXPLORATION

The Commission on Standards and its members were active in a number of related contributions growing out of Commission activities. Roy Edelfelt, University of North Carolina, and James Raths, University of Delaware, authored *A Brief History of Standards in Teacher Education* that was published by the Association of Teacher Educators. Joseph Vaughan, formerly with the U. S. Department of Education, wrote a stimulating conceptual paper on teacher educator standards that formed the basis for Commission discussions at two of its sessions but has not been published. When revising its standards for accreditation, NCATE used the ATE standards the basis for its faculty standards. Ronnie Stanford, University of Alabama, and Peggy Ishler, Northern Iowa University, designed a doctoral program based on the standards that provides a valid approach to preparing teacher educators.

Ralph Fessler and Rochelle Ingram, Johns Hopkins University, developed a doctoral program based on the ATE standards. Linda Adamson and Betsy Lowry, two students in its first cohort, described the program at the ATE annual meeting in February 2001. The program extended the ATE standards in three ways: it modified the standards to also include leadership in professional development, a strong emphasis on self reflection, and digitized electronic portfolios that not only chronicle activities and accomplishments but provide the substance for self-reflection. Other educators have proposed and initiated other innovative ways to base improved education on the standards.

The standards continue to be a "work in progress." Their full impact has yet to be realized. The activities described above provide some insight into the commitment of Commission members and other educators over a nine-year period and the potential impact the standards could make in our professional lives.

Where Are We Now?

Teacher educators have an obligation to be precise about what is entailed in being a teacher educator. The standards included herein are designed to ferment a continuing dialogue designed to sharpen our understanding of the multiple roles of teacher educators and the qualities that make them effective. Many challenges remain. We need to:

- Continue to improve the standards, decide how best to differentiate entry-level and master teacher educators, and refine the standards for the numerous roles of teacher educators.
- Provide tools to help universities, schools, and agencies use the standards move effectively.
- Generate broad-based support for using the standards system.
- Demonstrate how voluntary certification standards can be implemented and refined.

The Dutch Story

At the annual conference of the Dutch Association of Teacher Educators (VELON) in March 1997, the Dutch Minister of Education suggested that a plan of action for the development of a standard for the teacher education profession should be drawn up. Standards had already been developed for teachers in primary and secondary education and it seemed odd that there was no standard available for the 'teachers of teachers'. Beside that, the VELON considered the minister's suggestion an excellent challenge to improving the professional development of teacher educators as a group.

Teacher educators, as we identify them in Holland, are the same as in the United States, i.e., those educators who provide, either in institutes for teacher education or in schools, formal instruction for educating prospective and practicing teachers. In Holland we identify a teacher educator as a person who actually educates prospective teachers by providing teaching or instructional courses. So two main groups are teacher educators in our view: faculty in higher education who provide course work and personnel in schools who provide instruction or supervision of clinical experiences of prospective teachers. In our opinion a teacher educator has, at least for some time during his work, to deal with the actual education of student teachers.

Standards for Teacher Educators in Holland

EXPLORATION OF FUNCTIONS AND PRINCIPLES

An early decision was made to give the professional standard for Dutch teacher educators two important functions. The first is an internal function serving teacher educators as an instrument in their own professional development and improvement of their functioning as educators. The second is a more external function towards the government, students, clients, etc. which means that the standard serves as an instrument guaranteeing a certain level of professional competency and quality.

Four principles have guided the work of the development of the standard in Holland. First, a single set of standards would be written for all teacher educators. The content of the standard would have to be useful to teacher educators working in teacher education institutes as well as to school based teacher educators. It is also a general standard for all those teacher educators not connected to a specific subject or type of teacher education.

Second, the standard would focus on experienced teacher educators, because a standard focusing on quality development is a better guarantor of quality than a standard based on minimal requirements. This means that beginning teacher educators formulate their intention to acquire the competencies formulated in the standard and that experienced teacher educators can use the standard as a point of reference in their efforts to broaden or deepen their professional development. Third, the standards would apply to evolving situations as well as current needs, and fourth, the standards would consist of competencies that could be assessed.

WORKING GROUP FOR INITIAL SET OF STANDARDS

The launchpad chosen for the development of the professional standard for teacher educators in Holland were teacher educators themselves: they should feel that they (a) were the owners of the standard and the only way to realise that (b) was to develop the standard in collaboration with members of the professional group itself. If teacher educators feel they own the standard, they will value them when they see "what practitioners need to know and be able to do" (Ingvarson, 1998), and will be willing to use the standard as a point of reference for their own professional development. Development started with a working conference held in November 1997. Two documents were discussed: the standard for Dutch teachers and the standard for Master Teacher Educators (American Association of Teacher Educators/ATE, 1996). The plenary and working group discussions resulted in some general ideas about the content of a standard for teacher educators. In 1998, a development group of twenty teacher educators (from different types of teacher education institutions and backgrounds: institute-based teacher educators, school-based teacher educators, inservice educators, and those doing research into teacher education) formulated, reformulated, discussed and discussed over and over again different draft versions. They finally wrote the content of the first draft of the standard. About one hundred Dutch teacher educators discussed this first draft in a working conference in January 1999. The first public version of the standard was published in the middle of 1999 and sent to every teacher educator in Holland. Using the working conferences and the development group, the standard was thus developed by the teacher educators themselves, one of our basic starting points.

The student teachers spend a lot of their time doing teaching practice in the schools. The cooperating schoolteachers supervising them during their teaching practice play a crucial role in their development. That is why we call these teachers 'school-based teacher educators'. The standard is also a standard for them. They too were part of the 1998 group that developed the first draft version of the standard, and several of them are cooperating in our efforts to determine if the standard also benefits them.

THE FIRST VERSION OF THE STANDARD FOR DUTCH TEACHER EDUCATORS

The initial set of standards were analysed during the working conferences and the discussion and all the different remarks resulted in an intensive process of refining the content and description of the different elements of the standard. Three main changes took place. First, the foundations of instructional competencies were added and have become a very important part of our standard. Critical feedback on earlier drafts of the standard pointed out that "something is lacking" or "we miss the inspiration that is very important for teachers of teachers" in the standard. This addition became a major section in the standards.

The second main change resulted from the second working conference, when we invited some people from outside our own group to comment critically on the content of the standard. A representative of the union for student teachers in primary education made us aware that teacher educators must be prepared to work with their students to develop initiatives, yet this was not explicit in the standard for teacher educators. The third primary change occurred when several competencies, which were initially part of the pedagogical or communicative competencies were combined in a new competency area, "Developmental and Personal Growth Competencies" because we saw them as "meta-competencies" on which other competencies depend.

The standard for Dutch teacher educators is included in Table 5. The standard is presented in two parts: (a) the content of the foundations of instructional competencies and (b) an overview of the general competencies.

TABLE 5

The Dutch Standard for Teacher Educators

A. The Foundations of Instructional Competencies

Teacher educators provide educational services to a teacher education institute. The teacher educator's **core task** is *'to enable students to develop into competent teachers'*.

A teacher educator can also be expected to contribute towards the ongoing education of certified teachers or to contribute towards the research efforts on teaching and learning processes.

Teacher education is *vocational* education, in which the educator always works at the interface between his[2] own institute and the world of work and school. This is expressed in the following three levels: A good educator:

1. has insight into his pupils' development

2. facilitates and supervises the student teachers' development

3. takes charge of his own professional development.

Teacher educators formulate their own educational vision, one that is linked to the real world. They are able to adapt this vision to the pedagogical views of their institute, and to communicate this clearly to colleagues and students. Their educational vision must therefore be outward looking.

The work of professional teacher educators also demands a certain disposition. The following is true of all five competency areas described in the next section. A good educator:

• is open to others and is a good listener

---

[2]Where we write 'his', we also mean 'her'.

(continued on next page)

TABLE 5 (continued)

- dares to take risks and takes initiatives
- can offer feedback and is himself open to it
- stands by his views and can argue them convincingly
- is dedicated, committed and involved
- strives to solve problems with tact and diplomacy.

As a specific professional group, teacher educators work according to the following criteria:

- take, as a starting point, the specific practical problems and concerns experienced by teachers and student teachers, including those of the subject matter being taught

- is oriented towards the stimulation of systematic reflection (NB: this reflection is directed towards acquiring subject knowledge, establishing routines, seeking professional growth, etc.)

- makes deliberate use of both the interaction between the educator and individual students and between the students themselves

- works in an integrated manner, both with regard to the integration of theory and practice and the integration of different disciplines

- acquires and maintains knowledge from a variety of sources.

These criteria will also point to the kind of content of the competencies listed below.

These attitudes and criteria mean that the teacher educator must be prepared to take and develop initiatives together with his students in all competency areas. The educator considers the student as a partner qualified to contribute towards the development, implementation and evaluation of his own education and the ongoing development of the educator.

Teacher educators must also be models in all five competency areas. This means, for instance, that they must put into their own pedagogical behaviour all that they consider to be important.

(continued on next page)

TABLE 5 (continued)
B. General Competencies
The five competency areas are: 1. Content competencies 2. Pedagogical competencies 3. Organizational competencies 4. Group dynamic and communicative competencies 5. Developmental and personal growth competencies

The last competency area listed is a prerequisite for the first four; it is a 'meta-competency' on which the first four competencies depend. Each competency area comprises a number of specific skills. For those skills particularly characteristic of teacher education work (as opposed to teaching), the corresponding subsection numbers have been underlined. For two of the five areas of general competencies, i.e. pedagogical competencies and developmental and personal growth competencies, further details are listed in Table 6. (This version of the standard has been sent to every teacher educator in Holland in the middle of 1999.)

As in all professional walks of life, teacher educators must also be capable of integrating ICT into all their activities. This applies, for instance, to the creation of a digital learning environment for students (see 2.2), maintaining a network of contacts and keeping abreast of developments taking place in the profession itself (see 5.1).

FURTHER EXPLORATION OF THE STANDARD

During the yearly conference of the VELON workshops have informed teacher educators about the content of the standard and the possibilities to work with it. We have also worked with small groups of institute based and school based teacher educators to see if and how they can use the standard as an instrument in their own professional development and improvement of their functioning as a teacher educator. We found out that, for the school

TABLE 6

Pedagogical Competencies and Development and Personal Growth Competencies

B.2. Pedagogical Competencies

The teacher educator is able:

(Design)

2.1. to collaborate with colleagues on the preparation, implementation, evaluation, modification and renewal of course curricula

2.2. to create a stimulating learning environment for students and course participants

(Action)

2.3. to differentiate between different (student teacher and) course participants and monitor them along their specific developmental routes towards teaching competence

2.4. to link different teaching situations with the appropriate pedagogical insights

2.5. to make the used pedagogical approach transparent for the students and to discuss the pedagogical options with them

(Evaluation)

2.6. to develop and implement assessment tests of vocational skills, offer students feedback on their study progress, and assess students' capabilities for the teaching profession

2.7. to stimulate students to reflect on their experiences and to assess themselves on their own capabilities for the teaching profession

B.5. Developmental and Personal Growth Competencies

The teacher educator is able:

5.1. to evaluate with colleagues new developments in the field of education and in the area of teacher education and to incorporate these into his educational behaviour repertoire

5.2. to reflect systematically on his own pedagogical approach and (teaching) behaviour towards students, colleagues and others important to the teacher education institute

5.3. to make his own learning process visible to colleagues and students

based teacher educators, the content of the standard also is very helpful to make transparent

- to make transparent what you are doing as a teacher educator at the moment;
- what you consider as stronger and weaker points in the way you are functioning; and
- what professional development activities to undertake to improve your effectiveness as a teacher educator.

In the journal of the VELON we have published regularly about our experiences and experiences of others of working with the standard and the benefits it can have. The VELON journal regularly includes a discussion about the content of the standard and questions about its relevance for new developments in society and teacher education. Such an ongoing discussion is a valid part of professional development. As one of the people who advised us in the past once said: "A standard for teacher educators should never be finished and should be a document which is always discussed, dynamic, and in development." Our plan is to document all the discussions about the content of the standard and to publish a new (draft) version every two or three years.

The need to make the content of the standard more explicit very quickly became clear to us two reasons. First, the standard should not exceed two pages. Standards for teachers developed in Holland in the first half of the 90's were between 60 and 100 pages, very specific and detailed, and hardly anybody used them. Our task was to formulate a standard of a few pages. We succeeded, but some teacher educators asked for examples of the different elements of the standard, because they did not understand what is exactly meant by that element. The second need was for flexibility and the ability to add specific behaviours to every element of the standard. We did this by making an electronic version, a Web-version, of the standard. If a teacher educator wants some more information, he can click on a certain competency and more information is provided, what we call an authentic situation.

These authentic situations were developed by asking experienced teacher educators to select one or two elements of the standard. Then we asked them to describe a situation from their teaching practice in which they showed functional behaviour connected to that element. We also asked them to describe the context and the effect of their behaviour. Based on these interviews we are able: a) to describe an example of a situation connected to that element of the standard which is recognizable for many teacher educators; b) to analyze the functional behaviour of experienced teacher educators and describe that behaviour so other teacher educators can use that description to conclude "where they stand professionally," and c) show what the effect of using that behaviour is so it is clear what the improvement will be.

We believe that informing teacher educators through workshops and articles, stimulating the discussion about the content of the standard, and concretising the content of the standard are very important activities for the further exploration of the standard for Dutch teacher educators. But there is also another part of our mission: registration of teacher educators and developing a procedure of self-assessment for teacher educators. Activities like giving information or concretizing the standard are connected to the first function of the standard which is more internal, the development of the procedure of self assessment and the registration of teacher educators are activities to realize the second function of the standard, i.e. guaranteeing a certain level of professional competency and quality.

Registration of and Self Assessment by Dutch Teacher Educators

Currently we are developing an assessment procedure that is strongly appealing to the professional responsibility of individual teacher educators and setting up of a register for teacher educators.

The assessment procedure consists of five steps. In the first step, the teacher educator makes a self-analysis of strong and weak points. In the second step, the teacher educator, in a discussion with a peer coach, explains why he thinks the content of his analysis "is as it is." For example, he illustrates situations in which he demonstrates his strong points; or he describes situations where things did not go the way he planned; or he provides certain evidence that proves he is able to do certain things on an experienced level. This discussion results in the teacher educator formulating specific points on which he wants feedback from colleagues and student teachers. The third step in our self-assessment procedure is that we ask the participants to organise 360 degree feedback from colleagues on specific points (for example competencies as a member of a team in the institute) and from student teachers concerning specific points on which they have knowledge (for example pedagogical competencies).

The main purpose of the first three steps of this assessment procedure is to stimulate the teacher educators who want to register and to think in depth about the best goal they can select for their professional development. After they have formulated this goal they are asked to develop a plan for their professional development (step four) and to write in their portfolio about the execution of that plan (step five). The last step is that they apply for registration and peer assessors will discuss their portfolio with the teacher educator who wants to be registered and make a decision if he or she can.

For every step, one or two instruments are developed. For example, for the first step a format is developed which gives the participant the possibility to score all the different elements of the content of the standard (including the Foundation, which we have divided in twelve different elements) by answering the next question: "For this competency I am at the level of Beginner, Experienced, or Expert Teacher Educator." For the second step, a method is developed to identify the functional questions for the peer coach to use, and a systematic way to develop authentic situations.

Those who have gone through the assessment procedure and match some more formal criteria (for example enough work-experience) can be certified as a registered teacher educator. An organisation registers these teacher educators and selects and trains peer assessors for their roles in the registration procedure. In April 2001 a pilot of 30 teacher educators, who all want to be registered as a certificated teacher educator, will start. During that pilot we will find out how the five different steps of and the instruments for the self-assessment procedure work.

So far, one of the most important results of participation in the process of development and assessment is that it has made us realise that, for the teacher educators who participate in our project, clarifying and working with standards and continuously making an effort to achieve them is perhaps more important to the professional quality of these teacher educators than the mere possession of a fixed set of standards.

The world of education and teacher training is changing rapidly. We think this makes it necessary that professional standards be revised every few years and that certification continually change itself. In turn, members of the profession should be aware of the continuous need to screen and update their standards and professional competencies. Should they fail to do so, they will lose their right to ownership and before long others will impose standards on the profession.

Conclusions and Implications

The development of standards for teacher educators will help the larger community define the role of teacher educator. As with other standards initiatives, defining best practice brings out the subtleties of the concept being addressed. After decades of educating teachers, one would think that it would not be difficult to reach agreement on who are teacher educators. But this is to be expected since there is wide disagreement on the role of the teacher in educating children. Development of the standards should enable us to develop workable concepts about teacher educators.

The development of standards for teacher educators that apply to personnel in higher education as well as the schools holds promise for building better continuity in teacher education across the interface between school and university. Traditionally teacher education students learn about teaching in higher education and then go to the schools to practice what they have learned. Contemporary thinking and practice for teacher education blends the roles of the two institutions such that university faculty, along with school faculty, help students of teaching learn how to teach through school-based experiences. This can lead to a blending of roles and responsibilities for personnel of schools and universities. Defining the roles of teacher educators in both institutions should help improve the functioning of both types of personnel. It seems that there is just as much opportunity for school personnel to improve their role in educating teachers as there is for university personnel to learn how to function in the schools.

In the past two decades there has been significant advances in the knowledge base of educating teachers. Perhaps the development of standards for teacher educators will bring about a commensurate increase in the knowledge base for educating teacher educators. Just as there is still a thought that anyone can teach, there is also a belief that anyone can be a teacher educator. Many university faculty in the field of teacher education are specialists in such fields as reading, mathematics, or special education. Few university faculty, and fewer school personnel, have studied the field of teacher education. There is a growing awareness that doctoral programs that prepare personnel to work in the field of teacher education need to include study in such areas as adult learning, assessment of teachers, mentoring and supervision, and design of teacher education programs.

REFERENCES

Association of Teacher Educators. (1996). *Certification of Master Teacher Educators*. Final Report of the Task Force on the Certification of Teacher Educators. Reston, VA.

Ingvarson, L. (1998). Professional Development as the Pursuit of Professional Standards: The Standard-Based Professional Development System. *Teaching and Teacher Education, 14*(1). 127–140.

Koster, B., Korthagen, F., Wubbels, Th. & Hoornweg, J. (1996). Roles, competencies and training of teacher educators, a new challenge. In: E. Befring (Ed.) *Teacher Education for Equality*, Oslo College, Norway.

Turney, C. & Wright, C. (1990). *Where the buck stops the teacher educators.* Sydney: Sydney Academic Press.

Watts, D. (1984). Teacher educators should be certified. *Journal of Teacher Education, 35*(1) (pp. 30-33).

Wilson, J.D. (1994). Selecting and Training the Teacher Trainers. In M. Galton & B. Moon (Ed.) *Handbook of Teacher Training in Europe* (p. 109–127).

Summary and Implications

Gwendolyn H. Middlebrooks

The two chapters in this section chronicle extensive efforts of educators to develop and use standards for assessing the quality of teacher educators. They specifically detail the scholarly processes employed and document the extent to which expert educators utilized their knowledge and professional skills to develop and refine standards for teacher educators. The time required to participate in the process is testimony to the dedication of educators and their interest in ensuring that quality continues to exist in teacher education.

The merits of the standards developed by the Association of Teacher Educators (ATE) are presented in chapter two. Extensive examples are provided to demonstrate how teacher educators used team teaching as an instructional method or tool to adhere to the standards, while simultaneously modeling appropriate teaching practices for pre-service teachers. The authors provide detailed descriptions of the varied instructional roles teacher educators can assume while teaming. Clearly documenting that effective teaming requires increased collaboration and skills in planning and organization (Wenger and Hornyak 1999).

The first chapter discusses the rationale, and processes used to develop two sets of standards for teacher educators. The first set of standards was developed in the United States by the Association of Teacher Educators (ATE), and the second set was developed in Holland by the Dutch Association of Teacher Educators (VELON).

In the United States, the process was initiated in 1992, when ATE appointed a national Task Force on the certification of master teacher educators. Initially, the focus was on developing and using standards as a voluntary certification system for experienced teacher educators rather than licensure. Standards were conceptualized during the Fall 1993, developed at the ATE Conference in February 1994, and refined in later months.

However, in February 1996, based on the findings, the mission was expanded and the Commission on Teacher Educator Standards was formed. The Commission had a focus less on certification and more on standards by which teacher educators could be assessed. In 2000, eight years later, a set of standards for teacher educators was published.

In Holland, a standard for teacher educators was developed by the Dutch Association of Teacher Educators (VELON). The plan of action was initiated in March 1997 to develop a standard for the teacher education profession because a standard for teachers of teachers did not exist. It was believed that the development of a standard would improve the professional development, quality, and professional competence of teacher educators.

Following the lead of ATE, and incorporating the ATE standards for teacher educators into initial discussions, the standard developed in Holland through an intense process and the consistent work of teacher educators. The work was performed in a working conference and by teacher educators in a development group over a two-year period of time, from 1997–1999. The standard, published and distributed in the middle of 1999 to every teacher educator in Holland, listed five general areas of competencies that teacher educators must model. Special efforts were made to include teacher educators so they would develop a sense of ownership of the standard and an interest in its application.

Similarities

Although these processes were separate events, many similarities are evident.

- The definition of teacher educator included higher education faculty in teacher education and school-based teachers.
- The development of the standards was an initiative of a professional organization.
- The collaborative work by educators as members of the professional organizations to develop the standards.
- The absence of an existing standard for reviewing, assessing, or certifying teacher educators.
- The standards were refined and discussed at workshops and conferences of the professional organizations.
- Input from a large number of educators was obtained at varied stages of the process.
- Drafts of the standards were distributed to educators for review and recommendations.

The standards developed also share similarities.

- Modeling of instructional practices by teacher educators.
- Commitment and responsibility for professional development.
- Contribute to research and scholarly efforts in teaching and learning

Implications

ATE accepted the challenge of leadership when it established a Task Force to develop national standards for teacher educators. National standards are needed to guarantee that high quality preparation among teacher educators is required and maintained. (Wise and Liebbrand, 2001). The actions by ATE indicate that teacher educators support and encourage efforts to ensure that all education professionals are qualified.

Standards for teacher educators promote professional development and support the idea that the education of teacher educators is related to the improvement of teacher preparation and improvement in teaching and learning in schools. Consistent professional development is essential for teacher educators and the success of our schools (Fullan, Galluzzo, Morris, Watson,1998).

The standards are measures of excellence that can be utilized to ensure that teacher educators know and can demonstrate specific professional practices that enhance the preparation of teachers, and subsequently improve teaching and learning in schools. They specify the basic qualifications and competencies teacher educators must be able to model or demonstrate in order to produce qualified teachers. National standards for teacher educators assist educators in maintaining a high level of professionalism, scholarship, and competence in the eyes of the general public, in higher education, and specifically in the field of teacher education.

The authors of the first chapter suggested that the Association of Teacher Educators (ATE) provide tools to help universities, schools, and agencies use the standards more effectively. The "teaming" model presented in the second chapter serves as a model or a tool that can be used by teacher educators to comply with the requirements of the seven standards.

These chapters provide insights into the long and systematic process used to develop and validate national standards for teacher educators. According to Murray (2001) if teachers are expected to teach at high levels in our nations' schools, consensus must be reached on the qualifications for faculty members in teacher education programs. The national standards reflect the scholarly work of educators, serve to identify and clarify the roles, responsibilities, and competencies of teacher educators, and provide a platform of consensus concerning the qualifications of teacher educators.

REFERENCES

Fullan, M., Galluzzo, G., Morris, P. and Watson, N. (1998). *The rise and stall of teacher education reform.* Washington, DC: AACTE.

Murray, F. (2001). The overreliance of accreditors on consensus standards. *Journal of Teacher Education.* 52, 3, May/June, 211–222.

Wenger, M.S. and Hornyak, M.J. (1999). Team teaching for higher level learning: A framework of professional collaboration. *Journal of Management Education.* 23, 3, June, 311–327.

Wise, A. and Liebbrand, J.A, (2001) Standards in the new millennium: Where we are, where we're headed. *Journal of Teacher Education.* 52, 3, May/June, 244–255.

Division

2

Assessing the Impact of Standards

Overview and Framework

David M. Byrd and Peter Adamy

David M. Byrd is a professor at the University of Rhode Island and has a long-term research interest in programs for beginning teachers and teacher professional development. He is a graduate of the doctoral program in teacher education at Syracuse University. He has authored and co-authored over 30 articles, books and chapters including the textbook *Methods for Effective Teaching* published by Allyn and Bacon (1994, 1999) and chapters in both the *Handbook of Research on Teacher Education* (1996) and the *Handbook of Research on Supervision* (1998) both published by Macmillan. He has served as co-editor of the Association of Teacher Educators *Teacher Education Yearbook* series.

Peter Adamy is Assistant Professor of Education at the University of Rhode Island. His teaching and research are focused in the areas of improving teacher education through the integration of technology, the use of technology to enhance content area instruction and learning, and the development, implementation, and assessment of standards-based electronic portfolios for pre-service teachers.

Educational Reform in America

The history of education in this country is replete with moments of energetic attempts to determine what is of most value for people to learn, and to implement the most effective ways for people to learn it. Kliebard (1992) identifies a series of modern events that have resulted in criticisms of the effectiveness of our educational system, followed by the mobilization of resources in attempts to redefine teaching and learning. These events and subsequent reactions have been typically quite dramatic, and have resulted in what he refers to as the "pendulum swing" of educational reform.

For many, the modern rush to declare a state of emergency and mobilize resources in education really took hold in 1983, with the publication of the National Commission on Excellence in Education's *A Nation at Risk*. The report, which called for reform in education, included recommendations for stronger graduation requirements, K–16 standards (admission, academic, and graduation), standardized test administration at transition points in a student's career, and more time spent on the basics of education. It also included recommendations for improved standards for teachers. This in turn led to calls for reform of teacher education as a method for achieving broader school reform; better teachers will make better schools, and, subsequently, more capable graduates.

It is important to remember that in large part, the calls for reform of education, and more specifically teacher education, have tended to take shape through external mandates. In the mid 1980's, following directly on the heels of *A Nation at Risk*, a series of reports on teacher education reform were published by the National Commission on Excellence in Teacher Education (1985), the Holmes Group (1986), and the Carnegie Forum (1986). The publication of these reports led to an increased mix of reform calls in the '90's as well. The difficulty soon arose though, that the increase in teacher education reform documents from agencies outside of teacher education programs eventually watered down consensus on what that reform should look like (Valli & Rennert-Ariev, 2000). This general lack of agreement increases the importance of assessing the impact of these external mandates to improve teacher education and to achieve a thorough understanding of their effectiveness, feasibility, and cost.

As proponents of this particular brand of educational reform often point out, standards are designed to improve education through increased rigor, consistency, and accountability. Indeed, in theory, it is difficult to imagine who would not be in favor of their adoption (Brady, 2000; Shepard and Bliem, 1995). As with all educational reforms, however, we need to move beyond the rhetoric of standards. The four chapters in this section present possibilities for beginning to identify what is most valuable and most problematic about this movement before the pendulum begins to swing back in reaction to current reform efforts.

The Impact of Externally Mandated Standards

Cochran-Smith (2000) suggests that the content and future of teacher education have become political matters, and people outside the field are currently mandating how schools of education should structure their programs. She argues that while it is necessary to include those outside of teacher education in the debate around standards, the consequence of locating it externally is a lack of full understanding of the complexities involved in teaching someone how to teach others.

The difficulties of this situation are increased when you consider the different agendas that are brought to the table. While it may bolster conservative critics' claims of educational ineptitude to act as if things in our schools are worse than they have ever been, Rothstein (1998) points out that there is a long tradition of criticizing American schools. This tradition is repeatedly driven by the conservative game of looking backward to compare contemporary education to how it was in "the good old days." The difficulty, according to Rothstein, is that closer examination of the good old days reveals that even supposedly more idyllic times in the past had very vocal critics of the educational system; critics that pined for their own good old days when education was done properly. As Brady (2000; p. 651) puts it, "However, behind the standards juggernaut and impelling it forward is the single, primary, simplistic, and unexamined assumption that what the next generation most needs to know is what this generation knows". This attitude has most recently appeared in the form of a call for focusing on specific content area knowledge that is "basic" to being a literate, functional member of our society (e.g. Hirsch, 1988).

While few in the field of teacher education would argue against the pursuit of increasing the quality of education in this country, teacher educators also realize that the current manifestation of this agenda is too simplistic; content area knowledge is indeed very important for teachers to possess, but for the process of teacher education, pedagogical knowledge is also vital (Berliner, 2000). Apple (2001) argues that the determination of what "counts as common" is not a fair process. There is a differential among groups in our society in the ability to influence policy. Those who are more familiar with, or have more influence with the external mandating bodies have an unfair advantage in assuring that their children's needs are served. This means that in general, policies that are designed to raise scores result in the reinforcement of traditional social hierarchies and status.

Apple (2001) also focuses specifically on what he sees as not only a failure to improve education, but a resulting policy framework that reinforces traditional inequalities and results in a loss of multiculturalism. He states that the government views and makes decisions about teacher education based on results of standardized testing. This practice ignores the real-life experience of teaching in a complex, social environment: ". . . the reduction of education to scores on what are often inadequate measures—often used in technically and educationally inappropriate ways for comparative purposes—has some serious consequences" (p. 192).

Assessing the Impact of Standards in Teacher Education

In light of the disagreements over, and criticisms of the current focus of standards-based reform in teacher education, we are charged with the task of determining the most effective methods for creating and implementing standards, and for assessing their impact in the context of teacher education programs. This is, at best, difficult because there currently appears to be no consensus on what standards for teacher education should look like, and what it is teachers should know and/or be able to do after completing a credential program (Britzman & Dippo, 2000; Cochran-Smith, 2000; Valli & Rennert-Ariev, 2000). Groups like the National Council for Accreditation of Teacher Education and the Interstate New Teacher Assessment and Support Consortium have come to the fore as nationally recognized leaders in developing standards for teacher education, but their influence is not universal. Teacher education programs face differing accreditation procedures that are structured according to a mixture of national, state, and local policy.

Another difficulty is that teacher education programs, as units within the traditional world of higher education, tend to be "bastions of traditional practices" that perpetuate compartmentalization of the curriculum (Luke, Luke & Mayer, 2000). It is not possible, or necessarily desirable to eliminate standardized testing of specific content knowledge because the results of standardized testing do provide one type of outcome measure, and are perceived ultimately as important to administrators and legislators. State level assessments continue to be based largely on basic skills and a common core of knowledge. This places emphasis on decontextualized knowledge that will result in continued emphasis on standardized tests. Some researchers instead recommend that teacher education programs avoid viewing learning as a "linear path" that ends in mastery of specific behavioral objectives (Cochran-Smith, 2001), and instead develop educational practice that recognizes and incorporates the complexities and intricacies of what is essentially a socially interactive endeavor.

One option is performance-based assessment—the assessment of someone actively engaged in the complex and authentic process of teaching. This type of assessment is reflective of the recent move in teacher education from an input to an output model (Cochran-Smith, 2001), and results in an outcomes-based method that reduces the traditionally heavy emphasis on standardized testing. Performance-based assessment also has the benefit of precedent: it is how several other fields have traditionally trained their practitioners. Teacher education is focused on developing pedagogically sound behavior in interaction with students. It therefore makes sense to assess skill in these behaviors while they are being practiced and not in an abstract, mediated form.

Valli and Rennert-Ariev (2000) suggest that the lack of agreement as to what standards for teacher education should look like can be overcome by using performance-based assessment as a focal point for potential consensus. Sustained change should be a major goal of any reform effort, and it is incumbent upon those involved in teacher education to develop a body of standards and assessment methods that enhance the nature of the teacher education process in a meaningful and lasting way. Standardized tests are a reality that is not going away, and they serve as one outcome measure that should be combined with others like performance-based assessment. In the end, some combination of the two may be most useful for teacher educators (Shepard and Bliem, 1995).

Ultimately, teacher educators need to serve as leaders of the reform process in teacher education. As noted above, there is a call for greater participation and consensus from teacher educators, and the results of any form of assessment should be of equal, if not greater importance to them as front line implementers of standards for teacher education. This will encourage more informed participation from these key players in the process of standards development, implementation, and assessment.

The Chapters

The four chapters that make up this section all meet the need, identified by Cochran-Smith (2000), for educational researchers to take part in the debate over what standards for teacher education should look like, and how they should be implemented and assessed. In chapter 3, Grant and Klein do just this, with particular focus on the impact of implementing standards in a specific content area. In chapter 4, Bohn provides evidence supporting the claim that externally mandated standards impact how diversity is addressed in the classroom. Bergeron, in chapter 5, also addresses the impact of externally mandated standards, but does so in the context of a working relationship between a teacher education program and its professional development schools (PDS). Here Bergeron is stepping beyond the usual boundaries of researching ways of implementing and assessing standards to look specifically at the school of education/PDS relationship and its effect on how the standards implementation process can impact all levels of the teacher education process. Finally, in chapter 6, McDowell and Desmond provide us with a useful means for facilitating the implementation and assessment of standards: the use of dialogue between classroom teachers and teacher educators as a specific tool for exploring ways to put standards into practice in classrooms and universities.

REFERENCES

Apple, M. W. (2001). Markets, standards, teaching, and teacher education. *Journal of Teacher Education, 52*(3), 182–195.

Berliner, D. C. (2000). A personal response to those who bash teacher education. *Journal of Teacher Education, 51*(5), 358–371.

Brady, M. (2000). The standards juggernaut. *Phi Delta Kappan, 81*(9), 648–651.

Britzman, D. & Dippo, D. (2000). On the future of awful thoughts in teacher education. *Teaching Education, 11*(1), 31–37.

Carnegie Forum (1986). *A nation prepared: Teachers for the 21st century. A report of the task force on teaching as a profession.* New York: Carnegie Form on Education and the Economy.

Cochran-Smith, M. (2000). The future of teacher education: Framing the questions that matter. *Teaching Education, 11*(1), 13–24.

Cochran-Smith, M. (2001). Editorial: Higher standards for prospective teachers—what's missing from the discourse? *Journal of Teacher Education, 52*(3), 179–181.

Hirsch, E. D. (1988). *Cultural Literacy: What Every American Needs to Know.* New York: Vintage Books.

Holmes Group (1986). *Tomorrow's Teachers.* East Lansing, MI: Holmes Group.

Kliebard, H. M. (1992). *Forging the American Curriculum: Essays in Curriculum History and Theory.* New York: Routledge.

Luke, A., Luke, C., & Mayer, D. (2000). Redesigning teacher education. *Teaching Education, 11*(1), 5–11.

National Commission on Excellence in Education (1983). *A nation at risk.* Washington, DC: U. S. Department of Education.

National Commission on Excellence in Teacher Education (1985). *A call for change in teacher education.* Washington, DC: American Association of Colleges for Teacher Education.

Rothstein, R. (1998). *The Way We Were? The Myths and Realities of America's Student Achievement.* New York: Century Foundation Press.

Shepard, L. A. & Bliem, C. L. (1995). Parents' thinking about standardized tests and performance assessments. *Educational Researcher, 24*(8), 25–32.

Valli, L. & Rennert-Ariev, P. L. (2000). Identifying consensus in teacher education reform documents: A proposed framework and action implications. *Journal of Teacher Education, 51*(1), 5–17.

Developing Elementary Teachers' Knowledge of Content and Pedagogy Through Implementation of a Standards-Based Mathematics Curriculum

3.

Theresa J. Grant and Kate Kline

Theresa J. Grant and Kate Kline, Assistant Professors, Department of Mathematics and Statistics, Western Michigan University, are interested in how teachers learn in the context of implementing a reform curriculum and the challenges and rewards experienced by teachers as they learn to teach for understanding.

ABSTRACT

This study describes how primary teachers' knowledge about content and pedagogy developed as they implemented a standards-based elementary mathematics curriculum. Eighteen first and second grade teachers from a small rural school district in the Midwest were observed during professional development sessions, and they submitted written reflections. Four of these teachers were interviewed and observed teaching to provide additional insight into how they were interacting with the curriculum materials. The analysis of the data focuses on changes in teachers' goals for what their students should know about number and the resulting impact on instructional practice. Learning in this context of curriculum implementation proved to be a conducive environment for teachers. By the end of the first year, they reported major shifts in their goals from an emphasis on skills to understanding, and their classroom practice gradually shifted to focus on reasoning about mathematics.

The widely publicized *Curriculum and Evaluation Standards for School Mathematics* by the National Council of Teachers of Mathematics (NCTM, 1989) set forth a vision for mathematics education, through a discussion of content development in grades K–12. Further specificity of this vision came in later NCTM documents (e.g. 1991, 1995) and culminated in the revised compilation, *Principles and Standards for School Mathematics* (NCTM, 2000). These documents, taken as a whole, provide teachers with information on the mathematics content and teaching practices that shift the focus away from skill memorization and practice towards understanding mathematics. Enacting this vision in the classroom has remained a complex task, and the publication of a variety of complete standards-based curricular materials in the mid-1990's (twelve in total sponsored by the National Science Foundation) has provided contexts in which teachers are encouraged to learn about the Standards and witness first-hand the impact on their students.

Supporting teachers as they implement these standards-based curricula has presented many challenges in terms of professional development and appropriate learning opportunities for teachers. A major obstacle identified by analysts of the last major reform movement in mathematics ("New Math") is that the professional development opportunities were of limited availability, costly, and focused primarily on new content rather than pedagogical issues (Cohen & Barnes, 1993). Many teachers had only the textbook to guide them, within which there were "little to no philosophical or theoretical guidelines" (Bossé, 1995, p. 186). As a result, many of the current standards-based curricula specifically intended to help teachers learn as well as students, by including such information as descriptions of content development, samples of student reasoning, and examples of questioning techniques.

Recommendations for more thoughtful, long-term professional development that expands teachers' knowledge of content and content-specific pedagogy have also been made as a result of the past reform effort and research done since that time (Loucks-Horsley, Hewson, Love, & Stiles, 1998). Since the 1960's, we have learned a great deal about the complexities of changing teachers' beliefs and practice (e.g., Lloyd, 1999; Simon & Schifter, 1991; Wood, Cobb, & Yackel, 1991). This work has identified some of the inhibitors of change, which often relate to the organization of schooling and/or the teachers' personal characteristics, such as biography, beliefs, and knowledge (Richardson, 1990). While inhibitors have been identified, we are just beginning to understand how best to enable change in the climate of standards-based reform (Ball, 1996).

This study was designed to understand better the shifts in the thinking and practice made by teachers as they interact with a standards-based mathematics curriculum, both as a guide for day-to-day teaching and as a site for reflection in professional development sessions. The teachers' understanding of content and pedagogy as well as the types of exchanges they had with students in the classroom were analyzed in order to obtain a clearer picture of how teachers learn in the context of curriculum implementation.

Methodology

This study takes place in a rural school district during the first year of a three-year phased adoption plan for implementing a standards-based elementary mathematics curriculum, K–5. In the first year, all grades K–2 teachers in all three schools in the district implemented the curriculum. All K–2 teachers began with a selection of modules from their grade level that dealt mainly with number development. Modules for grades 3–5 as well as additional K–2 modules were added in subsequent years. While the researchers are involved long-term on this project, the data reported in this chapter are from the first year.

THE CURRICULUM

The standards-based curriculum used in this study, *Investigations in Number, Data and Space (Investigations)*, centers around four major strands: number, geometry and measurement, data, and change. There are six to eleven modules devoted to the development of these strands and the connections among them in each grade level, from kindergarten through grade five. The focus of the program is on reasoning and problem solving where students are required to explain their thinking orally and in writing. Students are encouraged to make sense of the mathematics they are learning and to use procedures that they understand, rather than those they may have memorized but may not fully understand. Successfully implementing Investigations requires that teachers understand the mathematical content, are prepared with questions to probe students' reasoning, and promote discussion and sharing of ideas in order to encourage construction of knowledge by students rather than dispensing of knowledge by the teacher (TERC, 1998).

A unique feature of this curriculum is the way mathematics content and pedagogy is communicated to teachers. The curriculum contains sections called "Teacher Notes" that may describe the importance of particular content, describe various strategies students may use and why they work, discuss connections among topics, etc. It also contains "Dialogue Boxes" that provide sample conversations a teacher may have with a student or group of students on a particular mathematical idea. These components provide helpful support for teachers as they shift to a standards-based focus on teaching mathematics for understanding.

PROFESSIONAL DEVELOPMENT

The researchers designed and facilitated all professional development. Five mandatory professional development release days, spread out across the year, were provided for the K–2 teachers during year one. The main goals for the professional development sessions were to develop teachers' understanding of the mathematics content in the program of effective teaching practices, and the of ways in which students learn. The curriculum materials themselves were the main "text" for these professional development sessions as each unit included: (a) an overview detailing the mathematical goals for the unit; and (b) specific sections that provide examples of student work on assessment items and sample conversations one may have with students to elicit explanations of reasoning. Each day was structured the same and involved discussing questions/sharing stories from the previous unit and preparing for the new unit by doing many of the activities together, discussing the mathematics, and discussing pedagogical implications.

DATA

All eighteen grades 1–2 teachers were asked to write about their goals for teaching number on the first and last days of professional development. At the end of the year, the teachers were provided with a copy of their first reflective writing and asked to write about the differences between their goals at the beginning of the year and those they had just written. Additional data collected on the entire group included field notes and audiotaped reflections by the researchers on the questions and concerns of the group during each professional development session and student work samples submitted by the teachers at each session. These data focused mainly on number as it is the mainstay of the elementary curriculum and the topic about which most elementary teachers are concerned.

Four of the eighteen teachers volunteered to participate in classroom observations and interviews to be spread out over the course of the school year. These four teachers, two in grade 1 and two in grade 2, were observed in the context of teaching each new module at their grade level. All lessons were videotaped or audiotaped and transcribed. Interviews typically took place after an observation and involved general questions on how effective the teachers thought the lessons were as well as specific questions on interchanges with their students. In addition, end-of-the-year interviews with the four teachers probed their personal reflections on how well they were implementing the standards-based curriculum. In one case, this included having the teacher view videotapes of her instruction throughout the year and comment on the changes in her practice that she witnessed. All interviews were audiotaped and/or videotaped and transcribed.

ANALYSIS

The reflective writings from the first and last professional development sessions on goals for teaching number were analyzed and sorted into categories. In most cases the categories were self-evident. If the description was unclear, and no explanation was provided, the item was taken at face value. Field notes of professional development sessions were used to provide further explanations for these findings. Transcripts of classroom episodes were analyzed for common themes within and among the four teachers. In particular, classroom exchanges that highlighted how teachers were eliciting and reacting to their students' thinking were identified and analyzed. A coding scheme was used that characterized the extent to which teacher-student exchanges focused on student thinking about important mathematical ideas. This distinguished exchanges where teachers requested answers only from those where student reasoning was elicited and pursued to highlight ideas or push ideas further.

Results

In this section, the discussion of the transformation in all of the teachers' understanding of important content related to whole numbers is discussed based upon their written reflections and discussions during professional development sessions. Next, the understanding of content and pedagogy displayed by the four volunteer teachers is described based upon observations of teaching and reflective interviews.

UNDERSTANDING THE CONTENT FOCUS

All eighteen grades 1 and 2 teachers identified what they thought was important for their students to know about number by the end of the year. They wrote about their ideas on this at the beginning of the year and after teaching *Investigations* for one full year. A summary of the results from the writing reflections is shown in Table 1.

TABLE 1

Beginning and End-of-Year Comparison
of Goals for Number

Beginning of Year (n = 17)		End of Year (n = 18)	
Adds and subtracts	76%	Number relationships	72%
Knows basic facts	65	Problem solving strategies	72
Recognizes coins	59	Higher level thinking	39
Number characteristics	59	Place value	39
Tells time	47	Explains strategies	33
Writes numerals	35	Counts by groups	28
Story problems	35	Understands addition/ subtraction	28
Patterns	35	Story problems	28
1-to-1 correspondence	29	Patterns	17
Knows how to count	29	Tells time	17
Place value	29	Adds and subtracts	11
Recognizes numerals	29	Knows how to count	11
Understands addition/ subtraction	24	Writes numerals	11
Problem solving strategies	18	Knows basic facts	6
Counts by groups	12	Recognizes coins	6
Number relationships	6	Number characteristics	6

In the beginning of the year, teachers' written comments were more skill-oriented, focusing on the typical goals of traditional instruction in mathematics. Teachers described the major goal, adding and subtracting, as 'regrouping,' suggesting a procedural interpretation of subtraction. In addition, their descriptions of other items on the list suggested a narrow interpretation of those items. For example, number characteristics in the broad sense could include substantial ideas about the ways numbers behave.

However, the teachers who identified number characteristics as important mainly described it as "identifying odd and even numbers."

Implementing the number modules in *Investigations* and using them as a site for reflection during the professional development sessions served to challenge both the teachers' goals for number and the relative emphases placed on those goals. While the majority of the teachers had expressed concerns about basic facts memorization and proficiency with standard algorithms in their early writing, the number strand in *Investigations* placed greater emphasis on fluency with basic facts, a rich understanding of the number system, and student-created procedures for computation based on reasoning. The researchers' notes on the early professional development sessions provided insight into some of the issues with which the group struggled. For example, in the beginning stages of implementation some teachers were concerned that they were no longer "teaching," since they were not supposed to provide students with a single method for solving computation problems. As they continued to bring in student work throughout the year and analyze the mathematical understandings evident in the students' invented procedures, many began to recognize the value of encouraging their students to develop and discuss their own procedures.

By the end of the year, the reflective writings provided further evidence of the shift the teachers were making in the way they viewed number. Many identified developing number relationships as one of the most important goals. This was characterized as involving landmark numbers, such as 10, 25, 50, etc., using these landmarks to move around the number system, and knowing what happens when you operate on numbers. All but two teachers recognized the importance of their students' abilities to solve problems in a variety of ways and/or explain their solution strategies. It was obvious that a major shift had occurred in their thinking about number toward an emphasis on understanding and away from skill development alone. Many of the teachers recognized this dramatic shift in their thinking when asked to look at their writing from the beginning of the year and compare it to what they wrote at the end of the year. They commented:

> "I see that I seemed more concerned with computation than understanding. I did not look toward the underlying need to see relationships and patterns that is necessary to total understanding when working math problems." (Grade 2 Teacher)

> "I now expect more from my students. Before I expected more rote learning but now I expect the children to think about what they are doing and then to explain what they are doing." (Grade 1 Teacher)

Enactment of the Standards-Based Curriculum in Practice

In the context of implementing the standards-based curriculum, the teachers learned about and came to value more reasoning-based goals for whole numbers. However, enacting these goals in the classroom proved more challenging. In the discussion that follows, data from the four teachers who volunteered to have their teaching videotaped in their first year provides snapshots of how the curriculum was enacted in the classroom. The issues that arose in teaching included balancing multiple mathematical emphases, sufficiently pursuing student thinking, and establishing mathematical reasoning as the focus during discussions.

Multiple Mathematical Emphases In the beginning of the year, some teachers struggled with balancing multiple mathematical emphases in a single lesson, particularly in the context of reasoning about number. For example, in a first-grade lesson, students were posed the following problem:

> Suppose I have 12 pets. Some of them are cats and some of them are dogs. How many of each could I have? How many cats? How many dogs? Remember, I have 12 things in all.

This is a common problem type used throughout the curriculum to encourage children to think about both the variety of ways that exist to make a number and about finding multiple solutions for a particular context. When the lesson was introduced, the teacher demonstrated an incomplete understanding of the mathematical emphasis. She referred to 12 as the "magic" number and that they were looking for ways to come up with combinations for 12. There was little reference to the context of the problem in the introduction or in the discussions with students while they were working. Not surprisingly, some students found combinations of three numbers to make 12, and one student proposed a subtraction equation ($13 - 1$). When these solutions, which clearly did not fit the context provided, were offered at the end of the lesson, the teacher accepted them whole-heartedly and did not question the students as to whether these solutions fit the problem.

When asked afterwards if these equations made sense for this lesson, the teacher commented, "They were looking for combinations, is what I said to them to do—find numbers that would equal 12." She seemed to have identified one important idea—that of thinking about combinations for any given number—yet had lost sight of the fact that this mathematical activity was embedded in a context that students should have had to consider.

Pursuing Student Thinking A common pedagogical struggle observed early in the year centered around the pursuit of student thinking. In the most extreme case, this takes the form of a failure to pursue student thinking altogether. In the lesson discussed above, for example, there was only one time in the entire whole group lesson where an explanation of how a solution was arrived at was requested. However, even when teachers understood the need to discuss the reasoning behind student solutions, they often had difficulty pursuing student thinking. For example, students would be asked to present answers only and then the teacher would offer her reasoning for how they could have arrived at particular solutions, rather than asking for the students' strategies. In addition, students were also provided with strategies often before they had even attempted the problems.

In the exchange below, second-grade students were using multilink cubes to find as many ways as they could to make 22. They wrote their findings on a recording sheet. The teacher came upon a pair of students who had 15 + 4 = 22 among many other correct equations written on their paper and the following exchange occurred.

Jake: Is this right? Are these right?

T: Well, I want you to check them and make sure they're right. Okay. [Focuses on 15 + 4 = 22.] Use your cubes and count them and see. Take 15 and add 4 to it. How else could you figure out if that was right instead of taking all the cubes? Well, if you had 15 and you wanted to figure out how much 4 more would be, what could you do? What's that strategy we talked about?

Jake: Count . . . . .

T: Yeah, counting . . . . . [motions upwards with her hands].

Jake: Numbers?

T: Counting . . . . .

Jake: Umm . . . . .

T: Counting up.

Jake: Up.

T: So, if I already have 15, I only have to count 4, don't I? So what would it be? 15, 16, 17, 18, 19. So, is that correct?

Jake: Yeah.

Jen: I'm way ahead (of him).

T: (to Jake) It is?

T: (to Jen) Oh, we need to stay together. Is that right? Would that be right?

Jen: [Nods her head.]

> T: 15 + 4? Oh, if I already have 15 and I add 4? 15, 16, 17, 18,
>   19? Oh, how many more do I need to get 22? [Jake, looking
>   confused, changes his paper to read 15 + 19 = 22.]

Notice that the teacher's initial reaction to the student's question about whether or not his equations were correct was to tell him that she wanted *him* to figure that out. She seemed to recognize the value in getting students to check their own answers and to figure out for themselves whether they were or were not correct. However, without hesitation she proceeded to walk him through a counting-up procedure to check the only incorrect equation on his paper. And based upon how he changed the equation to 15 + 19 = 22, it was clear that he did not learn from the exchange.

Focusing on Mathematical Reasoning By the end of the year, the teachers seemed more comfortable with standards-based teaching practices, as evidenced by their end-of-the-year interviews. They explained that they were "more open to having the children make choices in how they want to solve the problems" and "more patient about giving them time to work through it." They also explained the importance of letting students work through their answers to see if they really had the right answer and the importance of helping students become more willing to "take risks" and offer ideas for the rest of the class to consider. When the teacher in the above "Ways to Make 22" exchange was shown at the end of the year the video of her interaction with the pair of students, she exclaimed, "I'm doing it for him. He should be doing it! I should have had him figure out more!"

The excerpt below is an example of an exchange that focuses on reasoning. It took place in a first grade classroom at the end of the year. The students were measuring a strip of tape placed on the floor with their feet. One student (Jillian) had already walked along the strip to figure out that it took her 14 steps to cover the strip. The teacher then asks the class to think about how many feet it would take AJ (who has bigger feet than Jillian) and the following discussion ensues.

> T: AJ, let's see your feet. Hold a foot up in the air. O.K. It
>   might be a little bigger than yours [Jillian] right? Alright,
>   so if his foot is a little bit bigger, would he need more,
>   would we have more feet going down the row or less feet
>   going down?
> All: More...Less [Students yell out both answers.]
> T: Let me see a thumbs up for more. Let me see a thumbs up
>   for less. Where are the more's? Josh why do you say more?

Josh:	Because his feet are bigger.
T:	His feet are bigger so he would need more feet to go across? O.K. Where is someone that says less? Brittany why less?
Brittany:	Because um, Jillian's feet are smaller so, um it'll take less because it's like going back a little and his feet are bigger so it's going forward more.
T:	Hmmm.
Student:	I agree.
T:	Interesting. Did those arguments change anyone's mind? It changed your mind Matthew? Well, goodness, pretty good arguments then. Let's see it again. Give me a thumbs up if you think there's gonna take, if AJ is gonna need more steps to go across. Give me a thumbs up if it will take AJ less steps to get across. [Most students vote for less.] Well Brittany you are pretty convincing. [AJ walks along the strip and counts to 13. This is recorded on the board.]
Devon:	My feet are smaller.
T:	Thank you. So, your feet are smaller than Jillian's? So, would you be more than 14 or less than 13?
All:	More . . . less . . . more . . . no less . . . more . . . mine are smaller [Students yell out different answers.]
T:	O.K. Hold on . . . let's think. Devon says his feet are smaller than Jillian's.
Student:	And AJ's.
T:	If AJ's feet were big—not too big, just bigger than Jillian's. AJ's feet were bigger than Jillian's and he had less foot-steps. Jillian's feet were smaller than AJ's, so she needed more footsteps than AJ's. So would your number be higher than 14 or less than 14?
All:	More . . . less, less, less . . . more . . . more . . . less . . . more [Students yell out different answers.]
T:	You say more. What do you think Devon?
Devon:	More.
T:	Why more?
Devon:	Because my feet are smaller and um and 'cause her feet are bigger and it's just like . . . like AJ's feet are bigger than hers and he got one less.
T:	Are you convinced? [Said to the entire class.]

This was more indicative of the kind of exchange that occurred towards the end of the year when the teachers had a deeper understanding of the content as well as teaching techniques that focused on reasoning. It stands in contrast to data collected earlier in the year. In this interchange the teacher identified an important mathematical idea—the inverse relationship between the size of a unit and the quantity of units needed for the measurement—and pursued it. She also understood the importance of having the students pursue this idea themselves and engaged all students in this task by encouraging them to listen to each other's ideas to decide on their correctness.

Implications for Teacher Education

The current reform movement in mathematics education began with a vision first described in the *Curriculum and Evaluation Standards for School Mathematics* in 1989 and then clarified in later documents (e.g., 1991, 1995, 2000). These documents present a complex vision of teaching and learning mathematics that not only suggests alterations in *what* mathematics is taught and *how* that mathematics is taught, but goes further to highlight the interplay between content and pedagogical practices that lie at the heart of this reform movement. Thus, those involved in preparing current and future teachers to meet these standards are faced with the momentous undertaking of helping teachers understand the mathematics and the pedagogy, as well as the philosophy underlying this vision.

An inevitable result of efforts to comprehend all of the information in the Standards documents is that misinterpretations or incomplete interpretations have occurred. For example, some have focused on only a single aspect of the vision, such as simply adding certain content to the curriculum, and view it as the end of their work to improve mathematics education rather than the beginning. Others have taken certain aspects of the vision to unintended extremes, like assuming that "everything must be done in cooperative groups . . . and manipulatives are the basis of all learning" (Burrill, 1997, p. 62). The availability of standards-based curricula that make the vision of content and pedagogy more explicit gives professional development providers the wherewithal to avoid these more superficial interpretations of the Standards.

The implementation of standards-based curricula provide teachers with a real context in which to develop their understanding of content and content-specific pedagogy. With important mathematics identified and worthwhile tasks already created, teachers can concentrate on deepening their understanding of the mathematics as they work to change their role in the classroom to one that focuses on engaging with students' ideas and reasoning. Rather than approaching professional development in a step-by-step fashion, first having discussions about philosophy and what it means to teach mathematics for understanding before adopting a curriculum, it seems desirable to have these discussions in the context of implementation.

Enacting the curriculum, having students come up with powerful mathematical ideas, sharing their struggles with the mathematics and the teaching in a community of peers, and being encouraged by the professional development providers to reflect on these experiences somewhat simultaneously helps teachers move towards a better understanding of, and ability to implement, the vision of the Standards in their classrooms. Clearly this process must occur over an extended period of time to allow teachers to think about content and pedagogical issues individually and consider how in combination they form a cohesive vision of mathematics teaching and learning. As this project continues, efforts will continue to develop teachers' content knowledge and pedagogical approaches that support students' understanding of mathematics. This long-term approach to professional development is critical to enact the changes required to align practice with standards-based recommendations.

Conclusion

The changes that occurred in practice among the four teachers observed in this study suggest that change can occur as teachers negotiate through the myriad of ideas, beliefs, and attitudes that accompany an adoption of a standards-based curriculum. Although this study reports on only the first year of change, it is heartening that a substantial shift in teachers' goals regarding number and computation, the mainstay of the elementary curriculum, occurred. Furthermore, the teachers that were observed all improved in their ability to balance multiple mathematical goals, pursue student thinking, and keep mathematical reasoning as the focus of class discussions. While it is impossible to isolate the effect of the curriculum materials alone, it was evident in the professional development sessions and from interviews with teachers that the design of the lessons and the emphasis on standards-based goals continually encouraged the teachers to reflect upon appropriate mathematics content and effective instructional techniques. Thus, the curriculum, as an embodiment of the interconnectedness of content and pedagogical understandings essential to implementing the Standards, proved to be a powerful environment for teachers to learn about the Standards in the context of their work.

REFERENCES

Ball, D. L. (1996). Teacher learning and the mathematics reforms: What we think we know and what we need to learn. *Phi Delta Kappan, 77*(7), 500–508.

Bossé, M. J. (1995). The NCTM Standards in light of the New Math movement: A warning! *Journal of Mathematical Behavior, 14,* 171–201.

Burrill, G. (1997). Choices and Challenges. *Teaching Children Mathematics 4*(1), 58–63.

Cohen, D. K., & Barnes, C. A. (1993). Pedagogy and policy. In D. K. Cohen, M. W. McLaughlin, & J. E. Talbert (Eds.), *Teaching for understanding: Challenges for policy and practice* (pp. 207–239). San Francisco: Jossey-Bass Publishers.

Lloyd, G. M. (1999). Two teachers' conceptions of a reform-oriented curriculum: Implications for Mathematics Teacher Development. *Journal of Mathematics Teacher Education, 2*(3), 227–252.

Loucks-Horsley, S., Hewson, P.W., Love, N., & Stiles, K. E. (1998). *Designing professional development for teachers of science and mathematics.* Thousand Oaks, CA: The National Institute for Science Education.

National Council of Teachers of Mathematics. (1989). *Curriculum & evaluation standards for school mathematics.* Reston, VA: Author.

National Council of Teachers of Mathematics. (1991). *Professional standards for teaching mathematics.* Reston, VA: Author.

National Council of Teachers of Mathematics. (1995). *Assessment standards for school mathematics.* Reston, VA: Author.

National Council of Teachers of Mathematics. (2000). *Principles and standards for school mathematics.* Reston, VA: Author.

Richardson, V. (1990). Significant and worthwhile change in teaching practice. *Educational Researcher, 19*(7), 10–18.

Simon, M. A., & Schifter, D. (1991). Towards a constructivist perspective: An intervention study of mathematics teacher development. *Educational Studies in Mathematics, 22,* 309–331.

TERC. (1998). *Implementing Investigations in Number, Data, and Space, grades 1–2.* Palo Alto, CA: Dale Seymour Publications.

Wood, T., Cobb, P., & Yackel, E. (1991). Change in teaching mathematics: A case study. *American Educational Research Journal, 28*(3), 587–616.

Vanishing Act
The Effect of State-Mandated Content Standards on Multicultural Education

4.

Anita Perna Bohn

Anita Perna Bohn is an Assistant Professor in Curriculum and Instruction at Illinois State University's Department of Curriculum and Instruction. She has organized and presented at regional and national symposia on multicultural education in a standards era and published on this topic in the *Phi Delta Kappan* and *Education Digest* (with C. Sleeter).

ABSTRACT

A qualitative study documenting the impact of state-mandated standards and assessments on the multicultural education practices and dispositions of 14 elementary school teachers was conducted in an urban mid-western school district. Three apparent consequences of the district's standards policies and implementation plans were noted: a) a decline in teacher interest, time for, and concern about multicultural education during the first two years the standards were in effect; b) a policy shift away from site-based management and toward centralized control of pedagogy and content in the school district; and c) a silencing of community voices and an erosion of teacher agency. A call is made for teacher educators to speak out about the impediments to multicultural education reform that state-mandated standards can create and to support teachers in their efforts to deliver the benefits of our educational system equitably to all children.

Introduction

The current state standards movement in K–12 education is an unprecedented transformational force in American public schools, the real and lasting impact of which will not be understood completely for many years to come. The movement steadily gained momentum during the 1990s, as state-mandated standards and assessment programs proliferated across the nation. By 1997 every state in the Union, with the exception of Iowa, either had or was developing state standards. Most states also had or were developing mandatory standardized assessment programs to measure student performance against those standards (Gandal, 1997). These legally enforceable state standards for K–12 education, while varying enormously in both quality and design, nevertheless collectively constitute some of the most far-reaching educational policy changes America's schools have ever seen.

Although the machinery of legally enforceable content standards and assessment programs is well entrenched across the United States, only limited information exists on the effect of state standards upon another very critical goal: multicultural education. The multicultural education reform movement focuses on the educational significance and benefits of cultural pluralism and is dedicated to the goal of achieving equity and social justice for all groups within society.

The increasing diversity of America's classrooms demands that teachers be prepared and supported in the effort to deliver the benefits of our educational system equitably to all children. The mandate of legally enforceable state content standards also requires teachers' commitment to standardized content and uniform performance expectations for all students. A qualitative study was undertaken to understand how teachers and school districts addressed and reconciled these potentially conflicting reform goals.

OBJECTIVES OF THE STUDY

The qualitative study investigated the effect of newly mandated state standards upon elementary school teachers' multicultural attitudes and practices in an urban school district in the Midwest. It sought to illuminate the complexities, dilemmas, decision-making processes, and consequences that teachers experience when attempting to balance their multicultural beliefs and practices along with their obligation to deliver state-mandated curriculum standards and assessments. Two broad objectives guided the study:

1. To identify and analyze ways in which different teachers' multicultural education attitudes and practices were altered as a result of state or district policy related to implementation of new state standards and assessments.
2. To evaluate the consequences of those policies and practices upon the goals of the multicultural education movement.

A Brief Overview of Research on State Standards and Multicultural Education

Research and analysis of the effect of state standards on multicultural education reform to date have focused on two main areas of inquiry: a) the control and standardization of knowledge by the dominant culture, in terms of decisions about the content to be taught, and b) the punitive effect of high-stakes testing on marginalized groups, especially in light of the inequitable funding of public schools. Research in the first area examines situations such as those occurring in California and Oregon, where debates surrounding the development of mandated standards were manipulated politically and economically to assure control and standardization of knowledge by the dominant culture. (See, for example, Berlak, 1999; Bigelow, 1999; Sleeter, 2000; Vega-Castaneda, 2000.)

The second area of research documents the condition of unequal opportunity to learn in American public schools as an indication of the unfair impact of state mandated standards on marginalized groups, and also examines the deleterious effects of high-stakes testing on these groups. (See Apple, 1998; Heubert & Hauser, 1998; Kohn, 2000; Neill, 1997; Sacks, 2000; Whitty, 1997.)

Methodology and Data Sources

The study was part of a larger grounded theory research project investigating the conceptualizations and practices of multicultural education held by elementary school teachers, especially with regard to mathematics (Bohn, 1999). Research was conducted in an urban midwestern school district over a two-year period, from April, 1997 until May, 1999.

Phase One: Conceptualizations of Multicultural Education In the initial phase, data were collected from 14 kindergarten-through-fifth-grade teachers at two schools in the district. Participants were selected through the processes of theoretical and snowball sampling. Each was initially interviewed at least twice and observed teaching on two or more occasions wherever possible. Three teachers declined to be observed. Data were encoded via open coding methods and categorized according to common themes found in their beliefs and practices.

The categories were further analyzed via axial coding for reported influences or experiences that determined beliefs and practices. They were also compared to existing typologies of multicultural education, such as Sleeter and Grant's (1988) typology of approaches, and Banks' (1993) four approaches to teaching for multicultural education. In a continuously recursive process, teacher responses and evolving categories yielded understandings that were brought to bear in subsequent conversations and observations. Teachers' beliefs and practices of multicultural education could be relatively placed along a continuum suggested by Sleeter and Grant's typology. A number of theories were developed as tentative explanations for the observed phenomena.

A major finding in this initial phase was that participating teachers constructed very different conceptualizations of multicultural education, based upon their life experiences with race, social class, and gender issues. A second finding was that teachers whose life experiences had afforded them a deeper understanding and closer relationship with minority cultures possessed more advanced conceptualizations and practices of multicultural education and a deeper commitment to it than those not having those experiences. Four of the 14 participants described more intensive experiences and expressed multicultural education beliefs and values more advanced and more deeply committed to this reform movement.

Phase Two of the Study: State Standards Enacted During the two-year course of the study, some very significant educational policy changes took shape within the state and within the school district. During the first year (1997), the state passed into law a set of State Learning Standards that identified "goals for learning" every subject taught in the state's public schools. The state's official means for measuring attainment of these goals would be a new standardized test given to all third, fourth, fifth, seventh, eighth, tenth, and eleventh grade public school students in the state.

Anticipating the passage of these new state policies in the spring of 1997, the local school district already had decided to require that all elementary school teachers in the district use the same publishers' textbook series in each subject, beginning in the fall of 1997 with a new social studies series chosen by a district selection committee of administrators and teachers the previous spring. The committee had found the series to be the one closest aligned with proposed state standards in social studies. Following passage of the standards legislation in July of 1997, the district administration went on to dictate that teachers could not deviate from or substitute for these textbook lessons in any way.

Emergent questions about the impact of the new state standards on the curriculum and on teachers' practices led to a second set of questions and round of interviews and observations beginning in the fall of 1997 and continuing through the 1998–99 school year. Relying upon relationships and data established in the initial phase, the researcher collected additional data from the same 14 teachers, the two principals of the schools, and the district assistant superintendent in charge of curriculum. Specific attention was paid to ways in which teachers did or did not accommodate multicultural education within the constraints of the new state standards and proposed testing and the district's new textbook mandate. All participants were interviewed twice. Three teachers who evinced greater interests in the topic were interviewed an additional two times. Seven teachers were observed teaching during this phase, the rest declining to be observed again. Teachers' data were encoded, categorized by commonalties, and compared to their previously determined placements on the continuum of conceptualizations and practices of multicultural education.

The findings of this study are limited by its small sample size and the participants' restrictions on observations. The participants also were not asked to comment on the analysis and conclusions presented here. A third limitation of this study resides in the nature of grounded theory research, which is theory building and not theory testing. The extent to which any emergent theory may be true in general cannot be known from this study and remains to be tested in subsequent research studies.

Results

Three apparent consequences for multicultural education in the district were seen as resulting from the implementation of mandated state standards and the political decisions made by the school district. The consequences are summarized here, with a representative sampling of teacher and administrator voices preserved to reflect some of the complexities and nuances of the situations and attitudes with which they grappled.

DIMINISHED TIME, INTEREST, AND CONCERN

A marked decline in teacher interest, time for, and, in many cases, concern about multicultural education issues was noted over the two school years the standards were in effect. Within this category, teachers' different reactions to the same mandates were seen as related to their differing levels of understanding of and commitment to multicultural education, ascertained in the initial phase of the study.

For teachers who had earlier evinced limited understanding of the dimensions and implications of multicultural education, the standards and the commercial textbooks purchased to implement them gave the impression that multicultural education was "taken care of" by the standards and the mandated materials, thereby freeing teachers from the obligation of attending to it otherwise. As one teacher who had expressed interest but acknowledged knowing little about multicultural education said of the textbook's handling of multicultural education: "It's better than what I had before, which was nothing, really. Only teaching at this grade level for four years, with a lot of other important things to attend to, it was not something I had gotten around to yet, in all honesty."

A first grade teacher who had evinced little interest in multicultural education during her initial interviews, welcomed the new textbook mandate with these comments:

> I'm kind of thinking that it's going to be better if I have something I know I have to get through. For first grade anyway, ours [the first grade social studies curriculum] is by month, and like in December, it's [multicultural education] addressed in the new social studies Big Book and they tie it into cultures with lights, and it even has a big picture from India, Diwal Diwa—I don't know to say it [Diwali]—and Chanukah and, and what's the Black holiday? Kwanzaa. And Kwanzaa and Christmas tree lights, and so it ties all that in there, and then Thomas Edison is even mentioned! . . . For myself, I think it will help me touch the multicultural even better.

Teachers who were unsympathetic to multicultural education in the initial study seemed to find that the new policies legitimated their very limited exploration of these issues. One such teacher opined at the end of the second year that the decision of the district was really in everyone's best interest:

> I really think if we're ever going to get past looking at different colors of different skins, maybe instead of going, uh, 'It's White American month, or Black American month or Hispanic month,' we should just probably talk about famous people and just make sure that everybody's really well represented. Because otherwise, I just really do believe . . . I mean, we're still looking at skin color all the time and I'd like to get beyond that. That's really been a frustrating thing for me . . . it was getting to be, you know, everybody wants a history month. We should just have 'Famous Americans Month' and make sure we have a curriculum that includes all of that. Now, our new social studies series has Biographies of the Month . . . and they're just fabulous. They depict famous women, famous Blacks, famous Hispanics, just a whole gamut of different people, and it's just like one a month, and it's just a really neat idea. I'm really very happy with it.

For teachers who had previously been found to be aware and committed to the issues of multicultural education, the newly mandated instructional materials posed serious time constraints that interfered with their ability to deliver a multicultural curriculum or attend to culturally diverse instructional needs. As one teacher reported in the second year of the study:

I find that I'm not able to do as much as I used to because of the time—every-thing is so dictated right now. You have to be sensitive to the community that you teach in. We have a high African-American and Hispanic population here. You should teach certain multicultural topics and issues so that they at least get some exposure to them. I think it's important. [Now] you have to cut down on the amount of things you've done in the past and follow the district curriculum closer, and it's harder to find the time. Instead of having an hour or several hours for dealing with a certain topic, you have to condense it to twenty min-utes, or ten minutes here, fifteen minutes there. We don't have the large blocks of time we used to. You can work it in, if you really want to, but it's hard.

Three of the four teachers who possessed more advanced understanding and practices of multicultural education complained that the only way they were able to attend to a multicultural agenda under the new district policies was if they were willing to take the risk of non-compliance with the pre-scribed curriculum and the practice tests for state mandated testing. Only one of these teachers, however, openly admitted non-compliance with the textbook mandate and the practice tests. A second teacher intimated non-compliance only indirectly and then declined to comment or to be observed any further. A third teacher's non-compliance took the form of early retire-ment at the end of the 1998–99 school year, acknowledging that the new policies were at least partially responsible for his decision.

All teachers in grades tested to assess attainment of the standards com-plained that the increased time and attention required by the district to pre-pare students for the new state testing made it very difficult to deal effectively with multicultural issues. As one fifth grade teacher responded in February of 1999 when asked whether the first round of the newly devised state tests had significantly interfered with other curricular or instructional plans or possibilities in the classroom:

If you consider that it is now February, and that only now that the fifth grade tests are finally over have I, for the first time since the beginning of the year, been able to spend an entire day without preparing my students in some way to take these tests, going through the practice books, drilling them for material they have to know, giving practice tests and essays, all to prepare them for the fifth grade reading writing and math tests, I'd have to say yes, it has com-manded just a bit of our attention.

RESTORATION OF CENTRALIZED CONTROL OF SCHOOLS

A policy shift was witnessed in the district away from shared authority for policy-making and a substantial degree of teacher and site autonomy and back toward centralized control of both pedagogy and content. The school district had functioned under a site-based management policy for ten years prior to the passing of the state standards, and in a matter of six weeks, this was abolished without debate—in fact without any solicitation of teacher input into the decision. Teachers were eliminated from the power equation over the summer, after passage of the state standards legislation in July. The loss of teacher autonomy and decision-making power was presented as a fait accompli in the first district teacher institute of the fall of 1997. It was accepted without formal protest by teachers who explained in subsequent interviews that they saw the act as legally mandated and therefore beyond their or the district's control.

Curiously, official reasons for the necessity of this district policy shift varied with the administrator questioned, although all agreed it was necessary and unavoidable. One of the principals interviewed tied the decision to general trends of state and national accountability, stating: "The pendulum is swinging back." The principal of the second school in the study, however, presented the decision to centralize control of the curriculum as being only partially connected to the new state standards. She explained that local concerns about the lack of consistency in the curricula from school to school within the district precipitated the decision:

"... the desire to provide all of our students in the district with the same education wherever they happen to go to school, was also a deciding factor."

Interviews with the district assistant superintendent in charge of curriculum suggested that the school district had used the new standards as an opportunity to centralize control of the curriculum. She reported that the district actually had begun a curriculum review process two years before the state learning standards were passed, and "it was in this process that questions about site-based management and about the uneven quality of the education individual students were receiving in the district were raised." She went on to explain that "as much as anything, the upcoming standards gave us the opportunity to start from scratch, in terms of our curriculum, with a clear agenda." The district had explored a number of different avenues for aligning the curriculum with the standards. Ultimately they decided that the quickest impact they could have would be to purchase new materials. Significantly, a second interview with the assistant superintendent revealed that "the state gave us money to help with the purchase of the new textbooks." In a large district whose education dollars are stretched as tightly as this district's were known to be, the offer was apparently one they could not afford to refuse.

The assistant superintendent acknowledged that a desire for the district's students to score well on upcoming state assessment tests also guided their decision-making about the choice of new curriculum materials and the decision that they be used exactly as written. ". . . we wanted to be sure that the materials that we purchased supported our students achieving those goals. If our instructional materials are in line with what's being tested, then our students should necessarily do better." Of the mandate that teachers follow the materials closely and not deviate from them or eliminate any, the assistant superintendent commented; "I see that as essential."

DESKILLING TEACHERS, SILENCING COMMUNITY VOICES

Standardization of the curriculum with an off-the-shelf textbook curriculum deskilled teachers in several instances. Teachers were observed rushing through timed monthly material in order to stay on schedule, sometimes discouraging or ignoring the relevant lived experiences that children tried to offer in class discussions. Feeling rushed was a common complaint of teachers trying to adhere to the textbook curriculum. Teacher agency appeared to be hampered by a lack of time and opportunity to attend to the ethnic and social backgrounds of the students they currently taught, as witnessed in the earlier comments of the second grade teacher who found himself without time to address the diverse needs of his Latino and African-American students.

Teachers from non-traditional backgrounds with rich life experiences that might enhance the multicultural classroom expressed frustration at the heavily mandated content. One such teacher stated:

> I'm rather unique because I came in as a first year teacher at the age of 39, and I'd seen and done all kinds of things before I came in here. But, one of the reasons I didn't go into teaching right away was because when I student-taught, I just couldn't stand opening this textbook and just doing this regimented stuff. I just thought, this is not something where I feel like I have a lot of autonomy or a lot my own freedom, so I didn't do it. I mean, that's the only reason I never taught all those years. And then when my oldest son, who is now almost 22, was in school, just through his experiences I started realizing, because it was changing, that teachers had a lot more autonomy and a lot more opportunity for creativity than I had seen before. And that's when I decided that I wanted to do it. So I'm here a few years and all of the sudden, there it goes! And to be real honest about it, over the last couple of years I've thought maybe I didn't make the right decision here, because this is going right back to what I didn't want to do.

Finally, the limitations of the commercial curriculum silenced diverse community voices in deference to the singular view of history and culture offered by the publisher. In an example offered by another second grade teacher interviewed in the fall of 1998, a long-standing unit on Mexico that involved Latino families from the community was reluctantly abandoned, since Mexico was not in the second grade's textbook curriculum. The teacher explained in frustration:

> I liked it. I liked doing the Mexican unit. We all liked it, and got a lot out of it. We had families who made food for us and brought it in here, and taught us some Spanish, and told us about their lives, and even taught us a dance once. And that's, that's here! [meaning that it reflected the ethnic make-up of the town.] But I can't make the time now to fit it in, when it's not even in my curriculum. There's too much mandatory stuff to get through.

Discussion

The interaction of multicultural education and state standards is very complex. While standards per se should not necessarily be antithetical to multicultural education, the scenario played out in this large midwestern school district makes it clear that the interpretation, implementation methods, and assessment of state standards can result in acts very detrimental to the goals of multicultural education reform. If this school district's experiences with implementing state standards are indicative of the circumstances and options faced by teachers and administrators elsewhere, then for multicultural education to survive within the current standards movement, educators concerned about equity and social justice in our schools must be prepared to speak out. As teacher educators, our voices must be heard on the following issues:

1. The validity and the quality of state content standards and assessment instruments must continue to be interrogated vigorously and publicly from a multicultural perspective. State standards are known to vary enormously from state to state, in terms of quality and the effort put into in their construction (Finn & Petrilli, 2000; Mancuso & Kendall, 1998). Students and teachers alike are frequently tested and judged on their mastery of knowledge defined by the political agenda of state legislators and prominent state special interest groups. (Apple, 1998; Whitty, 1997). State testing methods generally rely upon isolated and decontextualized information bytes bearing no relationship to one

another or to the lives of the students they test (Neill, 1997), even if some test items do actually include "multicultural" information. Even more serious is the evidence that time allotted for students to practice test-taking is making ever larger inroads into the amount of classroom time available for more meaningful kinds of instruction.

2. Teachers, school districts, and state boards of education must be convinced that a commercial textbook series is not an effective path to multicultural education reform. The idiosyncratic nature of the different populations that textbook publishing companies serve, along with the commercial companies' desire for large market shares, preordain that textbook multicultural curricula will remain superficial and impersonal at best (Apple, 1986; Bohn & Sleeter, 2000). Yet, when schools are forced to tackle the daunting task of revamping an entire curriculum without simultaneously being given the time and resources necessary to develop a new one—and especially when the only offer of state financial assistance is toward the purchase of new textbooks—school districts will certainly resort to this solution to reform again and again. The inherent injustice of state standards without equitable state funding for education must continue to be publicly excoriated.

3. Administrators must be educated to see that excluding teachers from the power equation will never bring about meaningful school reform. Standardizing and centralizing the curriculum and turning teachers into dispensers of state-approved information deskills and dehumanizes the teaching profession. It alienates those from the profession whom we need the most—the best and the brightest whose insight and experiences allow them to think outside the box. Their loss would not serve any student well, but it would especially hurt students from marginalized groups in our society, whose support systems for social and economic success are the most fragile.

   We know that for the dream of equity and social justice for all students to be realized, teachers must be paramount agents of change. Teacher educators must therefore work to ensure that the recruitment and education of teachers produces teachers capable of carrying out that change and empowered to do so. We must also increase our collaboration with schools to support teachers in the decision-making responsibilities that are essential to their professional development (Darling-Hammond & McLauglin, 1995.)

4. In the current climate of standardized education, teachers need encouragement to continue drawing upon the wisdom of a growing body of literature that informs us about culturally relevant curriculum and instruction. They must continue to learn about and utilize their students' culturally determined preferences for thinking and interacting

and to examine the social conditions that perpetuate some groups' marginalization. Teacher educators must give teachers the direction and support they need to develop curricula and repertoires of instructional techniques that bring students' cultural experiences, values, and traditions into the classroom and facilitate the full and equitable participation of all students.

The findings of this qualitative study evoke genuine concern that state standards may cause schools to ignore decades of research and progress in the areas of teacher development, individualizing teaching and learning, and the promotion of equity and social justice in our schools. There is an urgent need for communities of teachers, administrators, and teacher educators to scrutinize the intent and the effect of state standards on diversity and equity, and for them to work together to staunch the flow of attention, energy, and resources away from multicultural education in the name of higher standards or accountability.

REFERENCES

Apple, M. (1986). *Teachers and texts.* New York: Routledge & Kegan Paul.

Apple, M. (1998). Are markets and standards democratic? *Educational Researcher, 27*(6), 24–28.

Banks, J.A. (1993). Integrating the curriculum with ethnic content: Approaches and guidelines. In J.A. Banks and C.A.M. Banks (Eds.), *Multicultural education: Issues and perspectives* (pp. 189–207). Boston: Allyn and Bacon.

Berlak, H. (1999). Standards and the control of knowledge. *Rethinking Schools, 13*(3), pp. 10–11, 29.

Bigelow, B. (1999). *Standards and multiculturalism. Rethinking Schools, 13*(4), 6–7.

Bohn, A.P. (1999). *Elementary school teachers' conceptualizations and practices of multicultural education.* Unpublished doctoral dissertation, Illinois State University, Normal.

Bohn, A.P., and Sleeter, C.E. (2000). Multicultural education and the state standards movement: A report from the field. *Phi Delta Kappan, 82*(2), 156–59.

Darling-Hammond, L., and McLauglin, M.. (1995). Policies that support professional development in an era of reform. *Phi Delta Kappan, 76*(8), 597–604

Finn, C. E., and Petrilli, M.J. (Eds.). (2000). *The state of state standards 2000.* Dayton, Ohio: The Thomas B. Fordham Foundation.

Gandal, M. (1997). *Making standards matter, 1997: An annual fifty-state report on efforts to raise academic standards.* Washington, DC: American Federation of Teachers.

Heubert, J.P., and Hauser, R.M., Editors. (1998), *High stakes: Testing for tracking, promotion, and graduation.* Washington, D.C.: National Research Commission.

Kohn, A. (2000). *The Case Against Standardized Testing.* Portsmouth, NH: Heinemann.

Mancuso, R.J., and Kendall, J.S. (1998) *The status of state standards.* Aurora, CO: Mid-continent Research for Education and Learning, Inc.

Neill, M. (1997). *Testing our children: A report card on state assessment systems.* Cambridge, MA: FairTest.

Sacks, P. (2000). *Standardized minds: The high price of America's testing culture and what we can do to change it.* Cambridge, MA: Perseus Books.

Sleeter, C.E. (2000, April). *Keeping the lid on: State standards and social studies curricula in California.* Paper given at the AREA Annual Convention in New Orleans.

Sleeter, C. and Grant, C. (1988). *Making choices for multicultural education: Five approaches to race, class, and gender.* New York: Merrill.

Vega-Castaneda. L. (2000, April). *A tale of politics and ideology—The real deal in state standardization.* Paper given at the AREA Annual Convention in New Orleans.

Whitty, G. (1997). Lessons from England: Charters, choice, and standards. *Rethinking Schools, 11*(3), 8–9.

Standards' Impact on Tomorrow's Teachers
Partnerships, Accountability, and Program Renewal

Bette S. Bergeron

Professor Bette S. Bergeron is currently the Head of Education at Arizona State University–East. Bergeron's current research endeavors focus on professional standards, school partnerships, and assessments. In addition to numerous journal articles on topics specific to teacher education, Bergeron has co-authored two books on elementary literacy practices.

ABSTRACT

The focus of this research is to investigate the impact of current national standards initiatives on the preparation of tomorrow's teachers. In light of the increased demands placed on teacher education units across the country to adopt mandated standards, this movement has had a potentially dramatic effect on every facet of program development and reform. As an additional strain on teacher education units, these changes are being enacted in a context demanding the implementation of Professional Development School (PDS) collaboratives.

Specifically, the purpose of this inquiry is to move the dialogue on standards from the current debate on "why standards?" to an informative exchange regarding how standards are transforming approaches to partnerships, accountability, and curriculum. This inquiry is presented through a case study of one large commuter campus and its response to state and accreditation standards mandates.

The education profession recently has been swept up in a national call for reform that can be characterized as a political combat zone (Cole, 1999). Teacher preparation has often been the focus of this targeted scrutiny. The demand for accountability in teacher education has been legislated clearly in the recently revised Higher Education Act, which outlines requirements for the publication of institutional "report cards" that include candidates' pass rates on standardized exams. Standards initiatives, driven by legislative mandates, have changed the very complexion of teacher education in part through the deletion of professional concentrations, shifting of faculty assignments, increased requirements for field experiences, and capping of education coursework (Scott & King, 1996).

It is evident that the development and use of standards alone cannot address teacher education's maladies. Blackwell (1997) considers standards as the "new medicine" in teacher education and suggests that "it remains to be seen whether or not this remedy will deal symptomatically or fundamentally with concerns we all have about the preparation of new teachers" (p. 3). This research report presents a case study of one institution's response to these external pressures and, in particular, the impact of legislated standards on the preparation of tomorrow's teachers.

A New Orthodoxy

In response to growing public and political concern, teacher preparation has turned to standards as a means for insuring the credibility and quality of the profession. Tozer (1999) notes that a "new orthodoxy," defined primarily through state and national standards, has been emerging throughout the 1990's. This new orthodoxy allows the profession to gain nation-wide consensus regarding definitions and assessments of good teaching (Corcoran & Tichenor, 1999). The widespread nature of this initiative is clearly indicated by states' overwhelming adoption of INTASC standards to redefine teacher education.

The development of standards does not guarantee quality, however. Critics of state standards worry that, when governments assume a prominent role in standards-setting, all the dysfunctional features of regulatory policy emerge (Sykes, 1998). The knowledge elites who construct national standards can use combinations of governmental inducements and mandates to secure both attention and compliance. A lack of focus at many teacher preparation institutions, public ambivalence for teachers in general, and lack of attention and status given to teacher education programs on most campuses work against the success of standards and substantive change. Blackwell (1997) fears that the standards approach to reforming the preparation of teachers will lead to superficial changes in education practices that make very little long-term difference in the lives of children.

This case study highlights one aspect of standards legislation: the effects of this "new orthodoxy" on Professional Development School (PDS) initiatives and resulting impact on the preparation of teachers. Zimpher (1997) suggests that PDS collaboratives provide reliable environments for teacher education students to learn about teaching and opportunities to engage expert teachers throughout the design and implementation of teacher education programs. Through these unique relationships, universities and schools jointly influence what occurs at each site, support the infusion of theory and practice, and expand opportunities for professional development for all participants (Yopp, Guillaume, & Yopp, 1998). These high stakes ventures expect that partners share responsibilities in areas where each formerly had independent control (NCATE, 1997). Despite their potential, however, some educators caution that much of the reported PDS work has had little systemic impact on the redesign of teacher preparation and has led instead to superficial modifications in existing traditional programs (Burstein, Kretschmer, Smith, & Gudoski, 1999).

In order to address the current educational crisis and assuage the critics of both higher education and its standards, it is evident that teacher preparation institutions must change both drastically and rapidly (Cole, 1999). While standards offer one possible avenue for defining effective teaching and assessment, it is within these new parameters that a number of compelling issues emerge and demand our attention.

The purpose of this research is to examine a variety of imbedded data sources, such as curriculum policy documents and various committee minutes, to determine what effect standards have had on one rapidly expanding teacher education program. Specifically, the inquiry centers on how standards have affected teacher preparation and its school partners, what next steps these changes imply, and what barriers may exist to standards-driven reform. From these data, implications can be drawn for other education units struggling to balance the demands of external standards with internal needs of its constituents.

Case Study: Midwest University

Although many teacher educators would concur that professional standards are a necessary component of reform efforts, the prevalent practice by states to mandate these standards is causing some perplexing dilemmas for teacher education. Three issues have emerged as critical to the national dialogue on standards: *partnerships, accountability,* and *curriculum reform.*

The following case report will overview these issues within the context of one large, commuter campus.

Midwest University (a pseudonym) is an urban campus with close ties to both suburban and rural adjoining communities. The student population is typically non-traditional and reflects the cultural diversity of the urban Midwest. The university's School of Education enrolls approximately 450 undergraduate elementary education students each semester. Like the campus student body, the School's population includes a large proportion of older adults who bring varied lived experiences to the classroom.

The School of Education has been facing the dual demands of increased enrollment and required field experiences that are offered prior to student teaching. Presently, preservice teachers have extensive field experiences related to five methods courses. The School is faced not only with acquiring appropriate numbers of classrooms for these multiple placements, but also finding sites that ensure quality experiences for the preservice teachers in diverse settings that appropriately reflect the demographics of the campus's multi-racial, multi-cultural communities.

State mandates have placed additional demands on the School's evolving education programs. In 1998, the state's Professional Standards Board approved teaching standards in 12 content and four developmental areas. In turn, the School of Education developed and adopted its own program standards specific to the mission of the School and reflective of the major themes found throughout the state's documents. Currently, the State Board is focusing its efforts on the implications of its standards on preparation programs, imbedded school-university partnerships, initial licensing, and continued certification. It has also collaborated with NCATE in a joint accreditation process that specifies the explicit adoption of standards. In light of these changes, the university is currently refocusing its preparation programs in order to effectively prepare the region's future educators within the state's newly defined contexts.

STUDY METHODOLOGY

The reported research utilizes case study methodology. Case studies, which include the intensive description and analysis of a single phenomenon or unit (Merriam, 1998), are anchored in real-life situations. Case study research results in rich and holistic accounts of the phenomenon and offers insights that can structure future research while advancing a field's knowledge base. Case studies are especially useful in studying educational innovations, evaluating programs, and informing policy. The phenomenon that provides the focus for the reported case study is the teacher education program at Midwest University and the impact of mandated standards on attempted reform at this institution. Data were collected over a five-year period, from 1994 to 1999. The study's author was the principal investigator for the research, and assumed the role of participant observer.

A variety of methods for data collection and analysis can be used in case study design. Data collected for the reported study are situated within the phenomenon and include minutes from PDS, curriculum, and School faculty meetings. Additional sources include anecdotal notes from state Board meetings, imbedded artifacts related to program and student assessments, and informal conversational interviews with School and PDS participants. Data were also collected from two interviews conducted with a key informant, who is a principal at one of the School's original PDS sites. Key informants are those participants who possess specialized knowledge and who contribute insights to study findings (Goetz & LeCompte, 1984).

Constant comparative analysis was used to examine data collected for the reported case study. This analysis involves comparing one segment of data with another to determine similarities and differences, group data on these similar dimensions, and form subsequent categories (Merriam, 1998). The overall object is to seek patterns in the data, which are analyzed in the building of grounded theory. In the reported case study, this analysis was used to uncover patterns regarding the impact and implications of externally driven standards on teacher preparation.

Limitations to case study design include the tendency to oversimplify or exaggerate the phenomenon being studied (Merriam, 1998). Additionally, case studies are limited by the sensitivity and integrity of the investigator and the possibility for bias to affect the final product. Because case studies focus on a single unit, there is also concern regarding the overall generalizability of these studies.

Findings

Close scrutiny of the reported case study revealed that standards impact three areas of teacher preparation: partnerships, accountability, and curriculum. One direct implication of these standards has been the development of school/university *partnerships*. The School of Education currently enjoys partnerships with 22 local school sites, wherein teacher leaders actively participate in the planning and delivery of methods coursework. The impetus on state standards is also directly related to expected changes in the *accountability* of both units and their candidates. Assessments must change in order to reflect not only the knowledges of future teachers, but their performances as well. A final implication of the state standards movement is on program *curriculum*. Together with its school partners, and informed by new accountability measures, Midwest is currently revising its teacher preparation curriculum to address the State's mandated standards.

PARTNERSHIPS

In order to actualize reform within teacher education, a variety of compelling partnerships must be formed. Griffith, Kovar, and Stoel (1996) note the interdependent nature of teacher education and the importance of viewing this preparation as a campus-wide responsibility. This responsibility also demands collaboration with community educators, policymakers, and all who are stakeholders in the education of today's youth.

The partnerships that have gained the most attention in teacher preparation have been those forged between universities and schools. Integral to these PDS initiatives is a heightened national focus on professional teaching standards. The complex layering of indicators related to PDS and teacher preparation includes standards developed by the National Council on Accreditation for Teacher Education (NCATE), Interstate New Teacher Assessment and Support Consortium (INTASC), and National Board for Professional Teaching Standards (NBPTS). In addition, NCATE is promulgating sets of standards specific to professional development schools. NCATE (1997) reports that PDS schools are an important part of the continuum that underlies professional teaching practices and therefore must be consistent with standards for both new and accomplished teachers. PDS partners are accountable for upholding professional standards for teaching and preparing new teachers in accordance with those standards.

Partnerships between school and universities are clearly being considered as much more than superficial collaborations of convenience. It is suggested that, without linking the renewal of teacher education with the renewal of schools, new teachers will likely be either swallowed up by mediocrity or become beacons in otherwise unengaged places (Blackwell, 1997). Sykes (1998) notes, "the professional agenda as articulated through such means as state licensure, content and teaching standards, and school restructuring ideas cannot prosper in the long run and across many locales without school-university partnerships dedicated to mutual renewal" (p. 12).

This development of state and national teacher preparation standards, and their infusion into locally-based teacher preparation program standards, are impacting the development of Midwest University's PDS partnerships as a whole and within specified content courses. One of the most marked areas of impact relates to the changes in participant roles at both the university and schools. Shifting the focus (and location) of teacher education programs requires lengthy conversations with university and school colleagues (Wall, Weisenbach, Rayl, Huffman-Joley, & Scannel, 1998), and the eventual redefinition of participant roles as interactions are increased between university faculty and classroom teachers. Inherent to performance-based programs is the expectation that courses become infused with extensive field experiences through team-taught instruction conducted by participants across settings. The collegiality and collaboration inherent to shared role responsibility represents a major step from the isolation and autonomy that have entrenched the conventional teaching cultures of both the university and school.

Prior to the inception of Midwest University's PDS partnerships, practitioners were considered a peripheral part of teacher preparation, with the exception of cooperating teachers who supervised student teaching. Field experiences in the elementary methods courses were sporadic, or even nonexistent. As the PDS partnerships developed and as the shift towards standards was made, it became apparent that clearly defined relationships with participants would be paramount to the collaboration's success. Currently, practicing educators can become involved in several ways with the teacher education programs. Through a truly collaborative partnership, standards can be infused effectively into course delivery, classroom experiences, and professional dialogue.

Within the Midwest teacher education programs, one of the primary classroom roles is that of *Host Teacher*. These practitioners host one to three methods students in their classrooms each semester. Additionally, an educator at each school site volunteers to be the *On-Site Coordinator*. This role's responsibilities include coordinating field placements within the school site and acting as a liaison between the university and school. In addition to the supervisory roles of Host Teachers and On-Site Coordinators, university faculty seek out the expertise of site-based educators to enhance the theory to practice link in the professional preparation courses. Often, university faculty invite *Seminar Leaders* to participate in the lecture portion of the methods course.

While these roles are critical to the success of the methods course experiences, Midwest University is also seeking avenues for more directly involving practitioners in the development and delivery of courses. This has been accomplished, in part, by creating the position of *Clinical Instructor*. Clinical Instructors, who are classroom teachers, share in all course responsibilities with a university faculty member and are paid a stipend by the university. Team-taught methods courses are held on-site and provide preservice students with multiple professional perspectives. In addition, the collaboration that occurs between the university and school-based instructors allows for extended dialogue concerning program and state teaching standards. These professional interactions have had effects beyond those impacting university students. For example, informal interviews with practitioners revealed an increased awareness regarding professional teaching standards and teachers' subsequent infusion of these standards into their own classroom instruction.

The role of Clinical Instructor has led to the development of a campus-based position that more clearly defines the relationship between theory and practice. This role has been formalized through the creation of a one-year *Clinical Professor* or Teacher-in-Residence position. A veteran teacher with extensive past experience in other PDS roles has a joint appointment by her/his school district and the university. As part of the university faculty, the Clinical Professor maintains a .75 FTE teaching load and serves on departmental committees. Because part of the salary comes directly from the partnering school district, the district also assigns the Clinical Professor to specialized staff development projects. At the conclusion of the academic year, the Clinical Professor resumes classroom teaching duties. It is anticipated that a cadre of Clinical Professors will be developed to serve as instructional leaders across the region and will become critical resources as the State's new standards-based licensing system is fully implemented.

ACCOUNTABILITY

Realignment of professional standards within teacher education necessitates major changes in how teacher candidates and the educational unit are assessed. In response to a the public's demand for accountability in education, many states have implemented standardized testing, which is relatively inexpensive, rapidly implemented, and quickly reported to the media through compelling soundbites (Brabeck, 1999). Massachusetts recently has been caught in the center of the nation's scrutiny over teacher testing, as a result of candidates' lack of success with the newly adopted state standardized exam. Despite concern from both educators and private citizen groups over the test's lack of validity and reliability, "the volume and vehemence of the teacher and teacher education bashing rhetoric in Massachusetts caught the country's attention" (Brabeck, 1999, p. 346).

In spite of this outcry, teacher education units are attempting to assuage the standardized testing rhetoric by developing multiple approaches to assessment more clearly aligned with teacher performance standards. One of the most popular tools for assessment, and one that has had considerable visibility within teacher preparation, is the portfolio. Teacher education portfolios have been in place at Midwest University since 1994 and provide students with the opportunity to demonstrate and reflect upon their proficiency in the School's nine program standards through self-selected entries. School-based PDS partners are involved with the portfolio process through their participation in "mock interviews" held during the student teaching semester. Through these interviews, small groups of preservice candidates meet with school administrators and teacher leaders to share their portfolios, discuss how their documentation reflects proficiency in the School's teacher education standards, and how to transform these "working" portfolios to "showcases" appropriate for job interviews.

Also under development is a means to infuse standards into the assessment of students' field experiences completed prior to student teaching. Previously, methods students were assessed solely on their written lesson plans and not on their actual performance in the classroom. With the emphasis on performance now so ingrained in professional teaching standards, it became apparent that significant changes in assessments must occur. A field experience rubric was developed that matches the expectations outlined in the School's teacher education program standards. The rubric is completed by the Host Teachers, thus expanding their role. This tool was developed cooperatively with school-based partners and has been implemented across all of the programs' field-based courses.

PROGRAM RENEWAL

The movement towards standards-driven teacher preparation centers on the call to renew program goals and curriculum. This shift must be considered as an ongoing process and not a singular event. Those immersed in this change process must be clear of their direction and identify incremental steps as program reform is articulated (Griffith et al., 1996).

Within the School's state, new standards initiatives mandate that a continuum be created from teacher preparation throughout the professional career. As a first step in addressing the continuum issue, Midwest University's School of Education faculty developed a set of standards unique to the institution and aligned with the primary areas of emphasis within the State's documents. The School's teaching standards outline the nine areas in which the faculty believe all graduates from the teacher preparation programs must be proficient (e.g., communication, problem-solving, educational research, technology). Data used to develop the standards included program evaluations, admissions interviews, the School of Education's stated mission, and feedback from school-based constituents. As evidenced through School and Curriculum Committee meetings, the faculty believed that it was crucial to develop their own standards, instead of a wholesale adoption of state or INTASC standards. By developing their own program standards, the School's faculty came to consensus through invigorating dialogue that articulated the program's focus and areas for renewal. The standards are reviewed on a cyclical basis, and provide the foundation for the programs' assessments and course development.

One of the most visible changes in Midwest University's teacher education programs has been the extension of methods courses into the K–12 classroom. Currently, elementary education majors must complete five methods courses that require a field practicum. As the program is being revised, these courses are moving towards site-based delivery and more direct participation of practitioners. For example, university faculty/clinical instructors meet with participating Host Teachers prior to the start of the semester to refine course syllabi and choose topics that directly relate to the teacher education standards. Courses meet twice a week, alternating between the university and selected PDS sites regionally recognized for leadership. Students spend approximately two hours a week in the classroom for each methods course, where they observe and implement lessons under the guidance of their Host Teachers.

The realignment of teacher education programs with professional standards has impacted directly the structure and delivery of the School's methods courses. This restructuring is dependent upon positive, open relationships with schools and practicing educators. Yopp et al. (1998) suggest that courses based in school sites allow future teachers to link theory and practice through various activities with teachers and children. Though this linkage has been met with structural resistance, to be discussed below, the collaborative potential has clearly been evident in the revised curriculum provided for the region's future teachers.

ADDRESSING THE CHALLENGES TO ALIGNMENT

The shift currently occurring in teacher education is moving the responsibility of teacher preparation out of the lecture hall and into the field of practice. This move has been met with some resistance, particularly when individual's role change. Specific challenges to the "new orthodoxy" in standards-based reform include the development of tools to assess students' teaching performances, limitations related to university scheduling and credit hours, and the lack of balance between participants' increased responsibilities and limited compensation.

As previously discussed, assessments based on standards are being developed within Midwest University's teacher education programs.

University participants report that the challenges inherent to these instruments include levels of validity and reliability and finding the staffing resources for their implementation. For example, a portfolio rubric is continually being refined in an attempt to reflect accurately students' proficiency in each of the program's nine standards. As the teacher education programs continue to grow, without the accompanying addition of new faculty, it is becoming increasingly difficult to coordinate portfolio reviews. It is apparent that this process will become more dependent on PDS partners. Similarly, the use of field assessments is a new addition to the Host Teachers' role. Concern already has been expressed that this expectation extends the role from one of mentor to that of an evaluator.

Some challenges that occur as a shift is made towards on-site instruction are caused by the culture of the university and schools. For example, the university defines professional experiences by setting rigid course credits and hours. This form of scheduling is problematic when attempting to move courses into the schools while coordinating students' other general education core classes held at the campus. Also problematic is scheduling methods course "lecture" times after school hours in order to allow Clinical Instructors to participate without violating their own districts' contracts, while balancing the field component of the course at times most convenient for the Host Teachers within the school day.

A similar challenge relates to issues of academic "turf" and curriculum change. At Midwest University, a Curriculum Committee was appointed that includes representation from the Schools of Education, Liberal Arts, and Math/Science. This committee jointly developed curriculums for both the elementary and secondary programs that, according to its participants, effectively infused the state and NCATE standards. However, when the curriculum documents were brought before the faculty at large within the discipline-specific departments, faculty voiced many concerns regarding what was perceived as the School of Education's attempts to overstep its boundaries and alter established patterns of liberal studies courses. For example, the revised curriculum eliminated three hours in foreign language and a course in global literature in lieu of new education courses specific to standards addressing diversity and assessment. While the newly proposed curriculum met the mandated state and NCATE standards, it failed to gain campus approval because traditional turf issues were not reconciled.

An additional challenge to collaboration is the lack of balance between increased participant responsibility and limited compensation. Currently at Midwest University, only the Clinical Instructors and Clinical Professors are paid positions. While school participants recognize the benefits inherent to having an extra pair of hands in the classroom and the infusion of new ideas from the methods students, there has been some resistance to added responsibilities. The system for relicensure currently proposed by the State does include provisions for professional activities, such as hosting teacher preparation students, that will be credited towards licensure renewal. The hope is that this future goal will provide concrete compensation for the many ways in which practicing teachers enrich and expand teacher preparation.

Implications and Conclusions

Standards-driven mandates have compelled teacher education units to take a closer look at issues related to collaboration, accountability, and program renewal. Perhaps integral to each of these elements are the school-university partnerships that have emerged in response to-and sometimes in spite of-mandated standards. As teacher preparation programs begin to align more closely with professional teaching standards and adopt performance assessment strategies inherent to these standards, the direct cooperation with school-based participants becomes paramount to the success of the program itself.

As school/university partners consider innovative ideas that enhance the preparation of teachers, it is essential to elicit the knowledgeable support of administrative leaders. Administrative support is critical in redesigning teacher education programs, particularly from those with the power to affect change in organizational structures (Burstein et al., 1999). At the university level, this includes the need to reconsider how courses are scheduled to allow for extended blocks of time for site-based courses and to model collaboration between departments to negate the potential effects of discipline-specific "turf." With open dialogue, creative flexibility, and administrative support, new models for organizational structuring can be actualized.

As participants from all levels of our profession and community come to the table to re-vision teacher preparation, there must also be regular and sustained dialogue regarding the standards that guide these endeavors. Partners must be made aware of initiatives occurring locally and how these standards are forming both inservice and preservice professional development. As standards are used to reform teacher education programs, classroom mentors need to be involved in the standards' implementation so that ensuing field experiences will support appropriately the professional growth of the preservice students. Specifically, teachers must use these standards to reflect upon their own practices, so that classrooms can be models of instruction that are immersed in the most current knowledge regarding children's learning. Sykes (1998) purports that, if standards are to have any real significance, local partners must engage in collaborative scrutiny, adoption, and adaptation of these standards.

Collaborative endeavors have the potential to assist education preparation programs as the "new orthodoxy" in our profession is enacted through legislated mandates and standards. Darling-Hammond (1994) purports that practice must be jointly constructed by all educational partners in order to push the edges of teaching knowledge forward while restructuring teacher education and schooling. By working collaboratively, college faculty, teachers, and policy makers can forge "a profound contribution to real and lasting educational reform" (p. 26).

REFERENCES

Blackwell, S. (1997, March). *The dilemma of standards-driven reform.* Paper presented at the Annual Meeting of the Conference on College Composition and Communication. Phoenix, AZ.

Brabeck, M. M. (1999). Between Scylla and Charybdis: Teacher education's odyssey. *Journal of Teacher Education, 50,* 346–351.

Burstein, N., Kretschmer, D., Smith, C., & Gudoski, P. (1999). Redesigning teacher education as a shared responsibility of schools and universities. *Journal of Teacher Education, 50,* 106–118.

Cole, N. S. (1999, February). *Assessment in today's environment.* Invited Address at the AACTE Annual Meeting, Washington, DC.

Corcoran, C. A., & Tichenor, M. S. (1999, February). *INTASC and effective teaching: Making connections for preservice teachers.* Paper presented at the ATE Annual Meeting, Chicago, IL.

Darling-Hammond, L. (1994). Developing professional development schools: Early lessons, challenge, and promise. In L. Darling-Hammond (Ed.), *Professional development schools: Schools for developing a profession* (pp. 1–27). NY: Teachers College.

Goetz, J. P., & LeCompte, M. D. (1984). *Ethnography and qualitative design in educational research.* Orlando, FL: Academic.

Griffith, F.A., Kovar, R., & Stoel, C. (1996, June). *Standards-based education: A framework for professionalizing teacher education.* Paper presented at AAHE Conference on Assessment and Quality, Washington, DC.

Merriam, S. B. (1998). *Qualitative research and case study applications in education.* San Francisco: Jossey-Bass.

NCATE. (1997). *Draft standards for identifying and supporting quality professional development schools.* Washington, DC: NCATE.

Scott, M. J., & King, D. A. (1996). State-mandated reforms. *KDP Record, 33,* 32–33.

Sykes, G. (1998). Worthy of the name: Standards for the professional development school. In. M. Levine (Ed.), *Designing standards that work for professional development schools* (pp. 11–32). Washington, DC: NCATE.

Tozer, S. E. (1999, February). *Professional standards, performance assessment, and the uncertain future of the social foundations of teacher education.* Paper presented at the ATE Annual Meeting, Chicago, IL.

Wall, F. E., Weisenbach, L., Rayl, S., Huffman-Joley, G., & Scannel, M. (1998, January). *Panel discussion.* Paper presented at IPSB January Invitational Conference, Indianapolis, IN.

Yopp, R. H., Guillaume, A. M., & Yopp, H. K. (1998). The reading consortium: A university-school collaborative (ad)venture. *Journal of Reading Education, 23*(2), 12–16.

Zimpher, N. (1997, Fall). A case for PDS: A speech by Dr. Nancy Zimpher. *New Educator.* MI: Michigan State University.

6.

Shaping the Standards
A Collaborative Approach for Professional Development

Linda L. McDowell and Cheryl T. Desmond

Linda McDowell is an associate professor in the Department of Educational Foundations at Millersville University, Millersville, Pennsylvania. Her research interests include teacher education reform, collaborative partnerships, and adolescent development.

Cheryl Desmond is a professor in the Department of Educational Foundations at Millersville University, Millersville, Pennsylvania. Her research interests include the history of education reform, women's studies, and teacher education.

ABSTRACT

This chapter explores the use of inquiry-based conversations in which teachers and teacher educators collaboratively reflected on standards-based reform as a means of professional development. In this study, the authors found that the conversations demonstrated the value of collaborative inquiry among teachers and teacher educators and their effectiveness as a means of professional development. An evaluation of the conversations indicated that they increased participants' knowledge about standards-based reforms; they provided a positive means for reflection on standards in learning and teaching; and they helped teachers construct understanding of the application and implications of standards in basic and teacher education. The authors conclude that creating opportunities for such conversations can increase teachers' sense of efficacy in the decision-making process and may help schools implement reform.

Introduction

The purpose of this chapter is to describe the implementation of critical conversations in an inquiry-based format where teachers and teacher educators collaboratively reflected on standards-based reform and constructed meaning of the directives and their application to teaching and learning (Dewey, 1933; Richardson, 1997; Yost, Sentner, & Forlenza-Bailey, 2000). The critical conversations were designed in an inquiry format, meaning in each conversation, participants used questions submitted by the researchers or questions the participants had constructed to probe the content of the text and its application to learning, teaching, schooling, and professional development. We begin by briefly discussing the challenges that come with implementing a movement that calls for rigorous, world-class standards (Doyle and Pimental, 1998), without sacrificing our commitments to equitable and authentic learning for all students or abandoning research that supports the importance of teacher power in the classroom. First we describe the organizational structure of these conversations and present an analysis of the data on the content and assessments of these conversations, data that is useful in understanding how teachers and teacher educators perceive the standards movement and its impact on children, learning, and schooling. Finally, we evaluate critical conversations as a means of negotiating the tensions that standards-based reforms create in classrooms and explore implications of their use for professional development.

Perspectives on the Problem

Over the past two decades, the strongest initiative implemented to ensure the accountability of educators has been the standards-based movement, designed to increase student achievement (David and Shields, 1999). Many educators and policymakers view the standards movement as a reform that will guarantee improved student learning. Within this group, many like Finn, Petrilli, and Vanourek (1998) press for even stronger standards, claiming that "most state standards don't cut the mustard" and that "most states have a long way to go before their academic standards will be strong enough to bear the considerable burden now being placed on them (p. 56).

Others like Goodlad (1999) and Noddings (1999) believe that the narrow definitions of student achievement promulgated by the standards and the growing use of standardized testing to measure student learning will only further undermine democratic education and equity and will diminish teacher autonomy in the classroom. Darling-Hammond and Falk (1997) cautions that standards "could serve to create higher rates of failure for those who are already least well-served by the education system" (p. 91). Cuban (2000) warns us that as individual and school wide performance, measured by test scores, have become the engines driving accountability plans in state after state, the temptation to engage in shady practices also runs strong.

Although the proponents of standards and high stakes assessments have been successful in advancing their agenda in most statehouses, such challenges continue to grow in educational circles as well as in the popular press. The challenges primarily focus on three areas; critics question the impact standards and high-stakes assessments have had and will have on a) the power over schooling, b) teaching and student learning within the classroom, and c) on equity for all learners and democratic education.

Standards and high-stakes assessments undermine teacher, student, and local district judgment and erode their power over the content of the curriculum, pedagogy, and the means of assessing students' knowledge of this curriculum. Fenstermacher (1998) articulated this clearly when he stated:

> What troubles me is the extent to which the authority for setting the criteria and standards for our work as educators, for envisioning the good and proper outcomes of our labors [is] moving upward . . . away from the site where the actual work takes place, away from schools and neighborhoods, campuses and communities, to state and federal governments and to national organizations and associations.

Others question the effect that standards-based reform will have on teaching and learning within the classroom. These critics (David & Shields, 1999; Gratz, 2000; Kohn, 1999; Pipho, 2000) object to a) narrowly defined statements of learning, b) the measurement of student achievement solely by high-stakes examinations and the consequences for children, and c) the suppression of teacher decision making and creativity in curriculum and instruction. Kohn (1999) asserts that this preoccupation with achievement is not only different from, but also often detrimental to, a focus on learning.

Critics are concerned that standards will adversely affect children in poorer school districts and contend that they assail the aims of democratic education. Recognizing that some children have access to greater resources that ultimately helps to ensure school success, Noddings (1997) fears that "national standards may create the illusion that everyone has a fair chance and that any resulting differences in outcomes, with regards to jobs or future education, are the fault of those who didn't try hard enough" (p. 186).

As educators and policymakers, regardless of our position on standards, we must respond seriously to these concerns as we consider that

K–12 students in forty-nine states are being schooled under the directives of standards. As those who must comply with state and national mandates on standards, it is important that we as teachers and teacher educators interpret, understand, and act on the standards in ways that meet equally important expectations for our profession; expectations that, ultimately, enhance student learning. In their implementation, we need to ensure that:

1. We are creative, active, and reflective practitioners as we construct our understandings of the standards and as we apply them to the curriculum and instruction;
2. The standards provide for equity for all students and promote the aims of democratic education (Noddings, 1999);
3. Student learning is broadly defined and is measured in authentic ways (Popham, 1999); and
4. The efforts of the past decade emphasizing the teacher as the responsible decision maker in the classroom and in the school continue.

In what ways, can we begin to educate teachers and teacher educators to assume leadership for the work? In the debate over standards and its implications for student learning, Noddings (1997) insists "if standards are to have meaning, the people who must meet them should be involved in their construction" (p. 188). She claims that if children are going to become "competent citizens in a democratic society as Dewey argued, then adults—educators, policymakers, parents, citizens—need to engage in conversation and in the cooperative construction of standards" (p. 189). Gibboney (1994) challenges us as teacher educators to educate ourselves on what do we rest our claim to educate others. Without intelligent conversation and reflection, "the grand strategies, national goals, and restrictive state standards imposed on an unthoughtful enterprise" will only "place boulders in the path" of meaningful reform (p. 12).

Objectives

1. To explore the use of collaborative teacher-teacher educator inquiry-based conversations centered on standards based reform as a means of professional development for teachers and teacher educators.
2. To increase understanding of the standards movement and its implications for all key stakeholders.
3. To encourage collaboration on shaping standards to meet the diverse needs of children and to promote equity among learners.

4. To describe the implementation of inquiry-based conversations where teachers and teacher educators collaboratively reflected on the standards based reform and constructed meaning of directives and their application to teaching and learning.

Methods

In response to the recommendations by Noddings (1999) and Gibboney (1994) for thoughtful conversations, we, two teacher educators at a state regional university with combined basic education teaching experience of 25 years, designed a network for critical conversations on standards-based reforms for K–16+ learning among teachers and teacher educators. Through a series of structured conversations, we engaged local stakeholders, i.e. teachers, teacher educators, citizens, students, and policymakers, in six local school districts and in one state university in thoughtful consideration of the standards movement. The purposes of these conversations were a) to break through the silencing of educators that occurs with compliance effecting mandates, b) to provide the space to reassert the power that is situated in each classroom, c) to increase our understanding of the standards and their implications for learning and teaching and d) to find the means for action that will enhance capacity for the standards for all learners.

We began with a steering committee of teachers, administrators, and university faculty from both teacher education and liberal arts who helped choose the focus, the structure, the participants, the locations, and the timeline for the conversations. As a result of our first meeting, we decided to implement a series of three conversations in five public school districts and one private school and at the university. The conversations occurred over a six-month period, centered on suggested common readings with optional guided questions, and culminated in a day long standards conference consisting of district, university, state, and community participants. We agreed to link the seven locations electronically through an electronic mail reflector list and met regularly with conversation facilitators.

During the initial meeting, it was made clear to us, as university educators, by our colleagues in the school districts that these conversations should not be considered a means for university faculty to "fix" K–12 teachers. School district participants also expressed their concern that academics have a tendency to dominate professional conversations. These concerns were not new to us. To nurture an equitable relationship of mutual respect and trust within the conversations, the group decided that K–12 teachers would lead the conversations in all six schools.

Facilitators were encouraged to choose a diverse mix of people from their school and community and to include a faculty member from the University in each one of their groups. Facilitators were provided with a) articles in support and in opposition to standards based reform, b) information on the Individuals with Disabilities Act 1997, c) the most recent state-adopted academic standards, d) copies of *Enhancing Professional Practice: A Framework for Teaching* (Danielson, 1996) as an example of a text of standards being proposed for teacher education, and e) guided questions on the readings to facilitate the conversations. These readings and questions were intended to serve as resources and as a way to create a common language among all groups. However, facilitators were free to use some or all of these readings and questions or select their own. All groups decided to select their own readings for the second conversation and chose to use the questions selectively. Each group named a recorder who posted the content of each conversation on the e-mail reflector list.

Data Source/Findings

The researchers did a qualitative analysis of the summaries of each of the conversations submitted by each group's facilitator through e-mail reflector to all participants and the researchers. Each conversation was coded according to topics generated in the response to the questions for the texts and to the topics participants contributed in addition to those directed by the questions. These topics were compiled and grouped around larger topics. These topics then were grouped into three general themes. An independent reviewer also read the conversations and coded sub and main topics. The researchers then correlated this independent review with their own analysis. In an analysis of the pages of content resulting from each groups' postings, three themes emerged: a) the potential value of the standards as they affected teaching and learning, b) improvements for the implementation of standards and c) basic problems with standards-based reform. The following are excerpts taken from individual group recorders' e-mail postings over a six-month period. These quotes reflect the thoughts and feelings of teachers, teacher educators, parents, school administrators, students, university faculty and community members; all who were participants in these conversations. Their words provide us with insight as they reflected on standards- based reform and all the challenges that come with this movement; they also further underscore the value of dialogue as a form of professional development and the importance of the coming together of all those involved in education, rather than just a select few.

Potential Value of Standards

When reflecting on the potential value of standards one high school facilitator stressed,

> Flexibility in interpreting the standards is needed because human beings are different and the accomplishment of the standard may look different in different circumstances.

A middle school facilitator shared similar concerns when he wrote,

> Standards can either help by raising the bar for expectations for kids who have been previously ignored or hinder the process if we use raising the bar as an excuse to leave them behind.

One school administrator shared,

> A significant plus of the standards movement has been the increase in student attention and success when teachers focus on the standard. Frequently, to help students demonstrate standards, teachers have had to implement new, different, or better teaching strategies. As a result, standards are driving some changes in instructional methods.

And finally a middle school facilitator wrote,

> Standards give us an opportunity to find the ways and resources to ensure that children experience success in so far as they are able.

Conversation participants generally recognized the value of standards as clear, common statements of expectations for student learning and their potential effectiveness in ensuring that all students meet common criteria for learning.

Improvements Regarding the Implementation of Standards

Teachers and teacher educators also offered some suggestions on possible improvements regarding the implementation of standards. One middle school facilitator remarked,

> There needs to be more emphasis on teachers gathering together in small groups and reflecting on the craft of standards implementation and sharing ideas on how to ensure student success.

They went on to say,

> They really miss the boat with regards to special education children. Performance seals on graduation diplomas are not available to those children. Isn't that discrimination? Someone needs to address this issue.

A local school administrator addressed teacher preparation and the implementation of standards,

> Teachers will need a strong background to teach to the standards. To do an effective job, teachers need to have knowledge beyond the standards in order to create learning that is meaningful for all students.

Within this theme, teachers emphasized that effective implementation of reform only occurs

> when teachers are knowledgeable about the reform and the expectations of the reform, are able to communicate actively and equally with each other and with all those involved with schooling about the reform, and have direct opportunity to guide the reform within their schools.

BASIC PROBLEMS ASSOCIATED WITH THE STANDARDS MOVEMENT

When addressing the basic problems associated with the standards movement one teacher educator remarked:

> It is no secret that standards are a combination of political agendas and a national movement. So much of their implementation comes down to how districts perceive their role—as lip service or as a real chance to rethink and redesign education.

Another basic problem addressed by a middle school teacher reflected the issue of change,

> There is fear out here in public education, maybe it is just the fear of change. Some teachers may fear sacrificing their individual style for the sake of standards. There is a fear that we are being asked to do too much. Do students really need to have all this knowledge or just be able to access it in a time where knowledge is increasing exponentially?

A teacher educator added,

> The caution expressed is that if teachers do not have the time to create depth of the understanding because they must complete every standard; standards could turn into a checklist of things to get done.

Several participants expressed their concerns about standardized tests and standardized curriculum. One middle school facilitator shared,

> Education that is just focused on standards will look differently somehow. If the standards are too rigorous, will we end up teaching to the test?

A high school administrator offered his concerns,

> Standards and their assessment will force more remediation. Students who fail to meet benchmark standards will not be passed on. How long will K–12 education become for some? More students will quit.

One teacher educator commented,

> I, too, am concerned about the uniformity of the curriculum through this movement. Whose interests are being served here? Certainly, those at the top and those who value social efficiency and who seek to maintain their class (and race) privilege can support standards.

As clearly indicated, teachers, school administrators and university faculty all had serious concerns about standards-based reform. They questioned the political motives behind standards and were concerned about their potential to maintain existing racial and social class privileges. They sensed the loss of teacher creativity and influence that come with standards and high-stakes assessment and are well aware of the constraints standards place on teacher time. They feared the standardization that comes with this movement and the ramifications on all students and student learning.

PARTICIPANTS' ASSESSMENT OF THE CONVERSATIONS

In order to assess the participants' perceptions in the value of increasing their knowledge of standards as a means of professional development, we asked them to a) complete a Likert scale questionnaire and b) and respond to an open response survey.

The Likert scale included the following six questions:

1. Did the conversations increase your understanding of the standards movement in basic education?
2. Did the conversations increase your understanding of the standards movement in teacher education?
3. Did the conversations provide an opportunity for active involvement in these issues?
4. Were the conversations an effective means of constructing a community of learners?
5. Were the conversations an effective means for learning about the standards movement?
6. Do you think the process of conversations with readings is an effective means for professional development?

The open-ended responses were grouped by question. The total responses to each question were analyzed for similarities and differences in the responses and for repetition of the responses that occurred in some questions. Similar responses were noted, grouped and combined. Idiosyncratic responses were also noted and weighed. For all six questions, 50 to 70 percent of the respondents indicated that they strongly agreed with each question. The remaining 30 to 50 percent agreed. There was a very positive response to the understandings developed through the conversations, to their active involvement in learning about standards through constructing a community of learners, and to the conversations as a means of professional development.

Participants also responded to open-ended questions on a) the gain in participants' knowledge on standards, b) the potential of conversations for reflection on daily teaching and learning practices, c) ways to improve the conversations, and d) whether the conversations should continue and if so, how. We found that all participants wanted the conversations to continue and valued them as a means of professional development. The participants had several suggestions for improvement. They recommended that more policy makers, especially those who helped to create the standards, be included, and that more student teachers be invited to attend. Teachers indicated that conversations between and across districts would provide opportunities, to learn more effective ways to cope with and implement the standards. They also strongly recommended that to reach all teachers, professional development credit should be provided by districts. They also stated using shorter readings would help them cope with time constraints.

When asked to respond to how the conversations enhanced their knowledge about standards based reform, participants overwhelmingly agreed that they had benefited from this experience. We include the following excerpts in participants' own words to illustrate the value of such conversations. One middle school facilitator shared,

> Our dialogue has made me aware of the 'attached strings' that come with standards. The conversations have forced me to think about what I teach and why I teach it. They also increased my awareness of the differences between postsecondary and K–12 educators. We need to continue the dialogue.

The majority of teacher and teacher educator respondents believed that the conversations provided them with an opportunity to reflect more critically on the daily practice of teaching and learning. An English supervisor and middle school teacher shared,

> As I work on curriculum the dialogue enhanced my thinking about how curriculum I tied to the standards movement.

The conversations caused several participants to reflect on their daily practice. Several middle school teachers shared,

> Our conversations caused me to reflect on the types of tests and assessments that I give in my classes. I also have been reflecting on what should be taught. The concept of internalizing teaching has caused me to reconsider my conception of how I think about myself as a teacher. I was reminded that simply reflecting on what we do results in growth.

One high school science teacher shared,

> I have become more aware of the kind of teacher I am. I am looking for ways to improve my classroom as a result of these conversations.

Most participants expressed their desire for the conversations to continue; however, several did have suggestions for improvement.

> Continue the conversations, but no more textbook readings.

> There were a lot of good ideas but we needed more time to receive feedback on making positive changes.

Most participants were very enthusiastic in their responses of support to continue the conversations. Remarks included,

I find this type of dialogue to be very stimulating and challenging intellectually.

I enjoyed participating in the conversations and hearing the thoughts of others.

The more we open the lines of communication the better our schools will be.

Conclusions

The findings overwhelmingly indicated that the critical collaborative conversations were an effective means of professional development by increasing all educators' knowledge about standards-based reforms, providing a positive means of reflection on their use in learning and teaching, and constructing understanding of the applications and implications of standards in basic and teacher education.

We learned that most teachers and teacher educators are not opposed to standards and understand their potential value. However, they are fearful of the numerous implications that have accompanied the implementation of standards. They are afraid that standards and high-stakes assessment reduce teachers' influence over curriculum and instruction and may cost some their jobs. They fear that they do not benefit all children in the classroom and that children with special needs will be left behind. They doubt statements that insist that standards will level the playing field; rather they predict that it will actually increase already existing inequities in schooling between the "haves" and the "have nots." They fear the standardization that comes with standards and that education will become a checklist. In essence, the conversations provided an opportunity for teachers and teacher educators to express openly their fears and to begin to work through critical questions to meet the challenges not only of standards but the wake of problems they may leave behind. Teachers know that they will be held accountable to manage any mess left behind when the policymakers move on.

The use of conversations as a means of professional development proved to be powerful. We found that teachers were eager to come together to talk about standards, effective teaching and learning, and the diverse needs of all learners. Almost all of the participants found that the structure of the conversations provided the impetus for meaningful conversations. Their eagerness underscored for us the lack of opportunities teachers have to discuss issues in schooling in an open, active and equitable manner. Teachers stated that most schools' professional development days are one-sided sessions where presenters talk at teachers about decontextualized solutions for presumed problems. They indicated that teachers are rarely given the opportunity to share views and ideas about professional topics. They concluded that the conversations went significantly beyond the chatter and complaints of the faculty room. They noted that teacher interactions within the school day are limited by time and energy and often focus on immediate issues. Several were excited by the intellectual stimulation of the conversations. All strongly affirmed the value of such dialogues for enhancing daily practice.

In conclusion, these conversations demonstrated that teachers value critical and collaborative inquiry among themselves and with teacher educators in a structured but informal environment. The structure and urgency of most school days provide few opportunities for teachers to engage in reflective conversations. We strongly recommend that some of professional development time be used for critical conversations and that these conversations be planned and implemented by teachers.

When teachers are given the opportunity to plan and conduct inquiry-based conversations, they are constructing the meaning of the reform and its application in their classrooms. They intellectually and actively engage in their own development and learning. The use of critical conversations as a part of district professional development has the potential of a) enhancing the implementation of standards-based reforms, or of any reform, b) deepening teacher understanding of the reform process, c) allowing teachers to see how the reforms may or may not work, and d) encouraging them to problem solve collaboratively on the adaptation of the reform in their own classroom and within their schools culture.

REFERENCES

Clark, R.W. & Wasley, P.A. (1999). Renewing schools and smarter kids: promises for democracy. *Phi Delta Kappan, 80*(8), 590–596.

Cuban, L. (2000). Watchdog agency needed for standardized test makers. *The State Education Standard, 1*(2), 36–38.

Danielson, C. (1996). *Enhancing professional practice: A framework for teaching.* Alexandria, VA: Association for Supervision and Curriculum Development.

Darling-Hammond, L. & Falk, B. (1997). Using standards and assessments to support student learning. *Phi Delta Kappan, 79*(3), 190–99.

David, J. L. & Shields, P. M. (1999). Standards are not magic. *Education Week,* April 14, 40, 42.

Dewey, J. (1933). *How we think: a restatement of relations of reflective thinking to the educative process* (2nd revised edition). Boston: D.C. Heath.

Doyle, D. P. & Pimental, S. (August 1998). How good is good enough? *Middle Ground*, 35–36.

Fenstermacher, G.D. (1998, February). *On accountability and accreditation in teacher education: A plea for alternatives*. Presentation at the annual meeting of the American Association of Colleges for Teacher Education, New Orleans, Louisiana.

Finn, C. E., Petrilli, M. J., & Vanourek, G. (1998). The state of state standards. *Education Week*, November 11, 39, 50.

Gibboney, R. A. (1994). *The stone trumpet: A story of practical school reform, 1960–1990*. Albany: SUNY Press.

Goodlad, J. I. (1999). Flow, eros, and ethos in educational renewal. *Phi Delta Kappan, 80*(8), 571–579.

Gratz, D.B. (2000). High standards for whom? *Phi Delta Kappan, 81*(9) 681–687.

Kohn, A. (1999). *The schools our children deserve: Moving beyond traditional classrooms and "tougher standards."* Boston: Houghton Miflin.

Noddings, N. (1997). Thinking about standards. *Phi Delta Kappan, 79*(3), 184–89.

Noddings, N. (1999.) Renewing democracy in schools. *Phi Delta Kappan, 80*(8), 579–583.

Pipho, C. (2000). The sting of high stakes testing and accountability. *Phi Delta Kappan, 81*(9), 645–646.

Richardson, V. (1997). Constructivist teaching and teacher education: theory and practice. In V. Richardson (Ed.), *Constructivist teacher education: building new understandings*, p. 22. Washington, DC: Falmer 3–14.

Yost, D.S., Sentner, S.M., & Forlenza-Bailey, A. (2000). An examination of the construct of critical reflection: Implications for teacher education programming in the 21st century. *Journal of Teacher Education, 51*(1), 39–49.

Standards
Changes in Curriculum, Teacher and Student Behaviors Summary

David M. Byrd and Peter Adamy

The process of standard setting is political. Standards emerge from a multitude of sources, each striving for notice and a prominent place in the national debate, each with its own focus and purpose. Special interest groups, research, professional associations, National Council for the Accreditation of Teacher Education (NCATE), Interstate New Teacher Assessment and Support Consortium (INTASC), New American Schools (NAS), federal initiatives, current issues of public interest and legislative pronouncement all effect and mix in the competition to influence the design of educational practice. This dynamic system has resulted in a patchwork of standards that have often left teachers with the role of implementer with little voice in design or direction.

The publication of *A Nation at Risk* (1983) nearly twenty years ago with its indictment of our nation's schools is often referenced as the impetus for our current reform agenda. Central to this agenda has been the development of standards or criteria for performance. This process began with the development of content standards in areas such as mathematics (National Council of Teachers of Mathematics, 1989) and science (American Association for the Advancement of Science, 1993). In tandem with this movement to content standards is a similar movement to develop criteria for the knowledge, skills and dispositions teachers need to promote student achievement (Ambach, 1996). These standards have been developed for both beginning teachers through the Interstate New Teacher Assessment and Support Consortium—INTASC (1992) and master teachers through the National Board for Professional Teaching Standards—NBPTS (1987). These standards are also being used as models for the development of state standards for beginning teachers and state program approval standards for teacher education programs and serve as a foundation for the National Council for Accreditation of Teacher Education's (NCATE, 2001) accreditation process. Clearly, Ed Pajak (2001) is right in his belief that current views on education reform stress the need for systematic change and it is this milieu that is the focus of this book.

Studying the Standards Environment

The theme that ties the four chapters in Division II of the Teacher Education Yearbook together is how individuals change to accommodate the standards movement. Central questions about the standards movement include: (a) will the standards movement improve education, (b) if so how is success achieved and sustained and (c) is student performance on state and national tests the only true measure of program success in a standards based environment?

Chapter 3 in this Division written by Theresa Grant and Kate Klien provides an overview of a study on how teachers' content knowledge and teaching style evolved as they implemented a standards-based mathematics curriculum. The curriculum focused on reasoning and problem solving with major emphasis on students being able to explain how they use mathematical concepts and procedures. The implementation of this curriculum, "Investigations in Number, Data and Space (Investigations)" requires teachers to utilize a range of student centered teaching strategies. The purpose being to provide a questioning and discussion rich environment in which students construct knowledge rather than having the teacher impart information. In short, teachers who were tied to a teacher-centered classroom had to make substantial changes if they were to implement this program. Comments such as "Do we teach" in this curriculum or just manage, referring to the student centered focus, were evident in the early stages of implementation. By the end of the year Grant and Klien report, through analysis of teacher comments, that teachers seemed to be gaining a comfort level with student reasoning and were beginning to "recognize the value of encouraging students to develop and discuss [their reasoning behaviors]." To their credit Grant and Klien didn't stop simply with interviews. While interviews give some indication of the value teachers placed on this curriculum – implementation in classrooms was the real goal of the project. From the analyses of videotapes of teachers attempting to implement the curriculum and teachers' reflections after viewing tapes, it is clear that early in the program teachers struggled with many of the concepts they were attempting to implement. In summary, while change took place the process of change was difficult and uneven. Some points of progress include identifying important mathematical concepts, realizing the importance of students struggling to master ideas, and engaging all students by encouraging them to listen to the rationales of others but to answer based on reflection.

A powerful two-phased model was utilized in this study. The first phase started with teachers having access to a fully developed curriculum. The assumption being that by providing a systematic overview of appropriate content and suggested instructional techniques "Investigations" allowed teachers to execute without the press of continually having to develop materials and lessons while still struggling to gain expertise on the subject of standards-based mathematics. This approach was based on the belief that all too often teachers are left to attempt implementation without adequate resources, time or the knowledge needed to develop them. The second phase of the model allowed teachers to practice with the type of immediate feedback that only students can provide and the ability to share their struggles with a community of peers while being pressed by the researches. Together this model allowed teachers to focus on implementation, receive feedback and reflect—the building blocks of change.

Progress has been shown with this study; perceptions changed, teacher behaviors changed, and student behaviors changed. However, the final step in the confirmation of this model will only come with implementation over time and the ability to assess what proponents of standards often point to as the true outcome measure for standards based education—the evaluation of student learning. Does implementation of this model cause state test scores on mathematics skills, concepts and problems solving to improve? This issue of the true measure of student performance is richly debated in a number of sources (see Brady, 2000, Education Week, 2001; Finn & Petrilli, 2000) which call for both more rigorous standards, assessment, and more balance and less reliance on single high stakes measures. Theresa Grant and Kate Klien should be encouraged to continue the search not only into the results of this curriculum on test scores but other more broadly defined measures of student success (e.g., continuation in advanced mathematics, career choice, attitudes toward mathematics, etc.).

Anita Perna Bohn in her chapter "Vanishing Act: The Effect of State-Mandated Content Standards on Multicultural Education" investigates an interesting issue—the impact content standards and assessments are having on the attitudes and practices of teachers regarding multicultural education. In short, are programs that are not covered by state and national assessment, such as multicultural education, being eroded by the pervasiveness of the standards movement?

As Bohn started to collect data some major changes were taking place. First, the state legislature passed into law a set of goals for student learning in each subject area. This led to a series of events, that the researcher believes, precipitated the decline in teachers' interest, time spent on, and concern for issues of multiculturalism and social justice. In addition, as the district administration moved to a tightly coupled relationship with state standards they moved away from site based management toward centralized control of content and teaching methods. Lastly, teaching was deskilled and teachers silenced. In moving to a structured commercial curriculum teachers lost control of their ability to make professional decisions regarding pace, objective and assessment. As explained by one teacher referring to a multicultural unit on Mexico which involved connecting with the local Latino community but was dropped due to the press of time, "I can't make time now to fit it in, when it's not even in my curriculum. There's too much mandatory stuff to get through."

Implications from this study are that highly structured state-mandated standards can serve as an impediment to other aspects of the curriculum such as multicultural education. This issue can be complex as Bohn points out, while commercial textbook series provide reference to multicultural topics the coverage is often superficial and impersonal (Bohn & Sleeter, 2000; Sleeter & Grant, 1991) and therefore lack the power to move students to understanding and action.

Bohn believes this move toward curriculum by textbook is particularly dangerous for areas like multicultural education where a majority of teachers are unprepared by education or experience. Preservice teacher education students do not enter teacher education programs with the skills, knowledge, and attitudes necessary to work successfully with a diverse population of students (Banks, 2001). In addition, while teachers can be educated to have greater awareness and understanding of issues regarding multicultural education they do not necessarily practice what they have learned. Furthermore, they need to be encouraged and supported in their analysis of the decisions they and others make as teachers and the effects these decisions have on students (McIntyre, Byrd & Foxx, 1996).

The kinds of personal transformations that are necessary to promote the elimination of racist attitudes and practices and peoples attitudes changing to an inclusive multicultural perspective can only be accomplished by an approach that goes beyond skill training and informational acquisition. Some of the best work in staff development for diversity involves teachers working intensely in communities. Moll (1992) has instituted a number of projects involving teachers and anthropologists working in Latino communities and in the homes of their students. Participating teachers gather information about "funds of knowledge" and invite parents and community members to make substantial contributions to their classrooms. Textbooks cannot duplicate the rich materials and personal connections that teachers gain when they contact with diversity in their communities. Bohn makes a strong case for teachers continuing to learn about students' communities, and for maintaining a focus on cultural preferences for learning and interacting, and to understand the conditions that "perpetuate some group's marginalization." We might add that understanding should also lead to teachers helping communities and children move toward action to improve their lives and communities.

In Chapter 5 Bette Bergeron studied the effect of national standards on the preparation of teachers. Interestingly, using a case study approach she investigates how standards are altering many of the practices related to Professional Development School (PDS) partnerships between schools and colleges of education and to the concept of teacher education program accountability. Frankes, Valli and Cooper (1998) reviewed research on the PDSs using four primary goals proposed by the Holmes Group (1990) for PDSs and compared the extent to which these goals have been achieved. The four goals used in this analysis were: teacher as researcher, teacher as decision maker, teacher as teacher educator, and teacher as political activist. Bergeron's study deals with the third primary goal for PDS teachers working more directly and collaboratively with colleges and universities as teacher educators and full partners in planning, teaching and supervision.

Prior to the development of PDS partnerships the teacher education program under study had little or no contact with school based educators with the exception of cooperating teachers. Since the development of standards-based PDS sites, the shift has been to clearly delineated roles to ensure the infusion of standards into the dialog among partnership participants and, therefore, into field based teacher education courses. In addition, roles for classroom teachers have been expanded to include: Host Teachers who work with up to three methods block students per semester, On-site Coordinators who form liaison and coordinate field placements in their school and Seminar Leaders who participate in the lecture portion of methods courses. However, the most important change may have been the creation of the concept of Clinical Instructors. Clinical Instructors share methods course responsibilities with campus faculty and receive a stipend. As Teachers in Residence they serve a one-year term and are jointly paid by the district and the university. During this yearlong activity they teach and serve on university committees and work on specialized professional development activities in their districts.

Bergeron also comments on the complex issue of accountability and how a standards-based teacher education requires changes in how students and programs are evaluated. Portfolios have become an archetypal device in teacher education for the measuring the multiple ways students' meet performance standards. Portfolios are reviewed in mock interviews with teachers and administrators which both provides for student evaluation and preparation for eventual job interviews.

Program renewal proved to be important as the university moved to standards-based teacher preparation field centers. The decisive issue, which marked a turning point for this, was the collaborative development for the School of Education's teaching standards. Through the development and ownership of standards, the community was invigorated and this proved extremely helpful as the process of standards driven curriculum development began. This finding is consistent with the research of Higgins (1999) in her work on learning communities and the four conditions which contributed to their emergence: trust, shared ownership, learning together, and reciprocal support.

This case provides important information on how one community moved to a standards-based curriculum. Its strength is in the details it provides on the evolutionary steps and role changes necessary to become more field based and accountable.

In Chapter 6 Linda McDowell and Sheryl Desmond provide a description of their efforts to involve teachers and teacher educators in critical conversations on the standards movement and its impact on the educational process. Three themes emerged from their work: a) the value of standards relative to teaching and learning, b) how implementation of standards progressed, and c) problems with standards-based reform. In general participants believed the value of the standards was that they provided a clear summary of commonly held expectations for student learning. Regarding the implementation of standards the teachers emphasized the importance of teachers being knowledgeable about the standards, being able to communicate this knowledge, and having direct opportunities to guide the standards movement in their schools. However, teachers, school administrators, and university faculty all saw problems in the implementation of standards driven instruction. Central to their concerns were questions of equity and excellence. All groups were concerned about the potential of the standards to perpetuate the existing unequal benefits of education based on race and class.

The conversational origin of this intervention was its strength—teachers valued the opportunity to investigate the standards movement—its meaning and applicability to their teaching. We encourage the authors to continue to collect data on the tribulations and victories teachers have as they move toward implementation of standards-based instruction and the impact these standards have on children and adolescents.

Conclusions

The standards movement, as it relates to teacher performance, received a major push in 1996 with the publication of *What Matters Most: Teaching for America's Future* by the National Commission on Teaching and America's Future. In addition to calling on policy makers to "get serious" about standards for students and teachers it promoted the notion that if all students are to be able to reach high standards then teachers must be supported as they develop the capacity to meet the learning needs of the wide range of diverse learners (Pajak, 2001). This transformation of a teacher education process based on standards is complex and will require significant changes in the way teacher education candidates are prepared and assessed. Without change and systematic reform high standards and high stakes testing could as its critics fear lead to more problems than it solves. Perhaps the greatest fear is that it could lead to even greater marginalization of those most in need (see Cuban, 1995; Kohn, 2000).

Clearly the continuing emphasis on state mandated testing, and the promise that if tests are only made rigorous enough and stakes are high enough then this will lead to teachers changing their behaviors and teaching strategies without the need to invest large amounts of money in curriculum or staff development, has not been fulfilled. Firestone, Mayrowetz and Fairman (1998) in a study of performance based assessment in Maryland and Maine found that while a moderately high stakes environment caused considerable activity focused on the test itself, the approach appeared to be less successful in changing teachers' basic instructional strategies. Furthermore, they conclude that teachers have to have a solid foundation in the subjects they teach and a clear understanding of how to assist children's learning. High stakes and concepts such as reconstitution (the closing of low performing schools) did seem to cause teachers and administrators to think more about how to change but the motivational effects appear limited even in the higher stakes environment of Maryland. Therefore, structures beyond the high stakes nature of tests are needed to ensure teachers are motivated to change their practice. Teachers need multiple opportunities to reflect on what mathematics is and how it should be taught to children. Colleges and universities, professional organizations, state and federally funded programs can all play a role in promoting information on how to change practice but as the studies in this Division show care should be taken in their design and implementation.

In chapter 3, Grant and Klein inform us about the importance of both content knowledge and pedagogical understanding to the teaching of standards-based mathematics. In chapter 4, Bohn provides evidence supporting the claim that state mandated standards may negatively affect other important aspects of the curriculum, specifically how multicultural education is valued and taught in classrooms. Bergeron, in chapter 5, also addresses the influence of standards, but in the context of a field based teacher education program (PDS). Bergeron informs us that the standards-based reform moves teacher education programs toward shared responsibility and greater accountability. Lastly, in chapter 6 McDowell and Desmond remind us of the importance facilitating dialogue and reflection as part of the implementation process for standards-based reform. The chapters in this Division of the Yearbook address the complexities, challenges and rewards that teachers and teacher educators can expect as they attempt to educate students in a standards-based educational environment. Each of these chapters provides major insights into how we should proceed.

REFERENCES

Ambach, G. (1996). Standards for teachers: Potential for improving schools. *Phi Delta Kappan. 78* (1), 207–210.

American Association for the Advancement of Science. (1993). *Benchmarks for science literacy.* New York: Oxford University Press.

Banks, J. A. (2001). Citizenship education and diversity: Implications for teacher education. *Journal of Teacher Education, 52* (1), 5–16.

Bohn, A. P., & Sleeter, C. E. (2000). Multicultural education and the standards movement: A report from the field. *Phi Delta Kappan 82* (2), 156–159.

Brady, M. (2000). The standards juggernaut. *Phi Delta Kappan, 81* (9), 648–651.

Cuban, L. (1995). A national curriculum and tests: Consequences for schools. In *The hidden consequences of a national curriculum* (pp. 47–62). Washington, DC: American Educational Research Association.

Education Week (2001). Quality Counts 2001: Seeking a Better Balance. *Education Week* [On-line]. Available: http://www.edweek.org/sreports/qc01/.

Finn, C. E., Jr., & Petrilli, M. J. (Eds.). (2000, January). *The state of state standards* [On-line]. Available: http://www.edexcellence.net/library/soss2000/2000soss.html.

Firestone, W. A., Mayrowetz, D., & Fairman, J. (1998). Performance-based assessment and instructional change: The effects of testing in Maine and Maryland. *Educational Evaluation and Policy Analysis, 20* (2), 95–113.

Frankes, L., Valli, L., & Cooper, D. (1998). Continuous learning for all adults in the professional development school: A review of the research. In D. J. McIntyre & D. M. Byrd (Eds.), *Strategies for Career-Long Teacher Education* (pp. 61–68). Thousand Oaks, CA: Corwin Press.

Sleeter, C., & Grant, C. E. (1991). Race, class, gender, and disability in current textbooks. In M. W. Apple and L. K. Christian-Smith (Eds.), *The politics of the textbook* (pp. 78–110). New York: Routledge.

Higgins, K. M. (1999). Building the layers of a learning community in a school-based teacher education program. In D. M. Byrd & D. J. McIntyre (Eds.) *Research on professional development schools* (pp. 218–233). Thousand Oaks, CA: Corwin/Sage.

Holmes Group (1990). *Tomorrow's schools*. East Lansing, MI: The Holmes Group. Inc.

Interstate New Teacher Assessment and Support Consortium (1992). *Model standards for beginning teacher and licensing and development: A model for state dialogue*. Washington, D.C. Council of Chief State School Officers.

Kohn, A. (2000, September 13). Standardized testing and its victims: Inconvenient facts and inequitable consequences. *Education Week, 20*(4), 46–47, 60.

McIntyre, D., J., Byrd, D., M., & Foxx, S. (1996). Field and laboratory experiences. In J. Sikula, T. Buttery, & E. Guyton (Eds.), *Handbook of research on teacher education* (2nd ed.), pp. 171–193. New York: Macmillan.

Moll, L. (1992). Literacy research in community and classrooms: a sociocultural approach. In R. Beach, J. L. Green, M. L. Kamil, & T. Shanalas (Eds.), *Multidisciplinary perspectives on literacy research* (pp. 211–244). Urbana, IL: National Council of Teachers of English.

Moll, Luis C.; and Others. (1992). Funds of Knowledge for Teaching: Using a qualitative approach to connect homes and classrooms. *Theory into Practice; 31*(1), 132–141.

National Board for Professional Teacher Standards. (1989). *What teachers should know and be able to do*. Detroit: Author.

National Commission on Excellence in Education (1983). *A nation at risk*. Washington, DC: U. S. Department of Education.

National Council for Accreditation of Teacher Education (2001). *Professional standards accreditation of schools, colleges, and departments of education*. Washington, DC: National Council for Accreditation of Teacher Education.

National Council of Teachers of Mathematics. (1989). *Curriculum and evaluation standards for school mathematics*. Reston, VA: Author.

Pajak, E. (2001). Clinical supervision in a standards-based environment: Opportunities and challenges. *Journal of Teacher Education 52*(3), 233–243.

Zeichner, K. M. & Hoeft, K. (1996). Teacher socialization for cultural diversity. In J. Sikula, T. Buttery, & E. Guyton (Eds.), *Handbook of research on teacher education* (2nd ed.), pp. 525–594. New York: Macmillan.

Division

3

Teacher
Education
Standards

Teacher Education Standards: Do They Really Matter?
Overview and Framework

Donna M. Gollnick

Donna Gollnick is Senior Vice President of NCATE where she is responsible for overall management of the accreditation process, including the training of Board of Examiners members who conduct onsite visits. Before joining the NCATE staff in 1986, she served as Director of Professional Development at the American Association of Colleges for Teacher Education and taught at the high school level in Indiana. Dr. Gollnick is the coauthor of two college textbooks: *Multicultural Education in a Pluralistic Society* and *Introduction to Foundations of American Education.* She was the third president of the National Association for Multicultural Education, an association of teachers and teacher educators who support equity, social justice, and multicultural education. She has been recognized as an outstanding alumna by Purdue University and is a recipient of AACTE's Advocates for Justice Award.

Everything is coming up standards. Student standards, teacher standards, program standards, and accreditation standards influence what is taught, tested, and learned across the country. The standards of the National Accreditation for Teacher Education (NCATE) themselves refer to at least 21 sets of standards that should influence the preparation of teachers and other school personnel. With no lack of standards to guide the work of faculty, the preeminent question is do they make a difference? Do they result in a higher quality educator who can help students in preschool through grade twelve learn?

Standards are touted as critical to ensuring high academic achievement of the nation's students. The National Commission on Teaching and America's

Future (1996) called for the preparation of teachers who could help all students perform at high levels:

> Clearly, if students are to achieve high standards, we can expect no less from their teachers and other educators. The first priority is reaching agreement on what teachers should know and be able to do in order to help students succeed. Unaddressed for decades, this task has recently been completed by three professional bodies, the National Council for Accreditation of Teacher Education (NCATE), the Interstate New Teacher Assessment and Support Consortium (INTASC), and the National Board for Professional Teaching Standards (The National Board). Their combined efforts to set standards for teacher education, beginning teacher licensing, and advanced certification outline a continuum of teacher development throughout the career. These standards offer the most powerful tools we have for reaching and rejuvenating the soul of the profession. (p. 18)

The standards used by over 600 colleges and universities that prepare teachers and other school personnel are those of the National Council for Accreditation of Teacher Education (NCATE). The 2001 version of the NCATE standards[1] requires programs to be performance-based, much more concerned with what candidates know and are able to do than in the past when the focus was on what candidates were taught. The centerpiece of the six standards is the first one on candidate knowledge, skills, and dispositions. The standard requires candidates to "know and demonstrate the content, pedagogical, and professional knowledge, skills, and dispositions necessary to help all students learn" (NCATE, 2001a). Although an education unit[2] identifies outcomes that emanate from its conceptual framework, it is also expected to prepare candidates to meet professional and state standards.

Principles of the Interstate New Teacher Assessment and Support Consortium (INTASC)[3] provide the basic foundation for knowledge, skills, and dispositions that are critical for new teachers. NCATE expects accredited units to assess whether teacher candidates have developed these proficiencies at the level expected for a novice teacher by the time they are recommended for state licensure. Most state standards have expectations very similar to the INTASC principles.

In addition to the generic principles on pedagogical and professional knowledge, skills, and dispositions, INTASC expects teachers to know the central concepts, tools of inquiry, and structure of their content field (INTASC, 1992). Other INTASC standards address the content and pedagogical content proficiencies for specific teaching fields. However, INTASC is not the only group that has written content standards. Most professional associations of educators have developed standards for P–12 students and teachers or other school personnel.[4] The standards for the preparation of teachers build on the association's P–12 standards, indicating what teachers should know and be able to do so that students learn. NCATE depends on the national professional associations such as the National Council for Teachers of Mathematics, the National Council for Social Studies, and the National Association of School Psychologists to identify the proficiencies that are important for professionals in their fields. Most states use the same professional standards as the framework for state standards.

NCATE also is concerned with the quality of master's programs for the continuing development of teachers and their ability to help teachers become better at their work. For this purpose, NCATE expects master's programs to be built on the propositions and standards of the National Board for Professional Teaching Standards (NBPTS, 1989).[5] Although these may appear to be another layer of standards to which teacher education faculty must respond, the propositions were the foundation for the development of the INTASC principles for performance-based licensure at the state level. Performance expectations, of course, are higher because the NBPTS uses its standards to certify experienced teachers nationally.

The other five NCATE standards address the unit's assessment system, field experiences and clinical practice, diversity, faculty, and governance and resources. Field experiences and clinical practice (Standard 3) provide the sites where candidates can demonstrate and develop the knowledge, skills, and dispositions necessary to help all students learn. This particular standard is grounded in the findings about quality clinical work from the pilot testing of NCATE's standards for professional development schools (PDS) (NCATE, 2001b). Standard 4 on diversity requires units to be clear about the proficiencies candidates should develop and demonstrate related to diversity and helping all students learn; they also must assess candidates to determine if they actually can work effectively with students from diverse ethnic, racial, socioeconomic, gender, language, religious, ability, and sexual orientation backgrounds. The standard on faculty expects education faculty to model best professional practices in teaching, scholarship, and service, including the use of performance assessment in their own teaching.

Teacher educators today must reflect many sets of standards in their work. One of the challenges is to integrate the requirements of the various standards. For the most part, the standards of professional associations, states, INTASC, NBPTS, and NCATE are related and supportive of one another. The authors of national standards have worked diligently to align the standards across groups, reaching consensus about the essential competencies expected of teachers and other school professionals. Meeting state standards often indicates that INTASC, professional, and NCATE standards have been addressed as well and vice versa.

Use of Standards in
Teacher Education Programs

The chapters in this section of the yearbook focus on how faculty at three institutions have used standards to change and evaluate programs. Interestingly, all three chapters examine programs for the preparation of elementary school teachers.

Faculty with responsibility for a seminar that accompanies the year-long internship at George Washington University redesigned the seminar to help candidates reflect on their teaching within the context of the unit's conceptual framework. Readings, reflections, and dialogues helped interns understand their own practice and the relationship to three themes of the conceptual framework: knowledge, individuality, and social responsibility. These faculty members have taken seriously NCATE's expectations that the conceptual framework be integrated throughout the preparation program.

Five faculty members who teach courses in the elementary education program at another institution describe their experiences in assisting each other in the development of rubrics—an NCATE expectation under its performance-based standards. This chapter outlines some of the issues that arose as the rubrics were developed and the discussions that ensued to clarify the meaning of performance assessment and rubrics.

In the last chapter of this section faculty involved in one of Illinois State University's professional development schools report on a formative evaluation of the effectiveness of the PDS and candidate's incorporation of the INTASC principles into their professional beliefs and work. The evaluation reported on the perceptions of teachers, candidates, students in the elementary school, and parents.

NOTES

1. The full text of the NCATE standards is available at *www.ncate.org/standards.*
2. The institution, college, school, department, or other administrative body with the responsibility for managing or coordinating all programs offered for the initial and continuing preparation of teachers and other school personnel, regardless of where these programs are administratively housed.
3. The INTASC principles, accompanied by knowledge, performance, and dispositions, are available at *www.ccsso.org/intasc.*

4. The program standards for the preparation of teachers and other school personnel can be downloaded from NCATE's website at *www.ncate.org/standards.*
5. The propositions and standards of the NBPTS are available at *www.nbpts.org.*

REFERENCES

Interstate New Teacher Assessment and Support Consortium. (1992). *Models standards for beginning teacher licensing and development: A resource for state dialogue.* Washington, DC: Council for Chief State School Officers.

National Board for Professional Teaching Standards. (1989). *Toward high and rigorous standards for the teaching profession.* Detroit, MI: Author.

National Commission on Teaching and America's Future. (1996). *What matters most: Teaching for America's future.* New York: Author.

National Council for Accreditation of Teacher Education. (2001). *Professional standards for the accreditation of schools, colleges, and departments of education.* Washington, DC: Author.

National Council for Accreditation of Teacher Education. (2001). *Standards for professional development schools.* Washington, DC: Author.

Meeting National Standards for the Program Conceptual Framework

7.

An Effective Model of a Powerful Teacher Education Program

Sylven S. Beck, Patricia S. Tate, and Ashley G. Giglio

Sylven S. Beck is Associate Professor and Director of Elementary Education in the Department of Teacher Preparation and Special Education at The George Washington University. Her research interests and teaching areas include educational foundations, elementary science education, and teacher development.

Patricia S. Tate is Assistant Professor of Elementary Education and Director of the Office of Laboratory Experiences in the Department of Teacher Preparation and Special Education at The George Washington University. Her research interests and teaching areas include pre-service supervision, teacher development, and elementary education.

Ashley G. Giglio is a graduate of the GWU Elementary Education Program and a fourth grade teacher at Bailey's Elementary School for the Arts and Sciences in Virginia. She is the recipient of the GWU Model Program Award and was nominated for a First-Year Teacher of the Year Award.

ABSTRACT

This article investigates the connections made by pre-service teacher candidates and their selected reading responses to the conceptual framework of their teacher preparation program. The conceptual framework that undergirds the Elementary Education Model Program at The George Washington University is anchored by three themes: knowledge, individuality, and social responsibility. Connections to the program's conceptual framework are made explicit in a series of seminars and a reading response paper designed to assess evidence of understanding. Several "gates for assessment" include Book Talk, a reader response activity involving group and individual responses to provocative readings about current issues in teaching, academic papers requiring reflection and analysis, and multiple opportunities to dialog and debrief by both faculty and students. The goal of this teacher education program is to link student responses of selected readings to a program conceptual framework that is standards-based, articulated, shared, and consistent with a high quality professional educational program.

Objectives

The authors present a strategy for facilitating teacher candidates' abilities to reflect through making connections to powerful ideas about teaching and learning that are embodied in a program's conceptual framework. The program pedagogy that is studied utilizes a year-long internship seminar as the central scaffold for helping teacher interns articulate and synthesize their beliefs and values about teaching and learning. This practical inquiry intends to show how a cohort group validated their beliefs and values through conceptual constructs of their teacher preparation program. Components of the seminar are described using examples of evidence from planned activities and assignments that provided windows into the nature of the interns' thinking and into the stances they held regarding the teaching and learning process.

Review of Previous Research

CONCEPTUAL FRAMEWORK AND STANDARDS OF PRACTICE

The most "vital mechanism" for linking elements of quality assurance in teacher education is the articulation of a conceptual framework that guides all components of a teacher preparation program (Dottin, 1998). Thus, the major cornerstone of the National Council for the Accreditation of Teacher Education (1997) accreditation standards is that teacher preparation programs need to specify a framework that provides the "philosophical and programmatic purposes" that undergird the course of study for students (Odell, 1997, p. 138). Howey (1996) explicates the power of conceptual frameworks to "serve as a road map" . . . "in deciding on those understandings and abilities, perhaps even dispositional behaviors for prospective teachers, framed by a clear vision of teaching and schooling" (p. 162). The conceptual framework provides the larger view of the essential elements of the teacher preparation program and shows how this view is based on standards articulated for the profession.

Conceptual frameworks that undergird teacher preparation programs are derived from agreements about what teachers should know and be able to do in order to help students succeed (National Commission on Teaching and America's Future, 1996). The Interstate New Teacher Assessment Support Consortium (INTASC, 1992) standards address initial teacher licensure qualifications and are built on the National Board for Professional Teaching Standards' (NBPTS, 1991) career continuum for teacher development. Taken as a whole INTASC standards encompass many ideologies or conceptual orientations (Calderhead & Schorrock, 1997) that represent aspects of essential preparation areas for teaching: academic, practical, technical, personal, and critical inquiry.

CONCEPTUAL FRAMEWORK AND THE INTERNSHIP EXPERIENCE

Encouraging teacher candidates to reflect on their field experiences over time and taking a broader view of teaching are key ways to facilitate teacher development (Knowles & Cole, 1996). Reflective thinking involves pondering dilemmas of practice (Schon, 1991) and requires weighing ethical, moral, and critical implications of one's work (Calderhead & Shorrock, 1997; LaBoskey, 1994). Kitchener (1983) maintains that reflective thinking cannot be taught as a discrete skill, but rather is developed from new analysis and assessment of personal assumptions related to the content.

Field-based program pedagogies (Carter & Anders, 1996) that assist in teacher development include: observation guides, reflective writing, seminars and conversations. Teacher candidates learn from and make theoretical connections to their field experiences through personal interpretations of events. Conceptual frameworks (Carter & Anders) as observation guides, provide the "intellectual context" within which a teacher candidate can interpret school experiences and engage in thinking "like a teacher" (p. 571). Reflective writing helps teacher candidates make their thoughts more explicit and tie those experiences to larger ideas about teaching and learning. Adding conversation and dialogue opportunities during the internship experience gives teacher candidates opportunities to reflect on practice. A seminar forum allows instructors to gauge how students make meaning and construct knowledge about their teacher preparation experience and uncovers alternative perspectives and/or misconceptions about their practice. These pedagogical approaches reflect a constructivist stance

(Guyton, Rainer & Wright, 1997) toward teacher preparation and the type of experiences that facilitate knowledge construction within a personal and social dimension.

Theoretical Framework

The conceptual framework that undergirds this program is anchored by three themes—knowledge, individuality, social responsibility—which reflect a multicultural as well as global perspective for teacher candidates as they pass through a series of clinical experiences. The conceptual framework's three themes are defined in the following manner:

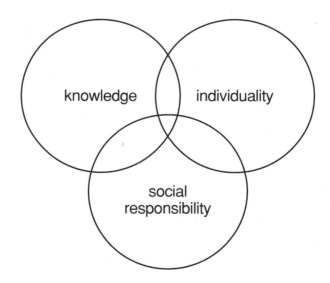

Knowledge. Good teachers know the subject matter they teach; they also understand the process of its construction and the impact of it in real world settings. Teachers help youngsters to understand their own thought processes and the significance of learning in their daily lives. Good teachers understand these active, underlying principles of knowledge in order to help students effectively think, communicate, and participate in the real world.

Individuality. Today's youngsters come from a rich array of cultural and experiential backgrounds. They bring to schools a diverse set of personal social, and academic expectations. Good teachers are attentive to students as individuals; they are also sensitive to the broader cultural context that gives shape to diversity. This awareness helps teachers design meaningful programs of study that maximize the development of each student's potential.

Social Responsibility. Teaching is a socially significant profession that calls for a wider, moral vision extending beyond the narrowness of personal gain and private intellectual development. The education of today's youngsters is connected to many crucial issues confronting the larger social order. Good teachers recognize and actively explore these important connections to critical issues that link school and society, classroom and community.

In sum, elementary school teaching is intellectually serious, personally enriching, and socially significant work for educators interested in the improvement of teaching and learning in today's schools. Coherence within the program curriculum is further strengthened in its alignment with INTASC and NBPTS standards that provide the framework for curriculum design and assessment.

Methodology

Program faculty redesigned the teaching internship seminar based on feedback from students, faculty, and cooperating teachers who have historically viewed the seminar as just an "add-on" class segment of the internship. The redesign provided a framework for interns to make connections between the program's conceptual framework and their internship experiences. Practical inquiry became the approach to study the what, why, and how of our pedagogical practices and to explore our views about the impact on our students during this process (Richardson, 1996).

DATA SOURCES

A cohort of thirteen graduate students responded to readings selected by faculty and their peers during a year-long internship (1998–1999) that included placements in urban, urban-fringe, and suburban partner schools. Students responded to their readings in two ways—as part of a large group process called Book Talk and through individual reading response papers. In collaboration with our study, one graduate from the cohort wrote a reflective paper of the impact of this experience during her first year of teaching.

Book Talks. Three Book Talk sessions were designed to develop interest in reading about other teachers' experiences and stimulate critical perspective on the important role teachers have in society. Reader response activities were built in to the large group sessions at the beginning, middle, and end of the semester to provide openness in discussion, reflective thinking, and exchange of perspective. Book Talk I grouped students in book-alike reader response groups. Students shared personal perspectives and reactions to book themes and their relationship to teaching experiences. Faculty supervisors functioned as facilitators connecting and summarizing what was discussed. Book Talk II gave students an opportunity to write their responses to books they had read on chart paper. Students were asked to consider what they liked or disliked about the book, the critical stance they believed the author was taking, and their evolving views about the teacher as professional. Faculty summarized apparent themes across commentaries while sharing their own perspectives. In Book Talk III students assembled in grade-alike groups and discussed readings in terms of the developmental ages of children with whom they were working. Self-selected readings were solicited at this point. Using examples from the group discussions, faculty modeled how students could begin synthesizing their thoughts for writing their reading response papers.

Reading response papers. A writing assignment required that students articulate their responses to their readings in terms of the program's conceptual framework, their beliefs about teaching and learning, and their perspectives on the essential themes of the texts. In a brief paper (5–6 pages) students critically examined, through their own interpretation and text analysis, what they read and how they connected their readings to the program's themes. Students considered the impact of their readings on their views about teaching and their professional roles.

Program graduate reflections. One graduate from this cohort participated in the presentation of our study at a national conference. She wrote about her seminar experience and, as a first-year teacher, reflected on the impact of the program's themes on her thinking and practice.

DATA ANALYSIS

The faculty authors co-taught the seminar and collaboratively worked together to study the data. One faculty member analyzed data from the book talk sessions according to Wiggins & McTighe's (1998) framework for assessing understanding. Evidence of understanding in the responses indicated students were: (a) making sense of things supported by their read-ings, (b) organizing information in disciplined ways, (c) using knowledge in thinking about the new situations posed about teaching, (d) building on ideas expressed by their peers, (e) taking critical and insightful points of view, and (f) getting inside another person's feelings and world view.

The other faculty author used a qualitative content analysis method to code statements taken from the reader response papers (Bogdan & Biklin, 1982; Strauss, 1987). Statements were coded according to how well they aligned with the program conceptual framework's three themes.

After separate coding faculty authors reread each other's analyses and developed agreements of categorizations and examples of evidence. Field notes taken by faculty during the seminar discussions were also consulted in reconstructing the significant events that occurred in the interactions observed among the students. The purpose of the data analysis was to find, in our practice, validity that each student was making meaningful connec-tions through engagement in group discussions, sharing of multiple per-spectives, and reflective writing around provocative readings.

Results and Discussion

The newly designed seminar format became the model for which students used their own voices to address their professional role of teacher. The sem-inar enabled the faculty to make the program's conceptual framework an explicit foundation upon which students could connect their thinking as developing teachers.

BOOK TALK

Book Talk I involved book-alike reader response groups. Students shared their thoughts about what they were reading and made connections to the program themes. The books chosen for discussion were *Up the Down Staircase* (Kaufman, 1965), *Growing Minds On Becoming A Teacher* (Kohl, 1984), *Among Schoolchildren* (Kidder, 1989), and *You Can't Say, You Can't Play* (Paley, 1992). The purpose of Book Talk I was to get interns to share what they were reading with one another and to articulate what was mean-ingful to them. Responses indicated that these readings: provoked "cogni-tive dissonance" about the fairness of classroom rules, captured the humor in the life of a teacher, presented examples of teachers who take on the sta-tus quo, and offered a safe haven for those students who identified with each literary role model.

Book Talk II expanded the book selections and asked students to consider critical stances and significant themes related to a teacher's professional life. Responses to *You Can't Say, You Can't Play* continued to create cognitive dissonance. Some found it too detailed and hard to grasp in a practical sense. Others were impressed with Vivian Paley studying her own practice and taking risks knowing that her approach would go against what was acceptable. *Among Schoolchildren* provided a secure sense that Chris Zajac was an effective teacher they could attach special memories to and think of when times got tough. *Up the Down Staircase* continued to provide the humorous relief the interns felt they needed through the eyes of Sylvia Barrett. However, there were also signs of anxiety as the interns' comments indicated similar difficult experiences could happen to them.

Book Talk II generated deeper thought about the influence of self/personal knowledge in one's approach to practice as well as the recognition of the political context controlling how schools operate in society. These selections included: *Savage Inequalities* (Kozol, 1991), *Pedagogy of the Oppressed* (Freire, 1993), *Other People's Children* (Delpit, 1995), *The Passionate Teacher* (Fried, 1995), and *A Tribe Apart* (Hersch, 1998). Interns' comments indicated they gained confidence in taking risks and making their own decisions about the best ways to use a curriculum, whether it was mandated or of their own creation. Many comments reiterated the larger vision of the teacher's role as the interns sorted out examples of ways the knowledge, individuality, and social responsibility constructs were played out in these real accounts of teaching and teachers' lives.

In Book Talk III students discussed reading selections in grade-alike groups which focused on the developmental needs of students and the individuality theme. It was evident that interns took initiative in knowing who their students were inside and outside of school. In particular their comments noted their perceptions had changed as they developed a clearer understanding about grade ranges and the appropriateness of expectations.

READING RESPONSE PAPERS

Students wrote reflective papers that synthesized and analyzed, through multiple interpretations, their own thinking linked with the program's conceptual framework. Examples of students' reflections by theme are classified here:

Knowledge. The students' responses to "knowledge" suggested that they valued a necessary knowledge base and its subsequent extension to their classroom teaching. Comments like "gained knowledge," "teaching repertoire," and constructivist classrooms" supported the theme in this way:

> This book deepened my thinking about my own knowledge and made me put myself in an arena much larger than just the classroom. It is ultimately the role of the teacher who plays a part in the big picture of a child's life—teachers see and understand children at their unique developmental level.

Understanding the dynamic, underlying principles of knowledge is also represented in phrases such as "the simplest techniques can bring a lesson to life" and "teaching methods appropriate to the reality of my students' lives." The students wrote of making "clear their children's thinking processes" in order to uncover the significance of learning in their daily lives, indicating they understood the necessity of communicating to their children that knowledge, both collective and individual, should be valid and meaningful.

Individuality. The students' responses to "individuality" revolved around the issue of diversity, bringing sensitivity to the broader cultural context. One student wrote of "working with students in the context of a larger environment" while another said, "I am more aware of the individual needs of my students, more so than I was this summer." This particular theme emphasized an awareness for teachers to maximize the development of each child's potential, an emphasis that is clearly represented with the statements, "[T]eachers must acknowledge and validate students' home language without using it to limit students' potential," and "[T]eaching is a way of encouraging individuality in students—helping students become who they really are." Written responses related to individuality showed a deeper understanding of why children bring to schools such a diverse set of personal, social, and academic expectations:

> As I continue to develop my thinking as a teacher, these texts remind me of the importance of listening, learning, and teaching in a way that relates to the many student perspectives I will encounter. My readings have further clarified that to achieve this is to do more than address and accept student experiences. Family life, classroom life, community life, and a larger, more ambiguous societal life all affect the academic success of students.

Social Responsibility. The most compelling statements that emerged from the students' reading response papers revolved around the theme of "social responsibility." They wrote of teaching to "keep an ongoing dialog" in developing a "guarantee of equal educational opportunity." The students' reflections on their roles as teachers were poignant and from the heart as they questioned their own motives, "One should want to teach in an environment where there is the most pressing need, correct?" Responses to the readings that "reminded me of all the reasons that made me want to teach" and to "think more about my responsibilities toward society" were also moving. For these selected readings, faculty noted those books which created some modicum of dissonance in the students' perception of themselves and of the teaching profession, one that calls for a wider moral vision. The responses to the theme of "social responsibility" indicated that the students were able to recognize the important connections that link school and society, classroom and community. For example, one student wrote:

> I am not sure how to justify avoiding the call to serve those in such dire need. The call to teach is in essence to touch those who need to be reached, to be led out, to be shown that opportunity exists where none has been seen before. Questions in my mind remain about the feasibility of surviving in such a setting as a first-year teacher.

PROGRAM GRADUATE REFLECTIONS

One cohort graduate who was teaching in a culturally diverse magnet school wrote about her reading selections and their connections to the program's conceptual framework. She also reflected on how the seminar experience impacted her own professional development. Excerpts from her written reflections follow:

> The seminar book discussions provided me with an opportunity to talk with my cohort about my student teaching experiences and connect the experiences to books we were reading. For example, Herbert Kohl, in his book, *Growing Minds On Becoming Teacher,* writes about finding a student's strengths first, then helping the student use these strengths to nurture growth. So often we focus on a student's weaknesses and overlook the positive attributes a student possesses. This made more sense to me when I thought about one of our graduate assignments: to list the names of every student in our first placement. Next to each name we were to list two strengths. I found this simple task challenging. I discovered that I had spent so much time trying to identify the areas where my students needed help that I overlooked the areas where they were strongest. This was Kohl's point.
>
> The objective of making text-to-self connections is to enhance reading comprehension; this did happen in our seminar book discussions . . . I needed the structure of a scheduled book talk to get me to take the time to do what teachers at my school call "get slow" or reflect beyond the daily details of my

teaching. I also thought it was helpful to include the faculty in our discussions so they could offer their own insight and share their experiences as well.

The book talk papers were also beneficial in helping me synthesize everything we discussed. Writing my thoughts helped me, as a visual learner, to pull together the different threads of our discussions and deal with it holistically. One of the most influential books I read during my experience in the Model Program was Herbert Kohl's, *Growing Minds On Becoming A Teacher*. In it, Kohl says that being a good teacher means, "being obsessed with helping others grow." I have learned that good teachers also focus on their own growth and seek opportunities to continue learning themselves. In fact, the issue of professional development was the determining factor in my decision to work in the school where I am currently teaching. I wanted to work in an environment where teachers were learners too.

Similar to the book talks at GW, interested teachers read a professional book together and meet monthly at my school to discuss its implications for the classroom. I was able to actively participate in these talks because I had done so in the Model Program. As a first-year teacher, my plate was overflowing just managing my classroom responsibilities. Initially, I wasn't sure I wanted to get involved in the book talks at Bailey's—I wasn't sure I could handle it. Then I remembered how much I got out of the book talks at GW (the ideas, the venting, the understanding . . .) and decided to read the first few chapters of the book, *Going Public* (Harwayne, 1999). After the first meeting I was hooked! I remember rushing back to my classroom to start implementing some of the things I had read.

Reflection is a vital part of the Model Program starting with the conceptual framework: Knowledge, Individuality, and Social Responsibility. Throughout the program we were asked to think about how these themes impacted on our developing philosophy of teaching. A year after graduation I must confess that I'm more likely to think about some of the content area strategies I learned during my training than the three themes. However, I do think the exercise of reflecting, a practice on which the Model Program is based, has changed my teaching. I have learned how important it is to take the time to think, talk or write about what goes on in the classroom. As a result, I think I know my students and their needs better than I would if I didn't take the time. I plan better and assess more authentically.

Conclusion

So, what can we say about the impact or sustaining influence of our program's conceptual framework on our interns? Did our program's approach to connecting this framework to standards of practice that embrace larger ideas about schooling influence our interns' beliefs and views as well as their willingness to engage in reflection? Did it have any sustaining power beyond these events? First, we know that the process of shared reader response activities motivated our students to read more and to take a larger perspective of the social and political contexts of schooling. This became evident as the readings expanded with the second Book Talk session. Second, the process of guided assistance helped the interns learn how to reflect on their readings over the course of the semester. During each phase of the Book Talk sessions a different set of books for discussion or type of grouping was targeted so that students experienced reflection in multiple ways. Third, the Book Talk discussions and the final written reflection assignment gave us insight into how the interns were: (a) constructing meaning and relating their readings to their school experiences, and (b) connecting their beliefs to knowledge, individuality, and social responsibility. Fourth, we opened up an affective avenue where interns could express a range of feelings that included enlightenment, fear, and frustration. Expressions about commitments to keeping memories of significant role models from their readings when "times got tough" were also evident in many of the responses. Lastly, we heard personal testimony from our graduate-turned-teacher of how insightful and influential the process of modeling reflection continues to be in her practice as well as in her continued participation in similar types of reflection activities.

Implications for Teachers and Teacher Educators

As a program pedagogy this approach is only a piece of the complex process for preparing teachers. The study of our practice does show how teacher interns had guided opportunities over time to be reflective about what they were learning through shared conceptual lenses. This seminar model is not elegant, but it is flexible enough so that the "examples of evidence" (Wiggins & McTighe, 1998) used can be applied to other teacher education programs. In this study we see how the conceptual framework created learning opportunities (Calderhead & Schorrock, 1997) and how the strategies used provided a way for the affective side of teacher development to be nurtured through the examination of the moral and ethical issues in the life of a teacher.

The power of these strategies used in combination with the reflective seminar format allowed pre-service teachers/professionals to initiate ideas of their own using their unique voices to reflect and connect with the current literature and research on American schools. Students inspired one another to think differently regarding their approaches to teaching, sharing invaluable insight during this part of their professional development. The seminar format provided interns time to understand their beliefs and opportunities to uncover their dispositions toward teaching.

These reflective experiences provided "new lenses" for our elementary teacher interns and elicited examples of oral and written dialogue that emerged from a community of learners (Howey & Zimpher, 1996). The study illustrates how teacher education programs can meet standards of best practice that empower students to approach their practice differently from the "status quo". We believe this can happen when students are given real experiences in schools coupled with thought-provoking notions about what teaching and learning can and should be.

REFERENCES

Bogdan, R. & Biklen, S. (1982). *Qualitative research for education: An introduction to theory and methods.* Boston, MA: Allyn & Bacon.

Calderhead J., & Shorrock, S. B. (1997). *Understanding teacher education.* Washington, DC: The Falmer Press.

Carter, K. & Anders, D. (1996). Program pedagogy. In F.B. Murray (Ed.), *The teacher educator's handbook: Building a knowledge base for the preparation of teachers* (pp. 557–592). San Francisco: Jossey-Bass.

Delpit, L. (1995). *Other people's children.* New York: The New Press.

Dottin, E. (1998). NCATE 2000: Continuing accreditation and beyond. Institutional orientation and professional development workshop. Sponsored by NCATE and AACTE, May 20–23, Washington, DC.

Freire, P. (1993). *Pedagogy of the oppressed.* New York: Continuum.

Fried, R. (1995). *The passionate teacher: A practical guide.* Boston, MA: Beacon Press.

Guyton, E. M., Rainer, J., & Wright, T. (1997). Developing a constructivist teacher education program. In D.M. Byrd & D.J. McIntyre (Eds.), *Research on the education of our nation's teachers* (pp. 149–171). Thousand Oaks: Corwin Press.

Harwayne, S. (1999). *Going public: Priorities & practice at the Manhattan New School.* Portsmouth, NH: Heinemann.

Hersch, P. (1998). *A tribe apart: A journey into the heart of American adolescence.* New York: Fawcett Columbine.

Howey, K. R. (1996). Designing coherent and effective teacher education programs. In J.Sikula, T. J. Buttery, and E.Guyton (Eds.), *Handbook of Research on Teacher Education* (pp. 143–170). New York: Macmillan Publishing.

Howey, K. R. & Zimpher, N. L. (1996). Pattern in prospective teachers: guides for designing pre-service programs. In F.B. Murray (Ed.), *The teacher educator's handbook: Building a knowledge base for the preparation of teachers* (pp. 465–505). San Francisco: Jossey-Bass.

Interstate New Teacher Assessment and Support Consortium (INTASC). (1992). *Model standards for beginning teacher licensing and development: A resource for state dialogue.* Washington, DC: Council for Chief State School Officers.

Kaufman, B. (1965). *Up the down staircase.* Englewood Cliffs, NJ: Prentice-Hall.

Kidder, T. (1989). *Among schoolchildren.* New York: Avon Books.

Kitchener, K. S. (1983). Educational goals and reflective thinking. *Educational Forum. 58* (1) 75–95.

Knowles, G. J., & Cole, A. L. (1996). Developing practice through field experiences. In F.B. Murray (Ed.), *The teacher educator's handbook: Building a knowledge base for the preparation of teachers* (pp. 648–688). San Francisco: Jossey-Bass.

Kohl, H. (1984). *Growing minds on becoming a teacher.* New York: Harper & Row.

Kozol, J. (1991). *Savage inequalities: Children in American schools.* New York: Crown.

LaBoskey, V. K. (1994). *Development of reflective practice: A study of pre-service teachers.* New York: Teachers College Press.

National Board for Professional Teaching Standards. (1991). *Toward high and rigorous standards for the teaching profession.* (2nd ed., summary). Detroit, MI: NBPTS.

National Commission on Teaching & America's Future. (1996). *What matters most: Teaching for America's future:* Summary Report. New York: Author.

National Council for Accreditation of Teacher Education. (1997). *Standards, procedures, and policies for the accreditation of professional education units.* Washington, DC: NCATE.

Odell, S. J. (1997). Curriculum: Overview and framework. In D.M. Byrd & D. J. McIntyre (Eds.), *Research on the education of our nation's teachers* (pp. 137–147). Thousand Oaks: Corwin Press.

Paley, V. G. (1992). *You can't say you can't play.* Cambridge, MA: Harvard University Press.

Richardson, V. (1996). The case for formal research and practical inquiry in teacher education. In F.B. Murray (Ed.), *The teacher educator's handbook: Building a knowledge base for the preparation of teachers* (pp. 715–737). San Francisco: Jossey-Bass.

Schon, D. (1991). *The reflective turn: Case studies in and on educational practice.* New York: Teachers College Press.

Strauss, A. (1987). *Qualitative analysis for social scientists.* New York: Cambridge University Press.

Wiggins, G. and McTighe, J. (1998). *Understanding by design.* Alexandria, VA: Association for Supervision and Curriculum Development.

Successes and Struggles in the Development of Performance Assessments

8.

Lori Olafson, Lisa D. Bendixen, Jeffrey C. Shih,
Kendall Hartley, Linda F. Quinn,
Merrie Schroeder (University of Nevada, Las Vegas)

Lori Olafson in an assistant professor of elementary education in the Department of Curriculum and Instruction at UNLV. Lori's research interests include pre-service teacher's beliefs about teaching and learning, subjectivity in adolescent girls, and school climate.

Lisa D. Bendixen is an assistant professor in the Department of Educational Psychology, at UNLV. Her research interests include epistemological beliefs and how they impact teaching and learning.

Jeffrey C. Shih is an assistant professor in elementary mathematics education at UNLV. His current research interests include developing frameworks of student understanding in fractions, professional development, and integrating mathematics with other content areas.

Kendall Hartley is an assistant professor of educational technology in the Curriculum and Instruction department at UNLV. Kendall's research interests focus on the potential of educational technology in learning and how it is used and perceived differently amongst learners with varying skills, attitudes and beliefs.

Linda F. Quinn is the Associate Dean at UNLV. Her areas of expertise include the professional development of teachers, curriculum, teaching strategies, classroom management, and international education. Linda has served on a number of ATE commissions and committees.

Merrie Schroeder is a graduate student in the Curriculum and Instruction doctoral program at UNLV. She is a faculty member at the University of Northern Iowa, Cedar Falls, Iowa. She has served as Professional Development Coordinator, Middle School Coordinator, and mathematics teacher at Malcolm Price Laboratory School, UNI.

ABSTRACT

This paper presents the results of a study conducted by five teacher educators who collaboratively developed performance assessments consistent with the revised National Council for Accreditation of Teacher Education (NCATE) Standard 5. We established a conceptual framework and designed performance assessments in the form of rubrics to be used in selected undergraduate teacher preparation courses. Our results demonstrate that our work with performance assessments had a direct impact on our teaching practices as we developed and communicated more clearly intended learning outcomes for teacher candidates. This study has had a significant impact on how we view our work as teacher educators. The implications for teacher education are clear. In order to best pre-pare candidates to authentically assess student learning, we must be prepared ourselves to be innovative in the ways we approach assessment.

The ripple effect created by changes in the National Council for Accreditation of Teacher Education (NCATE, 2000) perspective toward teacher education practices is stirring novice and experienced teacher educators to rethink the processes of teacher education. The new NCATE 2000 Standards call for performance assessment of teacher educa-tion candidates that verifies their knowledge of the content of their fields. These assessments must also give candidates an opportunity to demonstrate professional and pedagogical knowledge, skills and dispositions, and to apply them so that all students learn. This new emphasis on student learn-ing in place of teacher behavior when planning instructional episodes pre-sents, for some of us in the academy, a new way of thinking about how we train teachers. Faced with the prospect of creating assessment measures that emphasize student learning and performance, we began a program of research to design, implement, and evaluate performance-based assess-ments in our undergraduate courses. This paper describes the process of establishing a conceptual framework and developing performance assess-ments consistent with the framework.

Objectives

Our research had two main objectives. The first goal was to develop a common framework that would define key terms and establish criteria for performance assessments to be implemented in the courses we taught. We wanted to establish a shared vision for writing, implementing, and evaluating performance objectives. The second goal involved developing appropriate performance assessments within our undergraduate teacher preparation courses aligned with state and national directives and standards. In particular, we wanted to be consistent with the revised NCATE Standard 5. One element of this standard states that teaching at the university level should incorporate performance assessments as a way to model best professional practices in teaching (NCATE, 2000). Each of us prepared a performance task and an evaluation rubric for a course we were teaching.

Theoretical Framework

According to Eisner (1999), performance assessment is one of the "hot topics" on the agenda of educational reform. Although there has been an increasing realization that assessment practices need to be more authentic in our nation's classrooms, it appears that teacher training programs have failed to keep pace with assessment reforms. As Stiggins (1995) notes, "With a few notable exceptions, colleges of education continue to produce new teachers and administrators who are poorly prepared to face the increasingly complex challenges of classroom assessment" (p. 238). It is critical, therefore, for teacher educators to model sound assessment practices for teacher candidates. Diez and Hass (1997) maintain that "Teacher educators have a powerful reason to incorporate performance assessment as an essential component in preparing teacher candidates. Not only do such instruments provide documentation of the development of abilities, but the experience of the assessment process itself can contribute to candidate development" (p. 21). Our conceptual framework is based on the belief that we can best prepare teacher candidates to face the complex challenges of classroom assessment by integrating performance assessments into our instruction.

Despite the lack of a single definition, performance assessment is widely regarded as a practice "that requires students to create evidence through performance that will enable assessors to make valid judgements about 'what they know and can do' in situations that matter" (Eisner, 1999, p. 2). By performance-based assessment, we mean an activity that requires students to construct a response, create a product, or perform a demonstration that illustrates what they have learned. Assessment of these performance tasks may entail the use of rubrics, holistic scoring techniques, and teacher work sampling methodology. In our study, we decided to focus on the use of rubrics to assess our performance tasks, and we followed Huba and Freed's (2000) guidelines for developing useful rubrics.

Methods

Five teacher educators representing two departments within a College of Education at a large urban university were awarded a teaching initiative grant to design and implement performance-based assessments in their undergraduate courses. The faculty represented a variety of fields including mathematics education, developmental psychology, elementary teacher education and educational technology. We met twice monthly for six months to discuss the conceptual framework and to design and develop performance-based assessments for our undergraduate courses. Initial discussions centered on identifying the characteristics of an effective performance assessment. Six main characteristics were identified and served as a basis for performance assessments, rubric design and subsequent discussions. We agreed that performance-based assessments should:

- be clear in purpose,
- be student-centered and not teacher driven,
- be seen as informing teaching and learning,
- provide opportunity for success and growth through a developmental process,
- provide students multiple ways of representing knowledge, skills and dispositions,
- be as near to authentic as possible.

The identified characteristics closely match Ewell's (1997) principles of learning.

We began the design of our performance assessments by analyzing our syllabi and identifying specific tasks within our courses that would be appropriate for performance assessment. We then developed rubrics and draft assessments for the chosen tasks and shared our drafts with the group. After our pilot rubrics were shared, threaded on-line dialogues were created. Our dialogue in this process demonstrates the manner in which we asked questions, reflected on our own practices, and critiqued our colleagues' efforts. We then revised our assessments based upon the group comments. Throughout this process, we continued to meet as a group to discuss the conceptual framework and performance assessments.

Data Source and Analysis

Data were collected from three sources: threaded on-line dialogues from WebCT, field notes taken by a graduate student at our regular meetings, and individual interviews.

WebCT (i.e., Web Course Tools) is commonly used as a tool to assist instructors in utilizing the Internet to communicate with students. WebCT provides educational tools that facilitate interaction including bulletin boards, e-mail and document sharing tools. We used WebCT as a way to share and discuss our assessments.

A graduate research assistant attended all of the meetings as a participant observer and kept field notes of group interaction, goals, and progress towards the development of the performance assessments.

An individual interview was designed (see Appendix B), based on "Principles of Performance Assessment in Effective Teacher Education" (Murrell, in preparation). Murrell contends that teaching changes as one moves toward implementing performance assessments. We proposed questions that allowed us to monitor our own changes in teaching and assessing.

The threaded on-line dialogues, the interview data, and the field notes were analyzed using van Manen's (1990) approach for thematic analysis: that is, we reflected on these texts in order to uncover their thematic aspects or the elements that occurred frequently in the text. Employing the selective reading approach (van Manen, 1990), we read the texts several times as we asked the question "What statement(s) or phrase(s) seems particularly essential or revealing about the phenomenon being described?" (p. 93). These statements were highlighted, and, as we noted commonalities in the statements and gathered excerpts from the texts, we organized them into categories: the categories arose from the data (Seidman, 1991).

Results

For the purposes of this paper, we focus our results section on describing the pilot rubrics and on the issues and dilemmas that arose during our WebCT discussions. The richness and depth of the conversations that emerged were aspects of the research that we had not anticipated.

SUMMARY OF RUBRICS

The variety of courses, purposes, and criteria for which we developed our assessment rubrics is shown in Table 1. We include an example of one of the pilot rubrics (see Appendix A).

TABLE 1
Summary of Rubrics

Course	Purpose	Criteria
Elementary Math Methods	To assess students' knowledge of the development of children's mathematical thinking.	Writing word problems Identification of problem type Appropriate solution strategy Teacher assessment of what child understands.
Effective Strategies for Elementary School Teaching	To assess students' responses to reading required text.	Comprehending and Interpreting Intertextuality Making Connections Insight
Tests and Measurement	To assess students' reflections on readings, lectures, notes, and discussion.	Developing pertinent discussion questions Identifying concepts/issues that stood out and/or were not understood Practical application
Survey of Computer Uses in Education	To assess students' ability to design and develop an educational website.	Understanding of design principles Providing useful information Engaging Appropriate for target audience Reflects technical understanding Site navigation
Classroom Management in the Elementary School	To assess students' planning and implementation of management strategies.	Lesson plan format Relationship to assumptions and beliefs Objectives and rationale Learning activities Assessment

With feedback from our colleagues, we were able to refine further our individual rubrics. For example, Kendall's initial response to Jeff's rubric included the following suggestion: "My initial thought is that the characteristics should be more specific. The intent of the descriptors is to unambiguously describe the different levels of performance." For six weeks we posted and responded to messages on Web CT about the rubrics. Even when the rubrics were ready to be piloted, we recognized they were unfinished: "These will certainly be works in progress because I know I will discover more as I evaluate students' work."

EMERGENT THEMES

As we developed our rubrics and engaged in the revision process, several themes seemed to recur. These themes reflect primarily the "struggle for meaning" (Gore, 1993) that we encountered even though we were working from a common conceptual framework. Designing tasks/defining performance and judging with rubrics are examples of the activities with which we struggled. Professional development, the final section of our results, presents the discussions that are reflective of growth experienced in the first phase of our research.

DESIGNING TASKS/DEFINING PERFORMANCE

Designing the task and defining the performance seemed to be two sides of the same coin. The question "What do we mean by performance?" was continuously revisited during discussions of what our performance tasks should look like and what exactly they should measure. Defining "performance" in our specific contexts required clarification of the purpose of the assessment. We had to be able to articulate our instructional goals, what we wanted our students to know and be able to do. And then we had to identify the performances that would assure us that our students had, in fact, acquired the knowledge, skills and dispositions we felt were necessary for their success as preservice teachers.

Herman, Aschbacher & Winters (1992) suggest that in designing tasks it is important to think about both big ideas and specific skills, to focus on outcomes and on the process of the assessment. Jeff and Kendall recognize the link between designing the task and defining performance:

Jeff: I want my students to understand the development of children's thinking—to be able to solve problems as children

> do. The rubric I use to assess their performance must reflect what I ask them to do.
>
> *Kendall:* "IF" different levels of performance can be neatly described then I think we can rest assured that our students have acquired specific knowledge, skills and dispositions.

We recognized the need to define the criteria on which we would base our performance tasks. But we also found that it was not easy to state explicitly these standards in advance, as the following excerpts illustrate:

> *Linda:* I ask my students to write a plan for the beginning of the school year. This task gives them an opportunity to demonstrate their knowledge and skill in anticipating and planning for events that will promote success for their students. Specific strategies to be implemented in this plan are discussed in class. The task seems clear, but establishing criteria for evaluating the students' plans is difficult. What does a "fair standard" look like for something as creative as a lesson plan?
>
> *Kendall:* We are trying to design and evaluate more open-ended tasks but when we try to get a handle on some of the things we think are important but elusive (i.e., intangibles), we end up restricting the types of responses we deem acceptable.

We found that designing and defining tasks and their subsequent assessments linked purpose and performance in a more explicit and comprehensive manner. One question that remains is how we will document the impact of our performance assessments on student learning.

Judging with rubrics. A number of issues emerged regarding judging with rubrics. Primarily, our concerns centered around the rating scheme to be used because, in addition to specifying dimensions of quality, a useful rubric must also include labels describing the levels of student work (Huba & Freed, 2000). Each of our rubrics, then, specified levels of mastery. Four of the five rubrics used three levels of achievement representing excellent, acceptable, and unacceptable work, and one of the rubrics included four levels of achievement: exemplary, proficient, acceptable, and unacceptable (see Appendix A). Interestingly, two of the rubrics attached point values to each of the levels of achievement; for example, "unacceptable" level work was assigned a value of one point while "exceptional" work received three points. These two rubrics reflected a more analytic approach to rubrics, where a rating is given for each dimension of quality (Bullock & Hawk, 2001). The issue of whether or not to assign points to our rubrics and whether or not they should be point-driven or holistic generated a great deal of intense discussion as the following excerpt illustrates:

Lisa: I have one thought about points and their relationship to teaching and learning. Some would argue that points may give you more fine-grained information about what a student knows/doesn't know compared to pass/fail . . . the more information you have about a particular student the better able you are to teach them. I think good rubrics should be part of that but do they (points/rubrics) have to be mutually exclusive?

Lori: Assigning points for my rubric is untenable. According to Broad (1994), our work in performance assessment "has made the ground fertile for context, choice, difference, and multiplicity in the areas of students' evaluative input (but) we persist in stripping context and quashing difference when it comes to our evaluative output" (p. 266).

Lisa: Is it possible to have points or not have points and still have an effective rubric?

Lori: I think that points could be appropriate for some rubrics, depending on the purpose, what is being assessed, etc. Scoring seems to make sense where performance expectations are mastery in nature and the expectations are easily defined.

As we debated the issue of points, Jeff reminded us of the ultimate goal of our rubrics: "I think the important thing to keep in mind is the purpose of the assessment—the improvement of teaching and learning." Regardless of points, our rubrics needed to provide students with information they needed to improve the quality of their work. In the end, two of the pilot rubrics employed a point system, but all of the rubrics provided clear commentary describing the defining features of work at each level of mastery (Huba & Freed, 2000).

We did not believe, though, that this lack of consistency surrounding the points issue was a negative outcome. The conversations we engaged in about whether or not to assign points provided each of us the opportunity to articulate our beliefs about assessment. As Kendall noted, "The issue of points/grades has helped me to think about how I view assessment." When considering what rating scheme to use, Huba & Freed (2000) maintain that it needs to be done in a way that fits with each individual's grading philosophy. We were confident that the rating scheme for each rubric in the project was well-thought out and consistent with the grading philosophy of the individual. Additionally, we were confident that each rubric revealed the "scoring rules" of the performance task, explained to students the criteria against which their work would be judged, and made public key criteria that students could use in developing, revising, and judging their own work (Huba & Freed, 2000).

Professional growth. It was very clear that our growth as educators in the understanding and use of performance-based assessments was linked to the opportunity to grapple with the issues with our colleagues. We had never had a chance for others to examine our performance-based assessments. This experience coincides with Huba & Freed's (2000) notion that "A critical mass of individuals actually examining their assumptions and practices can provide mutual support for one another" (p. 274). Indeed, the supportive environment that was created within our group allowed us to take a hard look at our assessment practices and gain from that. This sentiment is echoed in the following dialogue:

> **Lisa:**   Thanks for all of the thoughtful, provoking feedback. As I had hoped this project forced me to think about my own assessment practices and where I stand on the important issues. I am trying to find comfortable ground that I can walk on.
>
> **Lori:**   I've had to do some research so that I can provide a rationale for my position. Without being "pushed" by my colleagues I probably wouldn't have done so. I really had to think about some key issues regarding the rubric: 1) What are the theoretical constructs that underlie the assessment, and 2) What is the purpose of the assessment.

In one of our face-to-face discussions we observed that in higher education there seems to be almost an unspoken secrecy surrounding assessment practices. They are viewed as a very personal choice that we are all entitled to as educators at this level. Working with our colleagues has broken down many of the existing walls that ultimately get in the way of growth and learning. As Kendall noted in regard to his own professional growth, "I am thinking about what I want the students to know in a completely different way. If I were to compare the syllabus of this class with what I have normally taught in the past, I would be appalled." Lisa speaks specifically about the rubric and how work on that led to changes: "The rubric is certainly a concrete piece of evidence concerning changes in my assessment practices. I think that this rubric still needs a lot of work but it is a start! So many issues came to the fore after I tried to put a rubric together."

Making major changes in assessment beliefs and practice on an individual basis has been described as a potentially "lonely" and "distancing" endeavor (Huba & Freed, 2000). It seemed that the risks in examining our own practice and trying new approaches was lessened, although not completely erased, by working together. However, because we truly trusted our colleagues and believed that this was going to be a learning experience, the mistakes, rough drafts, differing opinions, revisions, and the changing of beliefs were all expected and accepted.

Conclusions

As a team, we are still struggling with many of the issues inherent in moving from traditional assessments to performance assessments. According to Farr & Trumbill (1997), "It is virtually impossible for any single group of innovators to anticipate all of the pitfalls or missteps along the way" (p. 289). However, a look at our interaction over time also reveals several positive changes: 1) our team is definitely becoming more focused in what we know and what we believe is true about the role of assessments in teaching, 2) we have become more thoughtful in the design of our courses because keeping an eye to assessment requires knowing what skills and concepts we most value, 3) we are constantly reflecting and refining how we want students to demonstrate their knowledge and skills, using a variety of types of performances, 4) we are recognizing the need to communicate clear expectations to students, thus reinforcing the emphasis on student success, and 5) we recognize the power in modeling performance assessments for our students, with the goal that they will also teach using performance assessments.

Implications for Teachers and
Teacher Educators

We see two major implications arising from our work. One implication of our research is concerned with the connection between teacher beliefs and assessment practices. That teachers' beliefs influence their actions in the classroom is well-documented (Clark & Peterson, 1986) and that these beliefs act as filters when teachers have new experiences (Putnam & Borko, 2000). In addition, articulating teacher beliefs is an important first step for change (Cohen & Ball, 1990). It is critical, then, to identify preservice teachers' beliefs about assessment in general, and performance assessment in particular, if we hope to realize the potential for more effective use of assessment. In order to prepare teacher candidates to meet the complex challenges of classroom assessment, it is important to provide them with the opportunity to make their pre-existing beliefs explicit so that teacher educators may begin to challenge the adequacy of these beliefs. Participating in a variety of performance assessments in conjunction with discussions led by teacher educators allows teacher candidates to critically examine their beliefs about assessment, to modify their beliefs, and to expand their repertoire of assessment practices. We believe that it is vital for pre-service teachers to have these experiences if we expect them to include performance assessments in their future practice.

Secondly, as our results have demonstrated, our work with performance assessment had a direct impact on our teaching practice within the teacher preparation program. Eisner (1999) maintains that performance assessment "affords us an opportunity to secure information about learning that can help improve the quality of both curriculum and teaching" (p. 4). We believe this to be particularly true regarding undergraduate education, a view shared by Angelo (1999): "Assessment can be a powerful tool for improving—even transforming—undergraduate education" (p. 21–22). Using rubrics allowed us to develop and then communicate intended learning outcomes to ourselves and to our students. In essence, we began teaching more effectively with the use of rubrics. According to Johnston (1989) "The purpose of any educational assessment is ultimately to contribute to the improvement of teaching and learning" (p. 509). We will continue to develop our rubrics in order to improve both teaching and learning. In the next phase of our research we will be investigating the impact of our rubrics on student learning. Our hope is that we will be able to collect evidence that shows how our assessments have improved student learning.

Using rubrics to improve teaching and learning in our teacher preparation program has led us to rethink our practice. This has had a significant impact on how we view our work as teacher educators. The implications for teacher education are clear. In order to best prepare candidates to authentically assess student learning, we must be prepared ourselves to be innovative in the ways we approach assessment.

REFERENCES

Angelo, T. A. (1999). Doing assessment as if learning matters most. *American Association for Higher Education (AAHE) Bulletin,* May, 3–6.

Broad, R. (1994). "Portfolio scoring": A contradiction in terms. In Black, L., Darker, D., Sommers, J., & Stygall, G. (Eds). *New directions in portfolio assessment.* Portsmouth, NH : Heinemann.

Bullock, A. & Hawk, P. (2001). *Developing a teaching portfolio.* Upper Saddle River, NJ: Merrill Prentice-Hall.

Clark, C. M. & Peterson, P. L. (1986). Teachers' thought processes. In Wittrock, M.C. (Ed.), *Handbook of research on teaching,* 3rd Edition, 255–296. New York: Macmillan.

Cohen, D. K., & Ball, D. L. (1990). Relations between policy and practice: A commentary. *Educational Evaluation and Policy Analysis, 12,* 331–338.

Diez, M. & Hass, J. (1997). No more piecemeal reform: Using performance-based approaches to rethink teacher education. *Action in Teacher Education, 19*(2), 17–26.

Eisner, E. (1999). The uses and limits of performance assessment. *Phi Delta Kappan,* May, 1–6.

Ewell, P. T. (1997). Organizing for learning: A new imperative. *American Association for Higher Education (AAHE) Bulletin.* December, 1–4.

Farr, B., & Trumbill, E. (1997). *Assessment alternatives for diverse classrooms.* Norwood, MA: Christopher-Gordon.

Gore, J. (1993). *The struggle for pedagogies.* New York: Routledge.

Herman, J.L., Aschbacher, P.R., & Winters, L. (1992). *A practical guide to alternative assessment.* Alexandria, VA : Association for Supervision and Curriculum Development .

Huba, M. & Freed, J. (2000). *Learner-centered assessment on college campuses: Shifting the focus from teaching to learning.* Boston: Allyn & Bacon.

Johnston, P. (1989). Constructive evaluation and the improvement of teaching and learning. *Teachers College Record, 90* (4), 509–528.

Murrell, P.C., Jr. (in preparation). *Community teachers: Teacher preparation and the renewal of urban schools.* New York: Teachers College Press.

NCATE. (2000). NCATE 2000 standards [On-line]. Available: http://www.ncate.org/standards/m_stds.htm.

Putnam, R. T., & Borko, H. (2000). What do new views of knowledge and thinking have to say about research on teacher learning? *Educational Researcher, 29*(1), 4–15.

Seidman, I. (1991). *Interviewing as qualitative research: A guide for researchers in education and the social sciences.* New York: Teachers College Press.

Stiggins, R.J. (1995). Assessment literacy for the 21st century. *Phi Delta Kappan* (November), 238–245.

Van Manen, M. (1990). *Researching lived experience: Human science for an action sensitive pedagogy*. London: The Althouse Press.

Appendix A

SAMPLE RUBRIC FOR EPY 451—TESTS AND MEASUREMENT

This course is designed as an introduction to measurement and assessment related to instruction. All preservice teachers are required to take this class. One of the performance tasks is a weekly Learning Log that is designed to get students thinking about the material, including reflections on how the material is related to them as future educators. Entries are also used as the basis for small and large group discussions. Each entry (16 total for the semester) will be evaluated using the following rubric:

Criteria	Exemplary	Proficient	Acceptable	Unacceptable
One pertinent discussion question	Your entry contains a relevant, thought-provoking question	Your entry include a relevant question	Your entry includes a definition question	Your entry does not include a discussion question
Concepts/ issues that stood out to you OR that you did not understand	Your entry includes a detailed description of concepts that stood out to you OR were not understood	Your entry includes a detailed, surface description of concepts that stood out to you OR were not understood	Your entry includes a vague description of the concepts that stood out OR were not understood	Your entry does not describe any concepts that stood out OR were not understood
Brief discussion of how info. covered in class relates to YOUR future career as an educator	Your entry includes meaningful discussion and a personal and specific classroom example was given	Your entry meaningful discussion and a general classroom example was given	Your entry includes vague discussion and no examples given	Your entry include no discussion and no examples given

Appendix B

PROFESSOR INTERVIEW

1. Briefly describe the class you are piloting.
2. At what level of ability would you say you are with respect to implementing performance based learning?
3. How is preparing for this class different from preparing a traditional class (traditional to you)?
4. What changes do you see in your assessing practices so far?
5. What professional skills do you need to assess this way that you do not already possess (or that you didn't possess prior to this project)?
6. What professional knowledge do you need to assess this way that you do not already possess (or that you didn't possess prior to this project)?
7. What are some outcomes of this type of assessing or effects on your students that you hadn't expected?
8. How is this type of assessing affecting your teaching of students?
9. How are you assessing your own performance and growth during this term, as a result of this pilot?
10. In your perception, what is the value of performance assessment?
11. How do you feel about your pilot class so far?
12. What do you hope will be an outcome with respect to how you teach and assess students?

Meeting the Standards
Assessing an INTASC-Based Elementary Professional Development School

9.

Susan L. Nierstheimer, Wendy L. Black, Marilyn K. Moore, S. Rex Morrow, and Kenneth H. Strand

Susan Nierstheimer and Wendy Black have been directing this PDS project in collaboration with the faculty at Glenn Elementary and support from Marilyn Moore, assistant chair, and Rex Morrow, chair of the Department of C&I at Illinois State University. Ken Strand conducted the research and works in Educational Foundations.

ABSTRACT

In this chapter findings are presented from a mid-point evaluation of an INTASC-based, teacher preparation pilot project in the context of a professional development elementary school. The purpose of this evaluative research is to serve as a formative vehicle to help the project team identify challenges ahead as well as to determine the degree to which the objectives of the project are being met. Data were collected from various stakeholders: administrators of the project, classroom teachers, university students, children in the elementary school, and parents. Significant findings include a belief by the participants that the objectives of the project are being met, but that concern still exist. Improved communication between and among stakeholders, more teaching time in classrooms for interns, and better understanding among the children of the school as to why the student-interns are in their classrooms are some of the challenges facing the PDS team.

Professional Development School

Illinois State University is one of nine universities in the state of Illinois chosen to design and implement teacher preparation innovations based on the INTASC principles (Interstate New Teacher Assessment and Support Consortium). The nine universities were awarded initial funding by the state in order to support standards-based practices in the preparation of exemplary teachers. In Illinois State University's project, a cohort of twenty students is participating in one elementary school, Glenn Elementary School, Normal, Illinois, from their freshman year through their senior yearlong internship. The students' preparation experiences have been purposefully designed to underscore INTASC principles. The students are extensively involved in the school; some of their professional development coursework is taught on-site at the elementary school, referred to as Glenn Elementary Professional Development School (GEPDS).

Our collaborative—university faculty, administration, and classroom teachers—is working to infuse INTASC principles into the experiences of the preservice teachers engaged in the GEPDS undertaking. Some of the approaches the team used in the first two years were: required recurring student reflections, student seminars, inquiry projects, an electronic portfolio, and coursework instilling the principles. The ongoing electronic portfolio organized around INTASC principles and serves formative and summative functions. During students' preparation years it is formative in nature, a place for students to demonstrate their developing competencies as preservice teachers and to receive feedback from the elementary classroom teachers and the university faculty associated with the project. At the end of students' preparation years, the INTASC-based portfolios will be used as a summative tool to assess students' readiness to receive a preliminary license in the state of Illinois as an elementary teacher.

In addition to these standards-based teacher preparation opportunities, students try out what they are learning through two-hours per week, service work in the classrooms at Glenn School. Each semester, the future teachers are exposed to large- and small-group instruction as well as individual work with children, guided and supervised by the teachers at Glenn.

As well as the overarching goal of infusing INTASC principles into students' experiences, the objectives of the project follow those ascribed to by the Holmes Group (Holmes Group, 1993). Thus, our foremost objectives for this undertaking are: (a) to enhance the learning of pupils in Glenn School; (b) to provide high quality standards-based teacher education for preservice elementary education students; (c) to provide ongoing, continuous professional development of university and school faculty; and (d) to engage in professional inquiry/research as a community of learners. These four primary goals are referred to throughout this document as the Holmes' objectives.

At the midpoint of our undertaking the project team collected informal data that helped inform understandings of how beneficial the project was to its various stakeholders (Nierstheimer, Taylor, Lloyd, Moore, & Morrow, 2000). We describe these findings in the next section of this paper. However, we also wanted data collected and analyzed by an impartial observer, someone not involved in the project. To this end, we engaged a colleague who is a test/measurement-oriented professional from outside our department to conduct a formal evaluation of the pilot project mid-way through its existence. This "outsider" collected data, analyzed the findings, and made recommendations based on those findings. In this article, we report on what our researcher-colleague uncovered about the project now that our undergraduate students have just finished their sophomore years in the program. This evaluative research report is to serve as a formative vehicle that will help us identify challenges that need to be addressed as well as to determine the degree to which the objectives of the project are being met.

The guiding questions that underpinned this evaluative research are the following: a) To what degree are the objectives of the project being met? b) What are the strengths of the project and the benefits to the various stakeholders? and c) What are the challenges that need to be addressed?

Previous Research

When we conducted our first study of the project (Nierstheimer, Taylor, Lloyd, Moore, & Morrow, 2000), we took a constructivist stance as we attempted to understand the perspectives and views of the stakeholders and their professed benefits as a result of participation. In that study, teachers noted that they and the children in their classrooms benefited from help by the Illinois State University students with small-group and individual instruction, extra hands in the classroom, and struggling learners who received individual help. Our preservice teachers reported that they believed that the program was supplying unique, valuable, and early experiences that would prepare them for their future careers as teachers. The undergraduates also stated that they were learning from the teachers at Glenn School and having opportunities to be mentored on-the-job. The joint partners, university faculty and classroom teachers, believed that among the numerous benefits of professional development schools are the invaluable professional development opportunities for teacher educators. The team involved in this venture was and are encouraged about the work that we are doing to better prepare teachers.

Another goal of this research is to add to the body of information available about standards-based models for training teachers. Literature on standards-based teacher preparation models is scarce even though it is apparent that many universities are currently engaged in such enterprises and are taking their cues from such documents as NCATE (National Council for Accreditation of Teacher Education) and INTASC (Theobald & Rochon, 1999).

The teacher education field is paying attention to standards in this time of high-demand for quality teachers. Among the common goals of teacher educators is the mentoring of new teachers who have a positive impact on student achievement, are more attuned to students' needs, and are able to teach all children (Wise & Leibbrand, 2000). At the same time, as teacher educators we wrestle with reconciling our constructivist stance with some teacher preparation models where standards-driven curricula seem artificial. We question how to use standards in a student-centered, constructivist way (Hartzler-Miller, 1999). To that end, in addition to standards-related (INTASC) educational experiences, we are offering the students in this project early and systematic experiences in the field that are deemed so vital (e.g., Darling-Hammond, 1990; Haberman, 1996). In the report of the National Commission on Teaching and America's Future: What Matters Most, Teaching for America's Future (1996) the authors write, "Prospective teachers learn just as other students do: by studying, practicing, and reflecting; by collaborating with others; by looking closely at students [children] and their work; and by sharing what they see. For prospective teachers, this kind of learning cannot occur in college classrooms divorced from schools . . . (p. 31). Aiken and Day (1999) quote one of their former undergraduates who echoes this sentiment: "I really think we have to get college students out in the classroom [with early field experiences] . . . you need to get in there and start dealing with students because that is what education is, and until you do it, you have no idea what you're talking about" (p. 9).

Darling-Hammond (2000) notes that although debates continue about best practices for training teachers, the quality and extent of teacher education matters now more than ever. Teacher educators must strengthen their knowledge base and their abilities to connect theory to practice in order to equip and develop powerful teachers for our future. Darling-Hammond reports that teacher preparation and clinical experiences housed in professional developmental settings can be more purposefully and intentionally structured. She recalls the metaphor of teaching hospitals who prepare medical professionals in the kinds of settings where they will be expected to function with excellence when their formal education is complete. We heartily agree with this metaphor and are trying to replicate that model, apprenticing our students with exemplary classroom teachers (Fairbanks, Freedman, & Kahn, 2000).

Methods

DATA

The outside researcher employed both quantitative and qualitative methodology for this study. Primary data consisted of surveys created for the following groups: teachers at the elementary school, university preservice students, parents, and children from the school. Two surveys were created for each of the subgroups of Glenn Elementary teachers and the preservice teachers: one survey addressed the degree to which the objectives of the project were being met; the other addressed important components of the project, and measuring students' understandings concerning the INTASC principles (See Table 2).

The surveys constructed for the parents and children from the school were generated to understand those groups' perceptions of important components of the project. All surveys used in this research were specific to each of the various stakeholders. All groups except the children were required to react to each item on the unique instruments on a scale ranging from 5 (SA = strongly agree) to 1 (SD = strongly disagree). The children's instrument required them to answer 'Yes' or 'No.'

Secondary data were interviews held with both purposely and randomly selected individuals; these interviews were conducted using formal and informal interview questions for each subgroup. Interview protocols involving one-on-one conferences, designed and conducted by the outside researcher, were held with the university project director, the project manager, the Glenn principal, three Glenn teachers, three university students, and three children from the school. Interview information from the project director, the project manager, and the school principal informed the researcher about the background, logistics, and the operational issues related to the project; therefore, those interviews were not subjected to analysis. However, interviews conducted with classroom teachers, university students, and children were analyzed and were used to corroborate or disconfirm findings that emerged from the quantitative instruments. All data analyses were aimed at answering the guiding research questions.

DATA ANALYSIS

For the quantitative data collected through the use of survey instruments, means (M) and standard deviations (SD) were computed for each continuous variable. Frequencies were obtained and percentages were computed for each categorical variable. Content analyses were performed on the qualitative data that were collected: open-ended responses on surveys and interview rejoinders. Since the qualitative components of the survey instruments for the Glenn teachers and the university students were similar to the questions and/or statements communicated by the sample that was interviewed, the two sets of data were aggregated.

THE SETTING

The context for this evaluative study was a professional development school, located in a medium-size university community. The neighborhood school has approximately 260 students and two classes per grade K–6; it is within walking distance of the university.

PARTICIPANTS

The researcher collected data from multiple sources. The participants included university administrators, the school principal, elementary school teachers, preservice teachers, parents, and children from the school. Specifically, the participants were: the project director (the university faculty member who oversees the day-to-day planning and operation of the project for the university); the project manager (the university faculty member who has written and oversees the grant money for the project for the university and is an administrative coordinator); the principal of Glenn Elementary School; Glenn teachers (three who were randomly selected to be interviewed and four who responded to a survey instrument); undergraduate preservice students (four who were randomly selected to be interviewed and ten who responded to a survey instrument); Glenn parents (30 who responded to a parent survey instrument); children from the school (three who were selected to be interviewed and 253 who responded to a student survey. Of the 253 surveys that were obtained from the children, the researcher randomly selected ten surveys from each grade K–6 for analysis.)

TIMELINE

All survey information was gathered in May 2000. The Glenn Elementary teachers and children, the university students, and the university project manager were each interviewed in person between May and July 2000. Those interviews lasted about thirty minutes. The Glenn principal and the university project director were interviewed via telephone in June and July 2000; those interviews lasted approximately one hour each.

Results

The following results were noted after analyses of data from the following groups: Glenn teachers, university students, children at the school, and parents of the children.

GLENN TEACHERS

The results of a two-part survey completed by Glenn teachers reveal their perceptions about the progress being made in meeting the project's objectives and in fulfilling the goals of important components of the project. The first part of the survey assessed teacher perceptions of the degree to which the objectives of the GEPDS project were being met on a scale from 5 (strongly agree the objective was met) to 1 (strongly disagree). Overall, teachers agreed and strongly agreed that the four Holmes' objectives were being met, with response means ranging from 4.25 to 4.75.

Analysis of the surveys shows that Glenn teachers *strongly agreed* that Objective 2 and Objective 4 were met. They *agreed* that Objective 1 and Objective3 were met. Teacher comments accompanying the rating generally supported these results. The results should be considered with some caution, however, since the percent return of the surveys was low (29 percent).

The second portion of the survey, a questionnaire regarding *important components of the project*, asked teachers to similarly rate three components on a scale from 5 to 1. For each item Glenn teachers *strongly agreed*, with means ranging from 4.67 (SD = .58) to 4.75 (SD = .50). These items were:

1. As a result of my experiences with the partnership, I plan instruction based upon knowledge of subject matter, students, the community, and curriculum goals.
2. I have observed mutual respect between the partner institutions— Glenn School and ISU.
3. I take ownership in helping the ISU students to grow.

TABLE 1

**Glenn Teachers' Responses to Degree to
Which Project Objectives Were Met**

Objective	M	SD
1. to enhance the learning of pupils in Glenn School	4.25	.50
2. to provide high quality standards-based teacher education for preservice elementary education students	4.50	.58
3. to provide ongoing, continuous professional development of university and school faculty	4.25	.50
4. to engage in professional inquiry/research as a community of learners	4.75	.50

ILLINOIS STATE UNIVERSITY STUDENTS

The first section of results from two-part surveys completed by the university students at the end of their sophomore year reveal their perceptions about the degree to which the Holmes' objectives for the GEPDS project were being met. The response rate was 48 percent, again rating each item on a scale from 5 to 1. Analysis of the surveys shows that GEPDS students *agreed* that Objective 1, Objective 2, and Objective 3 were met. They *strongly agreed* that Objective 4 was met.

In the second portion of the survey, a questionnaire asked the ISU students to rate statements related to important components of the GEPDS project. The researcher based statements 1–10 on the INTASC Principles as can be observed in Table 2. Please note that the survey statements' language was purposely shortened for the purpose of brevity in this report.

Statements 1 through 7 relate to the degree to which the university students perceived they developed understandings of learning and teaching children, supporting learner needs and diversity, implementing a variety of instructional strategies and communication skills, and creating a positive learning environment. The students agreed that these seven important components were being met, with response means ranging from 3.90 to 4.40.

The university students also *agreed* with the statement regarding learning formal and informal assessment strategies, becoming reflective practitioners, and fostering relationships with school colleagues, parents and community.

TABLE 2

Statements Rated by the University Students Concerning the Important Components of the GEPDS Project

Statement	M	SD
1. I have developed an understanding of content knowledge . . .	3.90	.74
2. I have developed an understanding of development and learning . . .	4.00	.82
3. I have developed an understanding of diversity . . .	4.40	.97
4. I have developed an understanding of |instructional strategies . . .	4.00	1.15
5. I use my understanding of the learning environment . . .	3.90	1.10
6. I use my knowledge of communication in the classroom . . .	4.30	.95
7. I plan appropriate instruction . . .	4.00	.95
8. I have developed an understanding of assessment . . .	3.60	.97
9. I am becoming a reflective practitioner . . .	4.10	1.29
10. I am able to develop collaborative relationships . . .	4.00	.95

BENEFITS AND RECOMMENDATIONS FROM GLENN TEACHERS AND UNIVERSITY STUDENTS

Open-ended questions completed at the end of the surveys gave opportunities for the Glenn Elementary teachers and ISU students to write specific comments about the effects and benefits of the partnership on their teaching and to make recommendations for the program. Three teachers and three university students, selected randomly as a representative sample, participated in follow-up interviews on these issues: a) the major effects of the project, b) individuals' goals for the project, and c) benefits of and recommendations for the project. Below, in list form, are the major benefits of and recommendations for the project as noted by the three teachers and three university students.

BENEFITS

1. Close bonding with Glenn community, family
2. A chance to work with students early in their careers
3. A chance to try something new with GEPDS students
4. Observing growth in university students
5. Help students decide whether they want to be a teacher
6. An extra set of hands in the classroom
7. More one-on-one time for Glenn students

RECOMMENDATIONS

1. More student teaching time
2. Improve communication
3. Better organization
4. University professors should adapt more to partnership
5. Share information with high school students who want to go into teaching
6. Allocate more time to planning

THE CHILDREN AT GLENN SCHOOL

K–6 students at Glenn School expressed a mixed understanding of the role and relationship of student interns to the regular school environment. Each grade level, kindergarten through sixth grade, was asked a series of five questions in this survey study. The question-items that were repeated in each school grade level are listed in the chart below as well as the children's responses.

All surveyed Glenn children strongly agreed that the GEPDS student interns, referred to by the researcher as 'student teachers,' had been a positive influence in the school's teaching and learning environment. The one exception was question-item 3 in Grade Six, which reported by 75 percent agreement that the student intern did not help them learn. Ironically, the same survey group reported with 78 percent agreement, that the Illinois State student interns did help their regular classroom teachers. We are concerned by the trend reflected in Question 3 that as the researcher looked further up the grade levels (grades 4–6), the children perceived, in an increasing

TABLE 3
Questions Asked of the Children at the Elementary School

Questions:	Kindergarten	1st Grade	2nd Grade	3rd Grade	4th Grade	5th Grade	6th Grade
1. Did you know that there was an Illinois State University student teacher in your classroom?	67% yes 33% no	60% yes 40% no	90% yes 10% no	90% yes 10% no	100% yes	100% yes	100% yes
2. Did you like having the Illinois State student teacher in your classroom?	100% yes	100%	90% yes 10% no	90% yes 10% no	90% yes 10% no	100% yes	100% yes
3. Did the Illinois State student teacher help you to learn?	90% yes 10% no	80% yes 20% no	70% yes 30% no	70% yes 30% no	50% yes 50% no	44% yes 56 % no	25% yes 75% no
4. Did the Illinois State student teacher help your regular classroom teacher?	100% yes	89% yes 11% no	90% yes 10% no	90% yes 10% no	100% yes	100% yes	78% yes 22% no
5. Did the Illinois State student teacher learn to be a teacher?	100% yes	100% yes	70% yes 30% no	70% yes 30% no	80% yes 20% no		

numbers, that the student intern was there to help their teachers but not them. There was also some confusion, reflected in Question 5, whether or not the student interns were learning to become teachers.

PARENTS AT GLENN SCHOOL

Parents of Glenn School's K–6 students who responded to a survey expressed a strong understanding of the goals and components of the Glenn professional development school (GEPDS) as a part of a constructive school environment. Parents stated that the GEPDS partnership has been a positive experience for their child, a positive experience for the Illinois State University student interns, and a positive experience for the child's classroom teachers. However, these findings should be viewed with some caution because of the low response rate. Approximately 200 surveys were sent out to parents at the school and only 30 were returned.

A discussion of the findings that emerged from the groups of teachers, university students, children, and parents is presented next, along with implications for teacher education and further research.

Discussion and Implications

As the faculty, staff, and administrators from the Illinois State University/Glenn Elementary Professional Development School (GEPDS) designed a pilot program that infused INTASC principles into students' experiences, they adhered to the Holmes Group objectives for a professional development school (Anderson, 1993; Holmes Group, 1993; Pasch & Pugah, 1990). After conducting their own research on the effectiveness of their undertaking (Nierstheimer, et al, 2000), they engaged an impartial researcher to assess the project at its mid-point. The study described here allowed them to answer their guiding research questions.

Stakeholders agreed that the objectives of the project (the Holmes' objectives) are being met. Some of the strengths of the project were identified as early, meaningful in-school experiences for the undergraduates, working with teachers who are able to guide their understandings and skills. Further, the teachers have enjoyed trying new approaches in concert with their preservice mentees; both have enjoyed the relationships that have developed as university students interact with the Glenn Elementary "family." The learning environment has been enhanced for the children at Glenn by more one-on-one attention for the pupils and extra hands in the classroom. Each of these findings supports an earlier assessment of benefits to stakeholders (Nierstheimer, et al, 2000).

Additional information was forthcoming from this evaluation, however, when we examined this question: What are the challenges that need to be addressed? For example, we learned about teachers' and university students' desires to have more time in the classrooms actually teaching. In the last two years of the program, student interns should and will spend more time in the classrooms gaining valuable teaching experience as suggested by those who took part in this study. This finding relates to the very interesting finding that emerged from the responses of the children in the school. Few studies have actually addressed children's perceptions of student interns in their classrooms, making this discovery distinctive.

The children at Glenn Elementary School who were surveyed were very positive in their responses about liking the fact that they have a student intern in their classroom. However, some had negative responses when asked if the student interns helped them learn—increasingly negative as older children were asked. These responses underscore the responsibility of the classroom teachers and the Steering Committee to make sure that in the last two years of the project, the student interns are viewed more as teachers than helpers-to-teachers. It is logical that this will unfold as the undergraduates spend more time teaching individual children, along with small- and large-group interactions in their junior- and senior-years as the interns move toward student teaching.

Another noteworthy finding came forth concerning parents' perceptions; researchers have traditionally neglected parents' views of university-school partnerships. We learned that we need to give further attention to parents. Because the parent return rate on surveys was so low, it could be inferred that parents at Glenn School are not completely aware of the GEPDS partnership. Even if that is not the case, the Steering Committee should consider adding parent representatives as well as involving parents more in our endeavor, since they are valued and respected partners.

An additional challenge that emerged was Glenn teachers' desire to be more actively involved in decision-making. The Steering Committee must continually review the meaning of "partnership;" needs assessments should be done periodically ensuring that the partners never take shared governance for granted. In response, a Communication Committee was created this year to make certain that associates work diligently toward effective, regular, and honest communication so that expectations, clarifications, and problems can be conveyed.

At the midpoint of our pilot project and in the midst of the successes and challenges discussed in this paper, we come back to our efforts to infuse features of the INTASC principles into the experiences of the undergraduates.

However, as Hartzler-Miller (1999) points out, we need to think carefully about how standards-based teaching can be used effectively. Hartzler-Miller advocates using the standards as "vision statements," asking all stakeholders to engage in meaningful conversations that result in constructivist meaning-making in order that standards-based experiences might become more personalized to each individual engaged in the process. She also calls for more writing about how teacher educators can use "standards" in more educative ways. We concur and are attempting to add to teacher educators' understandings by sharing our experiences with a standards-based project and discerning the effectiveness of the undertaking.

The information gleaned from this study will be used to make adjustments in the remaining two years of our pilot project as well as informing future INTASC-related programs connected to our university. One of the celebrated by-products of our undertaking is the simultaneous renewal that classroom teachers and university faculty have experienced; we are all learning from each other. Classroom teachers are influencing the preparation of tomorrow's teachers. University faculty are receiving relevant and vital experience in the day-to-day workings of an elementary school; they are interacting with and sometimes teaching children in classrooms, updating skills and validating knowledge. Theobald and Rochon (1999) write, "The premise of simultaneous renewal is that the best chances of success are created when work to improve both schools and teacher education is undertaken simultaneously" (p. 584).

Few longitudinal studies of professional development school graduates or graduates of standards-based programs have been done. It is unclear if significant numbers of graduates of such programs remain in teaching or routinely employ innovative, research-based practices that they encounter in professional development school preparation. While some research substantiates that new teachers prepared in a professional development school are, in general, stronger upon their completion of their professional development school programs (e.g., Abdal-Haqq, 1998; Darling-Hammond, 1990, 2000), we believe that longitudinal studies that follow graduates into their first years of teaching need to be conducted in order to address the larger question alluded to earlier in this paper, Do teacher education programs based on standards produce better teachers?

REFERENCES

Abdal-Haqq, Ismat (1998). *Professional development schools: Weighing the evidence* (p. 16). Thousand Oaks, CA: Sage.

Aiken, I. P, & Day, B. D. (1999). Early field experiences in preservice teacher education: Research and student perspectives. *Action in Teacher Education, 21*(3), 7–12.

Anderson, R. (Ed.) (1993). *Voices of change: A report of the clinical schools project.* Washington, D.C.: American Association of Colleges for Teacher Education.

Darling-Hammond, L. (1990). Teachers and teaching: Signs of a changing profession. In R. Houston (Ed.), *Handbook of research on teacher education* (pp. 267–296). New York: MacMillan.

Darling-Hammond, L. (2000). How teacher education matters. *Journal of Teacher Education 51*(3), 166–173.

Faribanks, C. M., Freedman, D., & Kahn, C. (2000). The role of effective mentors in learning to teach. *Journal of Teacher Education, 51*(2), 102–112.

Haberman, M. J. (1996). The preparation of teachers for a diverse free society. In L. Kaplan & R. Edelfelt (Eds.), *Teachers for the new millineum: Aligning teacher development, national goals, and high standards for all students* (pp. 127–130). Thousand Oaks, CA: Corwin Press, Inc. Sage Publications.

Hartzler-Miller, C.D. (1999). Learning to teach teachers in a standards-based program: When experience isn't enough. *Action in Teacher Education, 21*(3), 88–101.

Holmes Group. (1993). *Tomorrow's schools: Principles for the designs of professional development schools.* East Lansing, MI: The Holmes Group.

National Commission on Teaching and America's Future (1996). *What matters most, teaching for America's future.* New York: New York.

Nierstheimer, S. L., Taylor, F., Lloyd, R., Moore, M., & Morrow, R. (2000). Infusing INTASC principles into teacher preparation at a professional development school: Assessing benefits to stakeholders. *Action in Teacher Education, 22*(3), 47–55.

Pasch, S. H., & Pugach, M.C. (1990). Collaborative planning for urban professional development schools. *Contemporary Education, 61*(3), 135–43.

Theobald, P., & Rochon, R. (1999). Orchestrating simultaneous renewal. *Phi Delta Kappan, 4,* 584–588.

Wise, A. E., & Leibbrand, J. A. (2000). Standards and teacher quality: Entering the new millennium. *Phi Delta Kappan, 4,* 612–621.

Reflection on the Use of Standards in Teacher Education: Summary

Donna M. Gollnick

T he three chapters in this section explore differences in practice occurring as the result of national standards. One described an internship seminar redesigned to assist candidates in relating their own teaching practice to the unit's conceptual framework. The second examined a team effort at incorporating performance assessment into their own teaching through the development and use of rubrics. The third evaluated the perceptions of participants regarding the effectiveness of implementing a professional development school based on the Holmes Group model and the integration of the INTASC principles in the preparation program.

Findings of the Three Studies

Faculty for the internship seminar at George Washington University were concerned with providing an inquiry approach to teaching and exploring beliefs about teaching. The seminar was redesigned to include academic papers, reader response activities, and multiple opportunities to dialog about texts on teaching, learning, and educational reform. In addition to relating the activities to the unit's conceptual framework focusing on knowledge, individuality, and social responsibility, the orientation was designed to help interns develop knowledge, skills, and dispositions related to selected INTASC standards. The seminar helped candidates reflect on "the effects of his/her choices and actions on others," understand different approaches to learning in diverse settings, and know about models of powerful teaching based on knowledge of the content field and developmental needs of students. Interns were asked to read selected texts and respond to the readings in a large group process and in individual written reports.

The process allowed the involved faculty "to make the program's conceptual framework an explicit foundation upon which students [i.e., candidates] could connect their thinking as developing teachers." The faculty concluded that the redesigned seminar motivated interns "to read more and to take a larger perspective of the social and political contexts of schooling." The guided reading process encouraged candidates to practice reflection over the semester. The discussions and written assignments helped faculty know "how the interns were: a) constructing meaning and relating their readings to what they were experiencing in the schools, and b) connecting their beliefs" to the conceptual framework. Candidates were able to express a range of feelings in the seminar. The authors suggest that the combination of internship experiences in a school setting with thought-provoking discussions among candidates can "empower students [i.e., teacher candidates] to approach their practice differently from the 'status quo.'"

The authors of the second chapter followed the development of rubrics by five professors and the changes that resulted in their own teaching as a result of using performance assessments. This group of professors approached the task with the belief that they could help teacher candidates use assessments by modeling performance assessment in the college classroom. The development of rubrics pushed the faculty members to be more explicit about the performances expected of candidates. Although different patterns for the rubrics evolved, one of the values of this project was the opportunity to work with colleagues to develop an understanding of performance assessment and rubrics. The five professors in this project reported that the project has influenced their own teaching practice. They have become more focused in their beliefs and knowledge about the role of assessment in teaching. The focus on performance assessment has made them more thoughtful in the design of courses and encouraged them to constantly reflect on and refine their knowledge of how candidates might demonstrate their knowledge and skills. The professors have not yet determined the impact of performance assessment in their teaching on candidate learning-an important next step in their development process.

An elementary professional development school with 20 teacher candidates from Illinois State University was the focus of the evaluation study reported in the third chapter of this section. The candidates had initiated their work in the school in their freshman year and were at the end of their sophomore year at the time of the study. The PDS was built on the Holmes Group model to enhance student learning, incorporate standards-based teacher education, provide professional development for university and school faculty, and engage in professional inquiry. In addition, it was a field site in which candidates were to develop the knowledge, skills, and dispositions outlined in the INTASC standards. The authors collected data from written surveys of teachers in the school, candidates, elementary students, and parents; they also compiled data from interviews of a sample of the survey participants. These data were supplemented by the observations of an independent researcher not directly connected to the PDS project. Based on the perceptions of the respondents, the PDS objectives were being met. Both teachers and candidates "believed that the standards-based approach [i.e., INTASC] was apparent." Teachers reported that they would like to be more involved in decision-making related to the PDS and preparation of candidates. The elementary school students saw the interns as teacher helpers, rather than co-teachers, especially at the upper elementary level. The few parents who responded to the survey saw the partnership as a positive experience for their children and others involved in the project.

Discussion

Changing teaching practice of P–12 teachers and higher education faculty is a challenging endeavor. Many enter the profession with misconceptions and myths about teaching and learning. Researcher Mary Kennedy (1997) claims that:

> The unusual nature of teacher learning is such that students entering teacher education already "know" a great deal about their chosen field. Moreover, they will use what they already know to interpret any new skills or new theories they acquire during the formal study of teaching. This fact means that the simple acquisition of new skills or theories is not adequate to alter teaching practices. Therefore, the central task of teacher learning must be to change these conceptions (p. 13).

Unless these misconceptions are confronted and other models presented, teaching will continue to be the presentation of information with little consideration of students' prior knowledge and experiences, ways of learning, and what we know from research.

The studies in this section provide an insight into how some faculty are beginning to examine their own beliefs about teaching and assessment, leading to changes in their own practices. They understand that it is not enough to talk about educational reform. Instead, they are learning the value of testing, refining, and modeling best practice based on theory and research as expected in NCATE's Standard 5 on faculty:

> Faculty are qualified and model best professional practices in scholarship, service, and teaching, including the assessment of their own effectiveness as

related to candidate performance. They also collaborate with colleagues in the disciplines and schools. The unit systematically evaluates faculty performance and facilitates professional development (NCATE, 2001, p. 11).

These three studies are a beginning. The first two chapters describe changes that faculty are making in their own practice; the third chapter describes participant perceptions of a PDS partnership and the incorporation of the INTASC standards in the clinical experience. None of the studies have reached the stage of determining whether these changes make a difference on the teaching practice of candidates in their field experiences, clinical practice, and later teaching careers. Do the candidates actually reflect on their own practice based on readings in the field, use performance assessments effectively and appropriately, participate in inquiry of their teaching and its relationship to student learning, and incorporate the INTASC principles into their work with P–12 students? Data have not yet been collected by the researchers in this section to report that the changes being made have a long-term effect on the teaching practice of the candidates they have taught. Follow-up studies can provide the missing information.

Do Standards Really Matter?

The Holmes Group, NCATE, and INTASC are the catalysts for the changes reported in this section. In two cases faculty have used the standards to change their own teaching practice; in one case the institution is participating in a state-supported project to incorporate the INTASC standards into the teacher education program within a professional development school. In all cases the researchers have been explicit about the standards that guide their work.

It is too early to know the depth of difference standards have made in the preparation of teachers and other school personnel. The beginning of this era of standards-based, performance-based teacher education would be an ideal time to collect some baseline data about what candidates know and are able to do today. Faculty journals and research of their own practice and changes that result as they model best practice will chronicle the evolution of our teaching. The serious undertaking of performance assessment related to standards will provide data for continued improvement of programs to ensure the preparation of the teachers we want in schools.

REFERENCES

Kennedy, M. (1997, April). *Defining an ideal teacher education program.* (Unpublished manuscript). Ann Arbor, MI: Michigan State University.

National Council for Accreditation of Teacher Education. (2001). *Professional standards for the accreditation of schools, colleges, and departments of education.* Washington, DC: Author.

Division

4

Perspectives from
Accrediting
Agencies

The Evolution of Standards for Teacher Preparation

10.

Arthur E. Wise and Jane A. Leibbrand

Arthur E. Wise is president of the National Council for Accreditation of Teacher Education in Washington, D.C. Wise formerly served as director of a center on the teaching profession at the RAND Corporation. He also served as associate dean at the University of Chicago. Wise is former chair of the board of the National Foundation for the Improvement of Education, and serves on the board of the National Board for Professional Teaching Standards and the National Commission on Teaching and America's Future. He is co-author of A License to Teach with Linda Darling-Hammond and Stephen Klein and has authored books and numerous articles.

Jane Leibbrand is vice president for communications at NCATE, and previously served as a senior manager at the George Washington University's Division of Continuing Education and as director of communications for the American Association of Adult and Continuing Education. She is also a former high school and college English teacher.

Introduction

This chapter describes the evolution of accreditation standards in teacher preparation from the mid-20th century to the present. It discusses standards for teacher preparation in light of the education policy environment, examining how the context of the times shapes the standards. The paper compares previous iterations of teacher preparation accreditation standards to standards at the dawn of the 21st century, showing a progression from a reliance on input factors, to a focus on curriculum, to a move emphasizing research-based knowledge, to the current place the standards reside—finding credible ways to show evidence of competent candidate performance.

The chapter also discusses NCATE's role as a key mechanism in the development of a quality assurance system for the teaching profession, and briefly traces the evolution of the interplay among accreditation and licensing, and the profession and the states. This brief overview shows how a changing society's needs have dramatically changed the standards for what all students should know and be able to do upon high school graduation, and how this change in expectations for students has led to a concomitant change in expectations for teacher knowledge and skill.

Teacher Preparation in a Historical Context

Until very recently, standards for teachers were usually set quite low. When normal schools began in the 1800s, teachers knew little more than their students did. Even with this rudimentary knowledge, teachers were generally respected even if not compensated well. Most of American society was still agriculturally based, and the bare basics of reading, computation, and writing were deemed satisfactory for the populace at large.

As American society moved from an agriculturally-based economy to an industrial one in the early 20th century, the need for workers who could follow directions and fit into life in a factory helped to transform education into a factory model itself. Students sat in neat rows, and the teacher imparted information at the head of the class. Students took notes, studied, and regurgitated what they had heard from the teacher and read in the textbooks. Standards were set fairly low for students and teachers alike. With the majority of American workers moving into jobs in industry, society needed many workers who had basic skills. Only a small percentage of workers would move into jobs as leaders of industry. High school dropouts and high school graduates could still succeed economically; basic skills, along with a solid work ethic, were enough to ensure a chance at a secure life working for the growing automobile and related industries, for example.

After World War II, servicemen took advantage of the GI Bill to enroll in higher education in record numbers. A college education, heretofore a remote chance for many, became a reality and a ticket to a burgeoning middle class life with new labor and time-saving conveniences. The number of Americans being educated at more than a rudimentary level was greater than ever before, and a new interest in education took root.

A Look Back—Teacher Preparation Standards in the 1950s and the 1960s

It is thus no accident that NCATE began as an independent accrediting body in 1954, supported by five organizations: the Council of Chief State School Officers, the National School Boards Association, the National Education Association, the American Association of Colleges for Teacher Education, and the National Association of State Directors of Teacher Education and Certification. Previously, it had been an arm of the American Association of Colleges of Teacher Education.

The first sets of accreditation standards produced by NCATE in the 1950s focused on inputs and processes. This was accepted practice in the accreditation industry at mid-century. Standard one required a statement of teacher preparation program objectives and assumptions. The standard stated that assumptions should cover such matters as "the level of basic intelligence required for effective teaching." A second standard focused on organization and administration of the unit. For example, colleges of education had to describe which persons or groups within the college had responsibility for decisions regarding amount and kind of general education, subject matter, and professional education. A third standard, student personnel programs and services, focused entirely on processes and the details of those services, including the expectation that the college "describe the system of records, noting the major items of information, where they are kept and to whom they are available." The standard did not focus on the candidates, but on the services surrounding them. A standard on faculty focused again on statistics. The standard on curricula required institutions to provide the minimum and maximum subject matter concentrations, the sequence of professional education, and the general education requirements. Each institution developed its curricula in the various teaching fields. Professional specialty organizations were not yet connected to the accrediting body nor had they produced standards. The last standard was entitled "Professional Laboratory Experiences." Institutions reported on the lab experiences, the number and location of lab schools used, the number of student teachers assigned to teach, the amount of credit given for student teaching, who had responsibility for assignment of student teachers to schools, and so on. Instead of focusing on student teacher performance, the standard asked for the proportion of time student teachers spent in the classroom of the supervising teacher and the proportion of time spent finding and organizing materials. A description of the kinds of classroom activities in which student teachers engaged was the closest the standards came to mentioning actual performance. A final standard focused on facilities and instructional materials. The standards contained only a one-sentence mention of program evaluation (NCATE, 1957).

THE 1970S

By the 1970s, the standards were divided into two sections—one addressing initial teacher preparation, the second addressing advanced preparation. Curricula had moved to standard one—the cornerstone of the standards. The length of this section within the standards indicates its prominence. The standard addressed general studies, professional studies, content, humanistic and behavioral studies, teaching and learning theory, practicum, curriculum design, and specialty association guidelines. The standard did encourage institutions to ensure that candidates received a well-rounded education; "at least one-third of each curriculum" was to be composed of general studies in languages, mathematics, logic, information theory, natural and behavioral sciences and the humanities. In terms of the content specialty to be taught, it was clear that the "instruction in the subject matter for the teaching specialties is the responsibility of the academic departments . . ." but "selecting courses is the joint responsibility of the academic departments and the teacher education faculty . . ." (NCATE, 1970).

The professional associations were beginning to make their presence felt in the accrediting body. For the first time, institutions were expected to give "due consideration" to the guidelines of those subject matter specialty associations that had developed them (NCATE, 1970). The institution was expected to acquaint itself with the guidelines and examine them in relation to the curricula. NCATE did not require institutions to actually use the guidelines. NCATE was still composed of the original five founding member organizations; none of the subject matter specialty groups had yet joined.

NCATE progressed in its expectations relating to program improvement and evaluation. The 1970 standards included evaluation, program review, and planning as a separate standard. The standard called for evaluation of teachers when they completed their programs of study and after they entered the teaching profession. But it did not specify any criteria or methods of making the evaluations; the standards recognized that "the means to make such evaluations are not fully adequate." No surveys of employers or self-report surveys were mentioned.

The standards still had the paternalistic view that the information flow is one-way, from higher education institution to P–12 school. "The specialized talent of the teacher education faculty is viewed as a potential resource for providing in-service assistance to the schools in the area . . ." (NCATE,

1970). The standard expected "continuing association with elementary and secondary schools," but did not specify type of commitment or involvement. It was extraordinarily vague.

While moving away from the input measures and details in previous iterations of the standards, this version provided little guidance or explanation of what is expected in the clinical program. A brief series of questions was posed in a separate section but was not included in the standards themselves, with the explanation that the questions are not to be construed as additional standards to be met, but as guides to address the standards. The questions posed included "what are the provisions for clinical experiences" and "what practices show a study of teaching and learning is required and is acquired by lab experience." No mention was made of P–12 schools. The lab experience discussed could have taken place on the campus.

The standards recognized that clinical experience could be enriched with the introduction of video, but there were no specific expectations. The standard on clinical experience noted that "the prospective teacher's efforts can be recorded, viewed, and reviewed," saying that it was now "feasible to give effective clinical experience outside the school classroom" (NCATE, 1970). Rather than focus on the P–12 school as the site of action, the standard focused on recording the teaching and viewing it at the university. The 1970s standards did not emphasize connection between P–12 school and university.

THE 1980s

In 1983, *A Nation at Risk* was published. Its appearance stimulated change in education policy for the remainder of the 20th century and continues to do so as we enter the 21st century. Its publication heralded the beginning of the standards movement, and two decades of fervent action on the part of the teaching profession and the states.

NCATE's constituents—policymakers and educators alike—called for change in accreditation and teacher preparation. In the mid-1980s, NCATE began to make just such a change, and by the late 1980s, NCATE had overhauled its standards and processes. The centerpiece of NCATE's 1987 redesign was the development of standards related to the knowledge base of teaching (NCATE, 1990). Colleges of education had to demonstrate that their programs were based on established and current research and best practice, and faculty and candidates alike were expected to be able to articulate the framework of knowledge. Research-guided practice became the focus. In addition, the specialty associations were now a growing focus within NCATE. The redesign acknowledged the importance of the subject matter specialty associations, and these associations joined the NCATE coalition. Accredited institutions were now expected to use the program standards (called guidelines) of the specialty associations in program design and delivery. This was a major step forward for the field. In the 1950s, each institution developed its own curriculum. By the 1970s, institutions were expected to give 'due consideration' to the specialty association guidelines for teacher preparation. In the 1980s, NCATE expected institutions to make the guidelines a cornerstone of program development.

If institutions did not meet the specialty association guidelines, they were cited with weaknesses. The examining team made a holistic judgment about the quality of the institution. If many of the programs did not meet the guidelines, the institution could be in jeopardy, but in general, examining teams looked at the conceptual framework and research base of the programs. Institutions could become accredited even if a number of programs did not meet professional subject matter standards. Indeed, the subject matter standards themselves were open to some criticism. A few associations were overly prescriptive with virtually only a handful of institutions meeting those sets of guidelines. NCATE halted the use of one association's guidelines for this reason, until the association revamped them.

In addition, the redesign addressed cultural diversity. For the first time, the standards included an expectation that the student body, the faculty, and the curriculum reflect diversity. However, the diversity expectation was included in the standards on student and faculty qualifications, and thus created a dilemma for evaluators. In the 1995 iteration, diversity in student body and faculty were separated into two standards, apart from qualifications.

During the first three years under the redesign, over 30 percent of the colleges of education were denied accreditation. Almost half of the colleges of education that were reviewed failed to meet standard one, the knowledge base standard. Given the prior emphasis on inputs, it is not surprising that institutions found change difficult.

As a result of the level of energy directed at education after the release of *A Nation at Risk,* the status quo in teacher preparation and licensing began to crumble, and the norms for teacher preparation began to change. Policymakers wanted to know exactly what teachers knew, and more states instituted teacher testing. In 1989, President Bush and the nation's governors agreed to establish national education goals, which began an odyssey of standards development followed by development of assessments to ensure that students were progressing toward the standards.

THE 1990s TO 2000

In 1993, NCATE outlined a continuum of teacher preparation and development (Figure 1) showing that important linkages between preservice preparation, licensure, and professional development were needed in order to formulate a more coherent system of quality assurance. Only through a coordinated system of standards and assessments for the three phases of teacher development can quality assurance for the profession of teaching become a reality. NCATE, as the profession's quality assurance mechanism, INTASC, a task force of the Council of Chief State School Officers, and the National Board for Professional Teaching Standards, have worked together for the past decade to develop a coherent and consistent set of expectations in preservice preparation, licensing, and continuing professional development.

Parts of the emerging system of quality assurance are in place and working well, while others are just beginning. *Standards* have been developed for P–12 students and for teacher preparation. Discipline-based professional education associations and national commissions have put much effort into standards setting during the past decade. In 1987–88, NCATE overhauled its accreditation standards for the preparation of teachers to emphasize research-based knowledge. In 1995, NCATE began the shift away from inputs to a system focused on candidate performance. In 2000, NCATE completed the job it had begun, this time developing a performance-based accreditation system. At the same time, states are developing state licensing standards for beginning teachers, and are drawing on the work of INTASC to do so. Likewise, the National Board for Professional Teaching standards has moved the field forward with the development of standards and assessments of experienced teachers. The teaching profession is reaping the benefits of the work of NBPTS, which has advanced the state of the art in assessing teaching performance. And assessment of teacher performance is exactly the place where the field is focused now. Policymakers want to know if teacher candidates know their subject matter and how to teach it effectively.

Linking the standards involves linking the systems that develop them: higher education, state departments of education/standards boards, the teaching field through professional associations, school district, and the National Board. Working together instead of independently involves new sets of meetings, new procedures, and new policies for all of the organizations. Attempting change in one part of the system (licensing requirements) will work only as well as changes made in other parts of the system (i.e. candidate preparation for new performance assessments).

Many states adapted the continuum of teacher preparation and development, creating tiered licensing systems. All grew aware of the need to link preparation and licensing standards. That has led to an unprecedented degree of consensus between the profession as delineated by NCATE in the accreditation standards, and many states.

The 1995 iteration of the standards differs significantly from the 1987 standards in that more attention is focused on the performance of graduates of teacher preparation programs. However, in 1995, NCATE still relied primarily on indirect evidence—course content—to examine the degree to which colleges of education assessed teacher competence. For example, examiners reviewed course syllabi to help determine whether the standards were met. The standards did call for assessments to monitor candidate progress. They also required explicit criteria for exit from the program, and appropriate assessments to determine whether the standards had been met.

NCATE in 1995 expected a college's teacher candidates to demonstrate specific skills—a departure from the standards in place prior to 1995. The indicators to NCATE's standard on professional and pedagogical knowledge are explicit. Teachers should be able to use strategies for developing critical thinking and problem solving. They should be able to use formal and informal assessment strategies to ensure continuing student learning. They should be able to use technology in instruction. Teachers should use research-based principles of proven effective practice. All of the above competencies were first included in INTASC's model state licensing standards. Thus in 1995, NCATE incorporated INTASC licensing standards into its own teacher preparation standards.

States recognized NCATE's standards through partnership agreements and began to match licensing requirements to the preparation standards. NCATE and the states now hold colleges of education accountable for producing candidates with the same knowledge and skills for which the states will hold individual candidates accountable through licensing. This relationship strengthens both accreditation and licensing, and joins preparation (profession) to licensing (state). Both now have similar, if not the same expectations, providing common ground for assessment development. In addition, upon initiation of NCATE, member subject matter professional associations are working with the Educational Testing Service to ensure that licensing assessments are aligned with the profession's standards in the various subject matter areas and developmental levels. This alignment will serve to further professionalize teaching, as the field engages in debate and comes to some resolve about what is important in teacher preparation today. The NCATE standards, the model state licensing principles, and the National Board standards are an expression of that resolve and consensus.

NCATE also adopted a policy calling for subject matter associations to revamp their program standards for teacher preparation to match the increasingly performance-based accreditation standards. Instead of focusing only on the topics to be covered in the curriculum, NCATE asked associations to formulate their standards in terms of candidate performance—what the candidate knows and is able to do in the classroom. Instead of deciding whether programs merit 'national recognition' on the basis of course content and experiences, associations are to judge whether candidates demonstrate proficiency in the standards through multiple performance assessments. This required a massive restructuring on the part of all associations that produce teacher preparation program standards. NCATE stimulated the movement with seed money from grants. Some associations are moving more quickly than others. The National Association of the Social Studies, for example, transformed its standards and requirements for evidence to emphasize candidate performance. This association has also created benchmark examples of acceptable performance. NCSS has served as an exemplar to other associations in the process of moving their standards to a focus on what the candidates know and how they are actually performing in the classroom.

In the 1990s, NCATE gradually gained a position of greater prominence in national and state education policy deliberations. The National Conference of State Legislatures issued a report that says NCATE "provides a means for states to upgrade teacher preparation" (NCSL, 1995). The blue-ribbon National Commission on Teaching and America's Future calls for all colleges of education to become professionally accredited (NCTAF, 1996). And the National Alliance of Business issued a 2001 report that calls for all teacher preparation programs to be accredited, encourages districts to hire graduates from accredited institutions, and highlights NCATE. (NAB, 2001).

Beginning in the late 1980s, NCATE initiated a State Partnership Program. NCATE progressed from having no relationship to the states to having 46 State/NCATE Partnerships by 2000. The partnerships were designed to increase the rigor of the teacher preparation experience. Partnership states have integrated NCATE's professional review of colleges of education with their own, thereby strengthening the review of teacher preparation at a growing number of institutions. The partnership program was designed to eliminate duplication of effort on the part of institutions that wanted to attain professional accreditation and that were required to host a state review. The partnership provides institutions and states with options for joint review with an NCATE/State team or a concurrent review with two teams. In both cases, the institution saves time, money and effort by preparing for only one visit every five years rather than two. A byproduct of the partnership program is the integration of state and national expectations for teacher candidates. Many states (28 as of this writing) have adopted or adapted NCATE unit standards as their own state standards. Additionally, institutions in 45 states and the District of Columbia are reviewed according to NCATE's program standards or standards that correlate closely with

NCATE's program standards. Thus NCATE has influenced the preparation of all teachers in those states, whether or not the institutions choose to undergo NCATE review. NCATE standards are increasingly the norm in teacher preparation.

The Standards in 2000 and Beyond

In 2000, the NCATE board ratified a new performance-based accreditation system and standards. With the advent of performance-based accreditation, teacher candidates are expected to show mastery of the content knowledge in their fields and to demonstrate that they can teach it effectively. Standard one moves candidate knowledge and skill to the forefront (NCATE, 2001). Specialty professional associations play a crucial role in accreditation now, as their subject matter standards are the focus for program design and delivery in professionally accredited institutions. Institutions are expected to meet the standards of the specialty associations.

In addition, the college must have a system in place to assess candidates. The system must include assessments at entry, throughout the program, and upon exit. As institutions develop better assessments of candidate performance, they are also expected to establish rubrics for acceptable versus unacceptable performance levels. Institutions must provide evidence that candidates who are completing their preparation have performed at acceptable levels.

Candidates know the criteria by which their competence will be evaluated. Multiple and longitudinal assessments of candidates help the institution form a judgment of candidate readiness to teach. The move to direct evidence of teacher proficiency, through examinations, on-demand tasks, and longitudinal assessment of performance, is the change wrought in the NCATE 2000 iteration of the standards. This shift to performance-oriented standards is just beginning to impact teacher preparation institutions, as they grapple with revisions in licensure and new accreditation expectations.

NCATE standards also expect teacher educators to model effective teaching. The traditional lecture alone is inadequate. Teacher educators must use strategies that they expect their candidates to use. Teacher educators should model expert teaching, because teachers teach as they are taught.

In addition, NCATE standards expect candidates to demonstrate that they can teach students of diverse backgrounds and prepare candidates who can help all students learn. The 1987 standards introduced diversity in the curriculum, faculty, and student body as an expectation; the 2000 iteration continues that theme by combining the strands into one standard and requiring evidence that teacher candidates have achieved the goal of helping all students learn.

NCATE standards also expect candidates to use technology as an instructional tool to help students learn. Technology expectations are woven throughout the standards. NCATE expects units to include technology implementation in their strategic plan. Technology has moved from the periphery to occupy a central place in the standards.

The new performance-based accreditation system expects university and P–12 faculty to function as joint *partners* in the education of teacher candidates. Collaboration in program design and delivery is expected. Cooperating P–12 teachers and supervisors have traditionally been treated as peripheral in the higher education area. Now they are to be included in the planning and design of teacher preparation programs. This alone will cause profound change in teacher preparation.

Teacher Shortages and the Effect on Preparation Policy

With all of these changes in the profession, it would seem that teaching as a profession would be advancing apace. Policymakers and the public are expecting more and more from those on the front lines in the classroom. The profession has initiated and developed standards for students and teachers. But in most of the U.S., salary and working conditions are much the same as they have been in the past. Therefore, many systems lack enough qualified teachers. As we enter the 21st century, the demand for teachers has grown to such a degree that district officials are using any means to cover classrooms. There are simply not enough teachers who meet the demanding new standards set by the profession and many states. Teachers who have been through in-depth, five-year programs with professional development schools may be teaching next door to someone who is a 'walk-in,' and may be expected to help mentor those with no background, experience, or preparation for the job. Yet both are paid the same salary and both are called 'teacher.'

It is time to stop this charade, which perpetually keeps teaching a quasi-profession. Schools should be required to disclose titles and qualifications to parents. Only those who meet increasingly rigorous state requirements— based on demonstrated performance and subject matter knowledge— should be given the title 'teacher.' Others whom school districts must hire to fill vacant classrooms or to teach courses for which they are not qualified should be known by a lesser title. Districts could develop a staffing structure

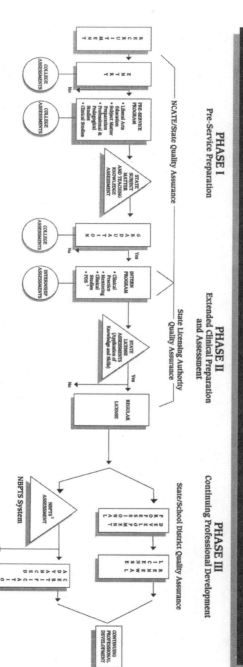

Teacher Preparation: A Continuum

PHASE I
Pre-Service Preparation

PHASE II
Extended Clinical Preparation and Assessment

PHASE III
Continuing Professional Development

NCATE/State Quality Assurance

State Licensing Authority Quality Assurance

State/School District Quality Assurance

RECRUITMENT

ENTRY

COLLEGE ASSESSMENTS
No

PRE-SERVICE PROGRAM
• Liberal Arts Education
• Subject Matter Preparation
• Professional & Pedagogical Studies
• Clinical Studies

COLLEGE ASSESSMENTS
No

STATE SUBJECT MATTER AND TEACHING KNOWLEDGE ASSESSMENT

GRADUATION
COLLEGE ASSESSMENTS
No

Yes

INTERN PROGRAM
• Clinical Practice
• Mentoring
• Clinical Studies
• TOS [1]

INTERNSHIP ASSESSMENTS

STATE LICENSE ASSESSMENTS (Application of Knowledge and Skills)
No   Yes

REGULAR LICENSE

PROFESSIONAL DEVELOPMENT

LICENSE RENEWAL

NBPTS [2] ASSESSMENT
No

ADVANCED CERTIFICATION

CONTINUING PROFESSIONAL DEVELOPMENT

NBPTS System

NCATE
The Standard of Excellence in Teacher Preparation

[1] Professional Development School
[2] National Board for Professional Teaching Standards

with corresponding levels of compensation in which qualified teachers would help supervise those without preparation. This is already occurring in a rudimentary way when teachers certified by the National Board for Professional Teaching Standards receive mentoring assignments. A teacher team could include Board certified teachers, licensed teachers, beginning interns, teacher candidates, and those with little or no preparation. Individuals would have district titles and different pay scales. This structure would provide a career ladder for highly qualified teachers and it gives districts a way to fulfill staffing needs with integrity.

The current strategy of regulating and deregulating teaching at the same time—through higher standards for preparation programs but allowing walk-ins in shortage areas—does not raise the overall quality of the teaching force. As teacher shortages grow, more unqualified people will fill classrooms. Disadvantaged students become even more disadvantaged, as the unqualified are invariably called to serve the already underserved. Let us work together to build a new system that will truly serve all of our students well.

REFERENCES

National Alliance of Business. (2001). *Investing in teaching.* Washington, D.C. Author.

National Commission on Teaching and America's Future (1996). *What matters most: Teaching for America's future.* N. Y. Author.

National Conference of State Legislatures (1996). *National accreditation of teacher education.* Boulder, CO. Author.

National Council for Accreditation of Teacher Education (1957). *Standards and guide for accreditation of teacher education.* Washington, D.C. Author.

National Council for Accreditation of Teacher Education (1970). *Standards for accreditation of teacher education.* Washington, D.C. Author.

National Council for Accreditation of Teacher Education. (1990). *Standards, procedures, and policies for the accreditation of professional education units.* Washington, D.C. Author.

National Council for Accreditation of Teacher Education. (1995). *Standards, procedures, and policies for the accreditation of professional education units.* Washington, D.C. Author.

National Council for Accreditation of Teacher Education (2001). *Professional standards for the accreditation of schools, colleges, and departments of education.* Washington, D.C. Author.

National Board Certification
What We Are Learning and What We Need to Know

11.

Elizabeth B. Castor and Gary R. Galluzzo

Betty Castor is president of the National Board for Professional Teaching Standards with offices in Arlington, Virginia and Southfield, Michigan. Prior, she was president of the University of South Florida from 1994–1999. Ms. Castor also served as Florida's Commissioner of Education 1986–1993, and earlier as a Florida state senator and Commissioner in Hillsborough County. She also taught at Holmes Elementary School in Dade County, Florida, and as a high school teacher for the British-American Aid for International Development program in Uganda, Africa. Ms. Castor has received numerous awards for leadership in education, good government, humanitarian efforts, mental health reform and women's issues. In addition, Ms. Castor has received honorary doctor's degrees in law from Stetson University, Rollins College and Florida Southern College, and an honorary doctor of humanities award from Rowan State College.

Gary R. Galluzzo (Ph.D., Syracuse University) is the Executive Vice-President of the National Board for Professional Teaching Standards. Dr. Galluzzo is also a member of the faculty of the Graduate School of Education at George Mason University in Fairfax, VA. Dr. Galluzzo was formerly Dean of the Graduate School of Education at George Mason University, and also formerly Professor and Dean of the College of Education at the University of Northern Colorado. He taught high school history and social studies in New York. He has served as the Director of the University of Northern Colorado Laboratory School and has been on the faculties at Western Kentucky University and Rowan University in New Jersey. He has sat as a member of the Board of Directors of the American Association of Colleges for Teacher Education (AACTE) and served as co-chair of the Colorado Teachers and Special Services Professional Standards Board. His research interests include investigations into how students become teachers, curriculum reform in teacher education, and program evaluation in teacher education. He was a member of the AACTE Research and Information Committee which conducted eight annual national studies of teacher education and which published the monograph series, Teaching Teachers: Facts and Figures. He is co-author of The Rise and Stall of Teacher Education Reform and is published widely in professional journals as well as in the Handbook of Research on Teacher Education, the International Encyclopedia of Education, and the Advances in Teacher Education series, among others.

Introduction

Since the publication of *A Nation at Risk* (1983), the standards movement in education is arguably the most enduring change on the education landscape of the last two decades. When the National Commission on Excellence in Education challenged the nation to improve the quality of education for our nation's children, it called for the creation of a far more demanding curriculum than it believed was offered at the time. From that challenge eventually emerged the standards-based education movement. So profound has this movement become that now all fifty states have adopted content standards detailing what students should know and be able to do to earn a high school diploma.

The challenge to create standards for the teaching profession was not far behind the movement to establish content standards for students. Led by the Carnegie Commission on Education and the Economy, the report *A Nation Prepared* (1986) issued a series of actions the nation must take to achieve the school reform outlined in *A Nation at Risk*. The authors of the Carnegie Commission report called for the standards movement to extend and to include standards for teaching. Teacher education was derided as a practice where there was more emphasis on the processes of becoming a teacher than the more important knowledge, skills, and dispositions that a teacher should actually possess. The Commission argued that if students were to achieve the lofty ideals of standards-based education, then their teachers needed to measure themselves against performance expectations. The Commission challenged the education community and the policy community to create a National Board for Professional Teaching Standards. Over the last fifteen years, both communities met the challenge and, we argue, the fruits of their labor carry the potential to raise teaching to the level of a profession which is grounded in principles of accomplished teaching, a body of literature which informs those principles, and a research agenda that substantiates the importance of these principles and the effects they can have on teachers, the profession, education reform, teacher preparation, and student achievement.

In this chapter, we strive to outline the agenda of the National Board for Professional Teaching Standards, not only as the profession's certifying board for accomplished teaching, but also as a catalyst for innovative thinking around which professional practitioners can organize to change the profession such that our system of education is re-shaped to reach all children. We do not revisit the history of the National Board, nor do we outline its mission and purposes. Such basic and introductory information can be gained by reading Buday and Kelly (1996) or the many materials found on our website *http://www.nbpts.org*.

Our purpose in this chapter is to speak to our colleagues in teacher education about the scholarship growing around the National Board and encouraging even wider study. Research in any field has the potential to make an innovation spread, to improve, and to leave a significant and positive mark on the field. We hope that discussing the emerging research on the National Board will inspire teacher educators to conduct further inquiries into the effects of National Board Certification on accomplished teaching, as well as to point the way for needed research on teacher education. By no means is this review meant to be exhaustive. Rather, we have chosen to use selected studies to highlight themes of research which examine the National Board, but which also can apply to the study of teacher education.

Evidence from early studies already suggests that completing the National Board's assessment processes immediately contributes to teachers' perceptions that their knowledge and skills are enhanced as an outcome. The results of a survey of 1150 California candidates completing the National Board assessment processes indicate that eighty-seven percent believe these processes have made them better teachers. Ninety percent of the respondents report that the National Board assessments are "the best professional development experience they've ever had." (Center for the Future of Teaching and Learning, 2000.) These data further are supported in an investigation conducted by Iovacchini (1998), who found National Board Certified Teachers sought National Board Certification for the reward inherent in the challenge of measuring oneself against external standards. The teachers in her study also reported that the assessment process strengthened their confidence as professionals and renewed their commitment to teaching. These results from independent surveys conducted for the National Board as well as from Iovacchini's study inform us that the five core propositions, the standards, and the assessments are sufficiently rigorous, as the National Board intends, and that they have profound effects on those who complete the assessment process. Candidates consistently report they were challenged to produce work at a level all too rare in their daily practice. These early inquiries into the intent of the National Board suggest that the substance and processes can serve to bring change to a teacher's practice in useful and productive ways, which speaks to the validity of the standards and assessments.

What We Know: Validity

With these early survey results as background for this chapter, the National Board steps back and self-imposes restrictions on its role in scholarship and program development. The National Board must be measured against its original three-part mission: to design the standards that guide the profession, to operate a voluntary system of national certification, and to advance related education reforms. The National Board has kept faith with its initial mission. The National Board is just what it purports, the standard setter for the profession. It prepares the standards, develops the assessments, and administers the certification system. It is not a think-tank, per se, for advancing specific school reforms. It is not simply a research and development arm of the profession seeking to unlock the deep truths about effective teaching. Nor is it not an agency that prepares teachers in competition with the nation's schools, colleges, and departments of education (SCDEs). The National Board launches ideas about teaching as we watch others gain inspiration to conduct research, advance education reforms, and prepare teachers. The National Board is a professional development effort to stimulate thoughtful introspection about teaching and to develop sophisticated, state-of-the-art performance assessments that essentially are available to others to use improve the quality of teaching and teacher education through both enhanced practice and inquiry.

As a result of these initiatives, we are observing a variety of impacts emanating from the work of the National Board. Local school districts, teachers' organizations and SCDEs are creating programs to support National Board Certification candidates as they go through the process. SCDEs are creating Master's degree programs grounded in the core propositions of the National Board. The National Council for Accreditation of Teacher Education (NCATE) now incorporates these core propositions into their unit review for advanced programs. School districts are including the propositions in their teacher evaluation schemes. Some SCDEs are extending the propositions into the preservice teacher education programs. National Board Certification is being adopted by states as the highest level of certification. We are pleased to have the intellectual property of the National Board used for these purposes, as they speak to the face validity and potential of the standards and assessments. But perhaps most importantly, we are pleased to observe a nascent research agenda growing around the National Board. We want this chapter to inspire others to develop a research agenda about accomplished teaching, including those areas we mention above.

While the survey results cited earlier address the face validity of the National Board's standards and assessments, they do not provide enough substance to serve as the kind of research that provides the deep and rich validity that demonstrates the effect of National Board Certification processes. To determine the consequential validity of these standards and assessments, Bond, Smith, Baker, and Hattie (2000) conducted a study to examine whether there were demonstrable differences between National Board Certified Teachers (NBCTs) and non-National Board Certified Teachers (non-NBCTs). These researchers created a sample of 65 teachers who completed all parts of the assessments and who received their scores on these assessments. These teachers were divided into two naturally formed groups, NBCTs (n = 31) and non-NBCTs (n = 35). For the next school year, these teachers were observed teaching in their classrooms and interviewed about their teaching. The researchers collected samples of the teachers' lessons, samples of the students' work and a variety of other writing assignments given to the students. The researchers interviewed three students in each teacher's classroom and conducted surveys of all children in the classroom. With this very rich portrayal of the teacher and the students during that year, the research team then began to analyze these data and to synthesize them to determine whether there were demonstrable differences between those teachers who achieved National Board Certification and those who did not.

The results are quite powerful. The scores of the NBCTs were statistically significantly higher than the scores of the non-NBCT comparison group on eleven of these thirteen attributes. Those dimensions include: 1) challenge; 2) climate; 3) deep representation; 4) deep understanding; 5) improvisation; 6) passion; 7) problem-solving; 8) respect; 9) sensitivity; 10) test hypotheses; 11) use of knowledge. The remaining two attributes on which NBCTs still had higher, but not significantly higher, scores were monitoring learning and multi-dimensional perception about their classes. These findings offer firm foundation for the claim that the children in the classrooms of NBCTs experienced a demonstrably richer curriculum than the children in the classrooms of those teachers who did not achieve National Board Certification. Perhaps even more gratifying and supportive of the survey results cited above, all teachers scored rather high on all thirteen attributes, suggesting again that just completing the entire assessment process enhances one's skills as a teaching professional. The National Board will continue to support research studies that test the validity of its standards and processes from multiple perspectives.

What we'd like to emphasize here, though, is that this seminal work by Bond, et. al., substantively and methodologically can serve as a model for the research agenda in teacher education at the SCDE site. Bond and his colleagues identified the data one needs to examine deeply whether any program designed to enhance teachers' knowledge and skills has had the intended effects. Certainly it provides a powerfully impressive substantiation of the processes of the National Board for Professional Teaching Standards at the same time it models a research design to measure program effects.

What we need to know about validity at the National Board is what the field needs to know generally, especially at the program level. With the increasing pressure on SCDEs to validate the effects of their programs, this study by Bond, et al. provides a research method template. Teacher educators can use these methods to assess the effects of their programs on beginning teachers as well as on teachers completing Master's degree programs. They can further be used to study the stability of teacher behavior over time. An important research question is whether National Board Certified Teachers, or any teachers who complete the entire assessment process, maintain the higher levels of confidence and skill they report in the studies cited above. That question interests the National Board, and it is also a useful question for teacher educators to ask of their programs as well.

With this much initial evidence about the consequential validity of NBPTS processes, we continue the theme of "what we know" and return to those areas of alignment and reform that appear linked to the National Board.

WHAT WE KNOW: SUPPORT PROGRAMS

Perhaps the most enervating phenomenon growing from the work of the National Board is the creation of cohort and support programs for candidates. These are programs, as noted above, offered by school districts, teachers' organizations, and SCDEs, among others to assist and guide teachers through the process. Often NBCTs lead these groups thereby demonstrating the NBPTS fifth proposition that "Teachers are members of learning communities." Support programs are as varied as the localities in which they are operated. Using a focus group methodology, Cramer and Cramer (2001)

interviewed National Board candidates who completed the NBPTS assessment in a support program but who were awaiting their results. The interviews were conducted in six sites (n = 81) with varied geographic
representation. They also conducted interviews with the facilitators of these
support programs.

The researchers identified three major attributes of successful support
groups. First, effective support groups require a knowledgeable and dedicated facilitator. Cramer and Cramer write, "candidates rely on their facilitators to be knowledgeable about the National Board process." (p. 17). They
expect the facilitators to be able to provide specific and focused feedback on
the development of the contents of the portfolio. Second, because of the
unique demands placed on candidates, the support program must include a
structured and sequenced curriculum. Facilitators must organize the curriculum so that the candidates learn to think and write about their teaching
and its effects in the deeply reflective ways expected of NBCTs. Candidates
seek that kind of support and guidance from their programs. This attribute
includes an atmosphere of shared learning, collaboration, and collegiality.
Candidates report learning about teaching by critiquing the work of others
in the support program. Creating a learning community, an ethos of egali-
tarianism in a high-stakes assessment environment, seems to advance
teacher growth and development.

We find the results of Cramer and Cramer quite informative. If we again
return to the survey results reported earlier in this chapter that the process
alone makes teachers better, it seems that these researchers identified three
attributes which facilitate that deeper and richer teacher professional development configuration. Like the Bond et al. study discussed above, Cramer
and Cramer provide a set of attributes for assessing continuing teacher professional development in Master's degree programs, even if they are unre-
lated to the National Board. We can ask the question, "do teachers in
Master's degree programs enjoy these three attributes when learning to
improve their teaching through graduate education?"

Rotberg, Futrell, and Holmes (1999), using a survey of candidates who
completed a local support program, found unequal access to information
concerning National Board Certification. They argued that the materials
available from the National Board could be more explicit in their expectations. They also called for more venues for providing such information. The
rapid increase in the number of support programs for National Board
Certification candidates can be the outlets in which teachers learn more
about accomplished teaching. More importantly, however, it is a way to make
more certain that all teachers have equal access to knowledge that would
ensure a broad and diverse group of National Board Certified Teachers.

There is genuine opportunity for teacher educators to become the providers of equal access to knowledge for National Board Certification candidates in their localities.

Along these lines, it is probably useful here to note that the NBPTS has no plan to enter into the practice of preparing teachers for National Board Certification. It is neither in the best interest of NBPTS, nor the profession. Rather, we remain hopeful that the standards, the disclosed assessment prompts, the portfolios, and the knowledge of effective practice in candidate support will strengthen the practices in any SCDE or school district that seeks to support candidates or improve its offerings in teacher professional development. One of the other events we are observing is the number of private companies venturing into teacher professional development. Using the intellectual property of the National Board, various for-profit businesses are building programs to reach teachers. We are hopeful that SCDE faculties will undertake similar types of activities over the next few years.

In another study of candidates Bohen (2000) compared the perceptions of candidates who participated in a cohort support program and those who did not. Both the cohort and non-cohort candidates found the NBPTS certification process a powerful professional development experience that transformed their views on their teaching. Both groups believed that completing the NBPTS processes in a structured and collegial environment did and would enhance the complete professional development experience. Bohen draws implications for the structure of Master's degree programs as well as the facilitation of support programs for National Board candidates. She concludes that teachers seem to welcome the opportunity to study their teaching and the teaching of others in such group settings where deep inquiry and reflection is valued and encouraged.

WHAT WE KNOW: MASTER'S PROGRAMS

As stated earlier in this chapter, we are observing the re-creation of Master's degree programs which are grounded in the National Board's core propositions, standards, and assessment processes. Two monographs by Blackwell and Diez (1998) and Diez and Blackwell (1999) outline in clear and direct language the opportunities available to the teacher education community by employing the substance of the National Board in programs at this level. However, we know very little as the field about the effects of Master's degree programs on teachers' knowledge and skill in the classroom. The research literature includes many calls for improving the Master's degree, but we could find few research accounts of effects beyond institution-specific satisfaction surveys. One research project is worth highlighting.

Dawkins and Penick (1999) conducted a survey of 300 teachers in North Carolina to assess their beliefs and attitudes about a proposed Master's degree program which was aligned with the fundamental principles of the National Board. As we might expect, the respondents were more supportive of program dimensions, including content and processes, which directly target their ability to improve their teaching and daily interactions with children. The respondents did not dismiss the philosophical dimensions found in most graduate programs for teachers. However, they wanted them grounded to their own professional development and improvement in teaching skill. Returning to the themes in the research we cited above, these are often aspects of the NBPTS process that teachers cite as critical as well.

We will use the remainder of this section then to ask a series of questions about the continuing professional development of teachers through graduate education. These questions, drawn from the research about the National Board, can be applied to any process designed to enhance teachers' knowledge and skills.

Does the graduate program produce demonstrably different teachers? On what dimensions?

What evidence does the faculty who teach in a Master's program accept that the program has had its intended effects on its graduates?

To what extent are teachers learning from one another's work, in contrast to learning as individuals ways that continue to treat teaching as an isolated practice?

Do the classes in a Master's degree program represent a community of learners?

Does the Master's program further develop teachers' understanding of the discipline(s) they teach? How is the effectiveness of that measured?

Are the faculty skilled at drawing out the best in their students and opening that for reflection on practice?

These sample questions, derived from the few studies cited above, suggest ways in which the new Master's degree programs proposed and discussed by Diez and Blackwell can be measured against external criteria of effectiveness and not solely against course-by-course or total program satisfaction surveys. The imperative facing the National Board, and we argue, the education of educators, is the ability to provide convincing evidence that our programs can be held against standards the profession accepts as high and rigorous. While we are heartened by the amount of activity we see in education schools across the country, we remain mindful of how much work we have ahead.

WHAT WE KNOW: CANDIDATE PERFORMANCE

Data collected from each administration of NBPTS assessments indicate the percentage of candidates achieving National Board Certification increases annually. In the 1999–2000 cycle, fifty-two percent of all first-time candidates achieved National Board Certification. However, within these data are differential achievement rates among racial and ethnic groups. Again, using data from the 1999–2000 cycle, fifty-four percent of white, non-Hispanic candidates achieved certification as did sixty percent of Asian-American candidates, thirty-six percent of Native-American candidates, forty-two percent of Hispanic candidates, and eighteen percent of African-American candidates. These data point to the need for much deeper inquiry into what we have labeled "adverse impact," or the differential and unintended effects of the assessments on groups of candidates. Bond and his colleagues, in a series of studies (1995, 1998a; 1998b), have been inquiring into the sources of adverse impact in an effort to establish a set of conditions which would reduce its effects. These studies have included an external panel review of the standards and assessments that found no bias inherent in either. They have included a study of the interaction of assessor race by candidate race, which also yielded no direct evidence of bias such that it would create wide-scale adverse impact. They have also included a study of candidates who did not achieve National Board Certification but who re-took exercises and who achieved National Board Certification on the next attempt. In this study, the candidates spoke of how they were underprepared for the amount of reflective thinking required and expected in the assessments, suggesting one part of addressing adverse impact is high quality preparation programs at the preservice, candidate support, and continuing professional development levels.

In a related study intended to locate other sources of adverse impact, Onafowora (1998) studied six African-American candidates who did not initially gain National Board Certification. Her findings are instructive to the National Board and to teacher educators who value the processes of reflective practice. Onafowora found that these African-American candidates were at a distinct disadvantage when the assessment task entailed writing extemporaneously. Further, she questioned whether the themes on which African-American candidates wrote and reflected are those valued in the

National Board assessment process. Rather than writing explicitly and directly about teaching, she found the entries of these African-American candidates tended to focus on philosophical themes, such as instilling "survival imperatives" in their students. She argues that African-American candidates wrestle with the writing style seemingly required of NBPTS assessment processes and labeled it "linguistic code switching." This small study suggests that the manner in which teachers view their roles as teachers powerfully influences where they believe the impact of their efforts are and how they reflect on that impact. Certainly, much more research needs to be conducted on such a theme. We believe, though, Onafowora raises a matter of professional substance which both NBPTS and teacher educators must spend more time considering.

The issue of adverse impact concerns the NBPTS staff and Board of Directors deeply. The issue is complex and demands more systematic and thoughtful inquiry. While NBPTS will continue to study this issue and direct its efforts appropriately to ensure there is no bias systematically creating adverse impact in these assessments, we welcome teacher education researchers to join us locating more ways to support candidates in ways which reduce adverse impact and enhance the conceptions of effective teaching implied in the core propositions and standards.

WHAT WE KNOW: STUDENT ACHIEVEMENT

At the time of its creation, NBPTS promulgated standards for a profession that lacked them. Its actions were considered demonstrative evidence that teaching was taking care of its shortcomings. Critics of the "education establishment" were no longer free to say that teaching had no standards for performance. In the fifteen years hence, having standards, and even assessments, has proven necessary but insufficient. The greatest pressure on the National Board, likely because of its high profile in the policy and political communities, is to measure its accomplishments against the ultimate outcome: student achievement.

In the spirit of this ATE annual yearbook, nothing would satisfy us more than reporting "what we know" about National Board Certification Teachers and their effects on student achievement. As gratifying as we find the results of the validation study of Bond and his colleagues, which included the analysis of 1500 student work samples from the classes of the 65 teachers, some policy quarters criticized the research as insufficient to tell the whole story. In all fairness to all who have touched or been touched by the National Board in some way in its history, these stakes are at a level for which they, we, and the field of education generally were not preparing.

Our history, notwithstanding, we can say in this chapter that the question of the effects of a teacher on student achievement is an unexplored area of inquiry for both the profession and the National Board. However, with a mission that includes the statement "to advance related education reform," the National Board is beginning to ask some of these hard questions. We are looking closely at the methods of William Sanders and his Tennessee Value-Added Assessment System. We hope to test his methodology with NBCTs, and we hope to test the teachers he identifies as effective against the National Board's standards. In the same spirit as we've treated the other studies, we hope to inspire others to consider the same questions in their venues. A sample of the questions we are considering include:

Do the students of NBCTs gain higher test scores than the teachers of non-NBCTs?

What are replicable methods for determining such effects?

How should student test scores be handled when using student achievement tests to assess teacher quality?

Are gain scores a better measure of the effects of NBCTs than annual test scores?

How might student work produced for the teacher be used to study the comparative effectiveness of NBCTs along these lines?

These questions can be used to study the effects of both preservice teacher education programs and Master's programs designed for the continuing professional development of teachers. They are not exclusive to the National Board, but they are questions away from which the National Board cannot shy. We know that our future in the policy community depends directly on how well we can make our case, and we believe the same metric applies to the teacher education community generally, of which we see ourselves as a part.

WHAT WE KNOW: ASSESSING ACCOMPLISHED TEACHING

In the area of measurement, the National Board has learned a great deal about measuring and scoring an activity as complex as teaching, but there is still much more to know. Results of studies reported by Jaeger (1998) and Bond (1998a) offer insights into the process of scoring multi-dimensional representations of teaching. It is not the purpose of this chapter to discuss in detail their findings, but to suggest the reader steep herself/himself in this literature. Likewise, Gitomer (1997) reviews five major challenges faced in the design, development, and implementation of the NBPTS assessment process, including: 1) defining scoring against independent standards; 2) handling a broad range of content and contexts; 3) resolving pedagogical, cultural, and contextual bias; 4) interpreting unfamiliar representations of content; and 5) identifying the cut-score. Each is a major theoretical and practical issue grounded in psychometrics, and those whose research agenda includes determining the effects of a program ought to wrestle with these issues.

Moss and Schutz (1999) offer a series of constructive questions which the National Board must address related to delving deeply into the issues of reliability and validity. They present a thoughtful discussion of what could be revealed by creating a more transparent process of standards design, assessment development, scoring, and judgment. Arguing from the perspective that the mission of the National Board is to operate a national and voluntary system of certification for accomplished teaching and to serve as a catalyst for change in the profession, Moss and Schutz question what can be interpreted from the processes and their results. They suggest a much richer and more collaborative assessment development process, where more teachers are included in the processes and broader representations of teaching and more refined and inclusive definitions of accomplished teaching result. As they note, the National Board would be closer to fulfilling its mission to advance teaching if it included such approaches. We agree with their observation that the assessment system can lead to one instantiation of teaching being valued over others. We look, however, to teacher educators to help teachers think more deeply about their teaching and how they represent it to others (including in NBPTS assessment process), and to the research community to experiment with more options for standards, assessments, scoring, and judgments. One of the limitations of the National Board, which Moss and Schutz include in their treatment of this topic, is the political nature of its obligations. Policymakers at all levels are invested in the National Board because of its adherence to high standards and a rigorous process. While we would acknowledge that any set of standards can be seen as arbitrary, we believe the processes employed to create this certification system, especially the strict commitment to including practicing teachers at all levels, as Gitomer (1997) notes, is critical to the validity of the National Board process. Moreover, the National Board welcomes researchers to conduct systematic analyses of the portfolios of the candidates to address this concern that some teachers are advantaged due to the choice of the teaching practices they present in their submissions. Let us close this section by acknowledging that we need to know much more about the assessment processes we employ and believe the authors cited in this section provide a very good sense of direction for the research community.

WHAT WE KNOW: CHANGING THE PROFESSION

The last area we'd like to explore is the effect National Board Certification is having on teachers' roles and responsibilities. In a recent, national, commissioned study of National Board Certified Teachers (NBCTs), Yankelovich and associates (National Board for Professional Teaching Standards, 2001), a national polling firm, surveyed all NBCTs concerning the effects of National Board Certification on their roles and responsibilities.

National Board Certified Teachers (NBCTs) report in significant numbers they are undertaking new roles and responsibilities in their schools and communities. For example, eighty-three percent of NBCTs report they are mentoring other teachers since gaining National Board Certification. Ninety percent report they now mentor or coach Certification candidates. These findings are not surprising. School administrators are seeing the value in having an NBCT in the school building who can work with other and new teachers. The data also suggest an emerging role for NBCTs as clinical faculty in teacher education programs. Over eighty percent of the respondents in this study express interest in teacher education. The data indicate that about one-half of the NBCTs have participated in teacher education programs in this way.

The overall purpose of this survey of NBCTs was to create baseline data on how NBPTS is shaping behavior within the profession. The data, as would be expected, indicate that change is widespread but not yet very deep. National Board Certified Teachers are working with peers in new ways. Many are working with local SCDEs in the preparation of new teachers. About sixty percent are writing professional development materials and about forty percent are becoming involved in issues of teacher licensure. These kinds of influences of teachers on the teaching profession fulfill the mission of the National Board. However, we call upon our colleagues in teacher education to study more closely the effects teachers have on other teachers, new teachers, and the profession generally. In the arena of the National Board as an agent of change, we need to know much more.

Closing Remarks

In so many ways, the National Board is fulfilling its mission to set the benchmark for accomplished teaching. It has overcome obstacles political, professional, and psychometric in nature. It has spawned a national inquiry into teacher quality, and its intellectual property is being used to revisit teacher licensure, teacher evaluation, and the profession in general. However, it still is a long way from having the kind of research evidence which solidifies its base. We are hopeful that by creating the broad categories we used to review this literature and through the selection of the literature we chose that our colleagues in teacher education will join in the quest for making teaching into the profession we believe it can be. That includes, but is not limited to, a set of standards and assessments which are generally acknowledged to capture the essence of the field and a conjoined research stream which substantiates and challenges the profession to continue to improve itself.

REFERENCES

Blackwell, P. and Diez, M. (1998). *Toward a new vision of Master's education for teachers.* Washington, DC: National Council for Accreditation of Teacher Education.

Bohen, D.B. (2000). *How teacher candidates view and value the certification process of the National Board for Professional Teaching Standards.* Unpublished doctoral dissertation: George Mason University.

Bond, L. (1995). Unintended consequences and performance assessment: Issues of bias and fairness. *Educational Measurement: Issues and Practice,* 14(4), 21–24.

Bond, L. (1998a). Disparate impact and teacher certification. *Journal of Personnel Evaluation in Education, 33*(3), 410–427.

Bond, L. (1998b). Culturally responsive pedagogy and the assessment of accomplished teaching. *Journal of Negro Education, 67*(3), 242–254.

Bond, L., Smith, T., Baker, W. & Hattie, J. (2000). Accomplished teaching: A validation of National Board Certification. Arlington, VA: National Board for Professional Teaching Standards.

Buday, M. & Kelly, J. (1996). National Board Certification and the teaching profession's commitment to quality assurance. *Phi Delta Kappan. 77*(2), 215–219.

Carnegie Commission on Education and the Economy (1986). *A nation prepared: Teachers for the 21st century.* Washington, DC: Author.

Center for the Future of Teaching and Learning. (2000). *In the teacher's voice: A survey of California teachers seeking and earning certification by the National Board for Professional Teaching Standards.* Santa Clara: Author.

Cramer, M. & Cramer, J. (2000). Candidates' perceptions of effective National Board for Professional Teaching Standards support programs. Unpublished manuscript. Conway, AR: Arkansas State University.

Dawkins, K. & Penick, J. (1999). "Teacher preferences for an advanced Master's degree based on NBPTS and NCATE standards." Chapel Hill: University of North Carolina, College of Education. (ERIC Document Reproduction Service No. ED443 673.

Diez, M. & Blackwell, P. (1999). *Achieving the new vision for Master's education for teachers.* Washington, DC: National Council for Accreditation of Teacher Education.

Gitomer, D. (1997). "Challenges for scoring performance assessments in the NBPTS system." Paper presented at the annual meeting of the American Educational Research Association.

Iovacchini, L.C. (1998). *National Board for Professional Teaching Standards: What teachers are learning.* University of South Carolina: Unpublished doctoral dissertation.

Jaeger, R. (1998). Evaluating the psychometric qualities of the National Board for Professional Teaching Standards, *Journal of Personnel Evaluation in Education, 12*(2), 189–210.

Moss, P. and Schutz, A. (1999). Risking frankness in educational assessment. *Phi Delta Kappan, 80,* (9), 680–687.

National Board for Professional Teaching Standards. (2001). *Leading from the classroom: The evolving roles of National Board Certified Teachers.* Unpublished manuscript. Arlington, VA: Author.

National Commission on Excellence and Education. (1983). *A nation at risk.* Washington, DC: Author.

Onafowora, L.L. (1998). Measurement consequences reconsidered: African-American performance and communication styles in the assessment for national teacher certification. University of North Carolina at Greensboro: Unpublished doctoral dissertation.

Rotberg, I., Futrell, M.H., & Holmes, A. (2000). Increasing access to National Board Certification. *Phi Delta Kappan, 81,* (5), 379–382.

Index